Christopher Gow is currently a tutor in the Department of Adult and Continuing Education at the University of Glasgow. He did his postgraduate research into New Iranian Cinema and émigré Iranian filmmaking at the School of Oriental and African Studies and at the University of Warwick. *From Iran to Hollywood and Some Places In-Between* is his first major publication.

'Incisive and insightful, Christopher Gow's book valuably enhances our understanding of the cinematic efflorescence that produced Kiarostami, Makhmalbaf, Panahi and others by expanding its boundaries both temporally and geographically. Looking back at Iran's remarkable pre-1979 cinema, examining the post-1979 work of important émigré directors Sohrab Shahid Saless and Amir Naderi, and considering such noteworthy films of the Iranian diaspora as Caveh Zahedi's *I Don't Hate Las Vegas Anymore* and Ramin Serry's *Maryam*, Gow gives us a protean Iranian cinema beset (or blessed) with all the tensions and possibilities of a rapidly globalizing world.'

– **Godfrey Cheshire**, film critic and filmmaker

'*From Iran to Hollywood and Some Places In-Between* makes an important contribution to studies of Iranian cinema by offering a much-needed nuanced approach that balances brilliantly the conceptual with the analytical. Opening with an exploration of the discursive paradigms that frame post-revolutionary Iranian cinema, Gow provides in the process a fascinating overview of Kiarostami's position in film criticism and history. By subsequently concentrating on émigré cinema, the book focuses its conceptual interrogation to questions of national cinema and identity and furthers critical arguments around exilic and diasporic filmmaking. The two case studies, the films of Amir Naderi and Sohrab Shahid Saless, are exemplary researched and presented, constituting in themselves valuable scholarship in a starkly under-researched area.'

– **Dimitris Eleftheriotis**, University of Glasgow

'Christopher Gow's book is a refreshing and innovative approach to Iranian films made in the wake of the 1979 revolution. Gow's meticulous and absorbing readings of the films support his argument and provide new vistas on Iranian films whether produced inside or outside Iran. In the process, Gow reveals hidden treasures rarely discussed in the context of Iranian cinema. In addition to having a solid theoretical grounding in film theory and criticism, the book is most lucidly written and a pleasure to read. The sound structure of the argument and the judiciously chosen examples make this into a stellar example of scholarship on Iranian cinema. This book will become an indispensable reference and guide for amateurs, students, and scholars of Iranian cinema.'

– **Nasrin Rahimieh**, University of California, Irvine

'Juxtaposing the rich and heterogeneous Iranian émigré films with those that are seen to constitute the New Iranian Cinema, Gow's lucidly written book offers fresh and nuanced insight into its subject matter. This is an essential book for both Iranian cinema enthusiasts and those interested in current debates about "national cinemas" in film studies.'

– **Saeed Zeydabadi-Nejad**, School of Oriental and African Studies

Published in 2011 by I.B.Tauris & Co Ltd

FROM IRAN TO HOLLYWOOD
AND SOME PLACES IN-BETWEEN
REFRAMING POST-REVOLUTIONARY IRANIAN CINEMA

CHRISTOPHER GOW

I.B. TAURIS
LONDON · NEW YORK

Published in 2011 by I.B.Tauris & Co Ltd
6 Salem Road, London W2 4BU
175 Fifth Avenue, New York NY 10010
www.ibtauris.com

Copyright © 2011 Christopher Gow

The right of Christopher Gow to be identified as author of this work has been asserted by him in accordance with the Copyright, Designs and Patent Act 1988.

All rights reserved. Except for brief quotations in a review, this book, or any part thereof, may not be reproduced, stored in or introduced into a retrieval system, or transmitted, in any form or by any means, electronic, mechanical, photocopying, recording or otherwise, without the prior written permission of the publisher.

International Library of Iranian Studies: 39

ISBN: 978 1 84885 526 7 (HB)
ISBN: 978 1 84885 527 4 (PB)

A full CIP record for this book is available from the British Library
A full CIP record is available from the Library of Congress

Library of Congress Catalog Card Number: available

*For my mother and father.
And for my friends Andrew, Ian and Neil.*

Contents

List of Illustrations   ix

Acknowledgements   xi

Introduction   1

1   Putting the 'New' in the New Iranian Cinema:
Post-Revolutionary Iranian Cinema as Art Cinema   9
     Iranian cinema after 1979   13
     The New Iranian Cinema as art cinema   17
     At the crossroads   39
     An 'Islamic' cinema?   45
     A cinema of resistance   54
     Reframing the New Iranian Cinema   57

2   From Iran to Hollywood and Some Places In-Between:
Iranian Émigré Filmmaking   61
     Naficy's 'accented cinema'   68
     'A journey without end': *The Mission, Guests of the Hotel Astoria* and *Nightsongs*   82
     Being in the moment: *I Don't Hate Las Vegas Anymore* and *Walls of Sand*   96
     The European connection: Reza Parsa and Susan Taslimi   107
     Children of the revolution: *Maryam* and *America So Beautiful*   114
     Recurring visions: *House of Sand and Fog*   120
     Tracking post-revolutionary Iranian cinema   123
     Postscript: back to Iran   125

3   Close Up 1 – Amir Naderi   127
     Sidewalks of despair: *A, B, C… Manhattan*   129
     Filling in the blanks: *Marathon*   139
     Iranian cinema in focus   144

4   Close Up 2 – Sohrab Shahid Saless   147
     Saless and the 'everyday'   152

    Hans: a film from Germany?   175
    Saless and Kiarostami: the Iranian connection   183
    Between the new waves   187

Conclusion: Iranian Cinema in Long Shot   191
    Postscript: Iranian Cinema after 9/11   199

Notes   203

Bibliography   215

Filmography   225

Index   229

List of Illustrations

1.	Stylistic signatures and obsessive motifs; from *Where Is the Friend's House?*	22
2.	Stylistic signatures and obsessive motifs; from *Through the Olive Trees*	23
3.	Stylistic signatures and obsessive motifs; from *Taste of Cherry*	23
4.	Stylistic signatures and obsessive motifs; from *The Wind Will Carry Us*	24
5.	*Marathon*	141
6.1–8.11.	*A Time of Maturity*	160–163
9.	*11'09"01 – September 11*	201

Acknowledgements

I wish to thank the following people: Francesca Capobianchi of Revolver Films in Italy, for providing me with a copy of Amir Naderi's film *Marathon*; Shahram Tabe, Director of the Diaspora Film Festival, and Klaus Volkmer of the München Film Museum, for their invaluable assistance in tracking down and obtaining copies of the German films of Sohrab Shahid Saless; Maani Petgar for his hospitality during my time in Iran and for providing me with copies of Naderi's *Water, Wind and Dust* and Saless's early films, in addition to other rare prerevolutionary works; and Reza Parza, for kindly sending me personal copies of his films and allowing me to interview him. Without the help of these individuals, it is no exaggeration to say that this book would simply not have been possible.

I also wish to thank the British Institute for Persian Studies, for the grant I received to cover my travel expenses to Iran in the summer of 2003, to undertake a ten-week Persian language course at the International Centre for Persian Studies. While I was there I also had the opportunity to speak with and benefit from the knowledge of filmmakers such as Maani Petgar and Bahman Farmanara. I also wish to thank the AHRC for the funding I received in my final year of postgraduate research at the University of Warwick.

Finally, I wish to express my deepest gratitude to the following people: Richard Tapper and Charlotte Brunsdon, for their excellent supervision and encouragement throughout the various stages of my postgraduate research; all the current and former staff and students of the Department of Film and Television Studies at the University of Warwick, who made me feel so welcome upon my transfer from SOAS; Negar Mottahedeh, for agreeing to review my work upon submitting my book proposal to I.B.Tauris; and my fellow PhD candidates during my postgraduate years, Saeed Zeydabadi-Nejad, Nacim Pak and Leon Gurevitch, for their friendship and good humour.

Introduction

My introduction to Iranian cinema, in the year 1999, will be similar I imagine to many a non-Iranian's introduction to this cinema – namely, via the films of Abbas Kiarostami. In my case, the film in question was *Through the Olive Trees* (1994). Upon my first viewing of this film I knew nothing of either its director or post-revolutionary Iranian cinema in general, and very little of the country Iran itself. I was equally ignorant of the fact that the film was the third and apparently final part of a loosely grouped series of films, its two predecessors being *Where Is the Friend's House?* (1987) and *And Life Goes On...* (also known as *Life and Nothing More* (1991)), based in and around the villages of Koker and Poshteh in northern Iran. I was aware, however, after viewing the film that it was quite different from any film I had ever seen before, though in truth I had struggled to engage with the film outside of its central focus on the budding relationship between its two main characters, Hossein and Tahereh. The famed final shot of the film especially – which shows in extreme long shot the two would-be lovers walking through a field and moving further and further into the distance to the strains of *Concerto for Oboe and Strings* by Domenico Cimarosa, until they become two tiny dots on screen – left a lasting impression on me. I shall return to this shot in the following chapter, but for the time being it suffices to say that the film's oblique manner of conveying the nature of Tahereh's response to Hossein's incessant marriage proposals, of saying everything and nothing at the same time as it were, was particularly striking in its audacious minimalism.

This single shot, or rather my reaction to it, in a sense provides the basis for this entire book. My considerable difficulty in following the film was in no small part due to its beguiling mixture of fact and fiction, its repetitive and non-linear mode of narration, as well as its complex film-within-a-film structure (which I eventually learned was an even more complex film-within-a-film-within-a-film *mise-en-abyme* structure). These features I soon discovered were characteristic of many of Kiarostami's other works, and of many post-revolutionary Iranian films. It was my desire to better understand this new, unfamiliar style of filmmaking that led me to watch more of Kiarostami's films, which in turn led me to watch many more award-winning films from Iran. This in turn led me to seek out other Iranian films (including those made before the 1978–79 Revolution) that were not quite so fortunate as to receive international recognition. Foremost amongst these films were, significantly, those directed by Sohrab Shahid Saless, which in turn led to my discovery of Iranian émigré filmmaking. With each successive stage on this cinematic journey I have moved further away from my original meeting point with the New Iranian Cinema, further away from the final shot of *Through the Olive Trees*. Yet at the same time I was moving closer to a better appreciation of this shot, of Kiarostami's films in general, and of the exact nature of my first encounter with the New Iranian Cinema itself.

On the one hand, I was simply going through a phase in my life when I was voraciously trying to consume as many films and discover as many 'new', interesting cinemas as I possibly could, having caught the film bug as an undergraduate at the University of Glasgow, where I had originally applied to study English Literature with History, randomly selecting Film and Television Studies as an obligatory third subject, foolishly believing that kicking back and watching a few movies every now and again would provide some welcome relief from my more 'serious' studies. On the other hand, there was a conscious desire on my part to gain a better understanding of Kiarostami's films, and a better overall perspective of Iranian filmmaking, so as to be able to place the New Iranian Cinema within its various contexts, an objective which is perhaps the overriding concern of this book. As my own knowledge of the New Iranian Cinema expanded over the years, so too has the amount of literature on the topic, especially following Kiarostami's victory at the 1997 Cannes Film Festival with *Taste of Cherry* (1997). Since then a variety of studies have emerged, from those examining broadly the social, cultural and political significance of the New Iranian Cinema, both internationally and domestically (most notably, *The New Iranian Cinema*, edited by Richard Tapper), to publications focusing on the works of particular filmmakers (such as Eric Egan's *Films of Makhmalbaf*). Despite the far-reaching scope of these studies, however, for even the most ardent of foreign film enthusiasts, Iranian cinema remains largely synonymous with the works of Kiarostami. Moreover, it is usually defined solely by those films that were made following the Revolution, or to be more exact, following the success of Kiarostami's *Where Is the Friend's House?* at the 1989 Locarno Film Festival. This is despite the fact that the beginnings of the so-called Iranian new wave can be traced as far back as the early 1960s, in particular to Farough Farrokhzad's *The House Is Black* (1962).

The reasons for this are numerous and are interlinked to a considerable extent. First, and perhaps foremost among these reasons, is the way in which post-revolutionary Iranian cinema has been regarded as a quintessential 'art' cinema in Europe and North America. Following the social and political upheaval of the Revolution, Iranian cinema, like many European cinemas in the aftermath of the Second World War, experienced an artistic revival, along with a commensurate rise in international prestige. One of the effects of these various cinematic resurgences, however, is that in most instances the rich filmmaking traditions and influences that preceded them are frequently overlooked. Indeed in Iran's case they are not so much overlooked as they are virtually forgotten. More often than not the Revolution is perceived as a catalyst for, rather than an interruption of, Iranian cinema's creative renaissance. As a result, many pre-revolutionary films which serve as precursors to the best examples of contemporary Iranian filmmaking are excluded from consideration, simply because they fall out with the restrictive timeline artificially imposed upon the evolution of the *New* Iranian Cinema.

Second, there has been an inordinate focus upon an elite group of internationally acclaimed Iranian auteurs (Kiarostami and Mohsen Makhmalbaf being foremost among these), which is also counterproductive to a wider, more nuanced and inclusive appreciation of contemporary Iranian filmmaking. Indeed the emphasis on individual directors so prevalent in much of the writing on the New Iranian Cinema is also heavily informed by notions of authorship that are themselves intimately bound up with, and derived from, traditional concepts of art cinema. This will inevitably change over time, as more scholars revise the official history of the New Iranian Cinema and the established canon of films that are considered to comprise it. But for the time being the New Iranian Cinema, as was the case with other cinematic movements such as the French New Wave, is a closely guarded club, where only an exclusive few are permitted entry.

Third, little attempt has been made to account for the emergence over the past three decades of a prolific and diverse Iranian émigré cinema, produced not only by second-generation Iranian émigrés, but also by prominent pre-revolutionary filmmakers such as Saless, Amir Naderi and Susan Taslimi. In this respect Hamid Naficy's *An Accented Cinema*, an immense analytical overview of exilic and diasporic film-making in general, is important insofar as it sheds light on the existence of a diffuse and itinerant Iranian cinema produced outside of Iran by filmmakers living and working all over the world. The existence of such a cinema represents a significant challenge, not only to the historical and geographical integrity of the New Iranian Cinema, once again as it has been constructed as an archetypal art cinema within Europe and North America, but also to traditional methods of organising national cinemas along purely geographical boundaries.

The overall perception of the New Iranian Cinema in Europe and North America, therefore, is artistically, historically and geographically blinkered. By being transposed into the framework of European art cinema, the New Iranian Cinema has been gradually removed and cut off from the particular contexts not only wherein it has developed, but also in which it presently resides, in relation to pre-revolutionary Iranian cinema and Iranian émigré filmmaking. To a certain extent the term 'New Iranian Cinema' is itself reflective of this transposition, and of the severance of post-revolutionary Iranian cinema from its historical roots and other contemporary incarnations, serving as it does to impose an indeterminate period of artistic relevancy upon this cinema, dictating certain avenues of discussion while restricting others.

Indeed, there is a sense in which the New Iranian Cinema has been a victim of its own success. As the international profile of the New Iranian Cinema gradually increased, so too has the number of international co-productions between Iran and other countries. Since *Where Is the Friend's House?* for instance, nearly all of Kiarostami's subsequent films have been co-financed by French partners. As Shohini Chaudhuri has noted, international co-productions, often conceived as a collaborative means of countering the apparent global dominance of Hollywood, are frequently misrepresentative of the

INTRODUCTION

sum total of the cinematic output of the particular countries involved. These disparities, furthermore, are often carried over into an academic context relatively unchallenged:

> International co-productions also contribute to uneven power relations; for example, Middle Eastern films co-produced with European partners often obtain international video or repertory distribution, while mainstream local production often remains unseen by foreign audiences. Film studies has yet to address properly the extent to which current critical coverage manifests the inequalities of global film distribution.[1]

International co-productions, somewhat ironically, can thus serve to skew the overall picture of Iranian filmmaking, by actually restricting the variety of Iranian films made available to foreign audiences around the world. Traditionally, one of the most common ways of countering such misperceptions and imbalances has been to focus on popular indigenous cinema within a given country. Such an approach, however, is not so easily available to me as a non-Iranian. Indeed one aspect of contemporary Iranian filmmaking that is conspicuous by its absence in this book is popular cinema within Iran, or what Chaudhuri would call 'mainstream local production', a definition which does not account for cinema that is popular abroad. The disparities between art cinema and popular cinema, and their specificity (or rather lack thereof) to the Iranian context, will be addressed at greater length in the next chapter. At this early stage, however, I would simply draw the reader's attention to the original title of my postgraduate thesis, *Iranian Cinema in Long Shot*, which, besides referring to the wider, more comprehensive panorama of Iranian cinema that I attempt to outline, in addition to the autobiographical information contained in the opening paragraphs above, hints at my own critical distance from this cinema as a non-Iranian. Which is not to say that I am necessarily any more or less qualified than any Iranian to comment upon this cinema (many Iranians have found Kiarostami's films just as challenging and problematic as I have, for instance). Rather it is to recognise that there are definite limits to my own knowledge of what is ultimately for me a foreign cinema. I am, after all, a *khariji* (Persian for foreigner). In this respect, my original title was also intended to evoke memories of Hamid Dabashi's acutely personal and in-depth study of Iranian cinema, *Close Up*. The title *Iranian Cinema in Long Shot* by contrast points to my own status as an outsider.

It is this very status, however, that hopefully enables me to bring a different perspective to the study of the New Iranian Cinema, an area of research that has thus far been dominated, for better or for worse, by the writings of Iranian academics working in the West, and a perspective that would most likely not be possible had I grown up watching Iranian films. Far from wishing to define my research in opposition to Dabashi's work, I would say that this book can hopefully be understood as existing in relation to Dabashi's work, as well as Naficy's, though I certainly take issue with many of their arguments throughout.

The central aim of this book, therefore, is to recontextualize the New Iranian Cinema, or to consider what happens to the concept of the New Iranian Cinema when it is viewed in relation to Iranian émigré filmmaking. What transformations, if any, does the concept of the New Iranian Cinema undergo when considered in such a light? Not only that, but also what implications does such a consideration have for our understanding of several key theoretical paradigms within film studies, such as art cinema, authorship and national cinema, in particular as they have been employed and/or deployed as a means of engaging with post-revolutionary Iranian cinema? Given the evident concern of this book with re-evaluating certain theoretical paradigms as they have been used traditionally in film studies, it is perhaps unsurprising that the means by which I attempt to answer the above questions are methodologically differentiated from each other throughout. This diversity is also reflective of the sheer heterogeneity and eclectic nature of the films considered in this book.

Chapter 1, therefore, examines how the New Iranian Cinema has been constructed as an art cinema in Europe and North America. This has been achieved to a great extent by frequent and largely superficial analogies with European art cinema, most notably the French New Wave. Accusations of pandering to Western tastes for Third World exoticism and a 'cinema of poverty' aside, in what ways do post-revolutionary Iranian films lend themselves on an aesthetic level to their repositioning within a European art cinema framework?

How and to what extent is this at odds with the Iranian government's own attempts to 'Islamize' Iranian cinema following the Revolution? How have Iranian filmmakers resisted the attempts by foreign audiences to define their films as examples of an exemplary alternative art cinema or their own government's efforts to project their films as examples of an ideologically infused 'Islamic' cinema?

Chapter 2 by contrast examines the development of Iranian émigré filmmaking. What are the connections between this cinema and the New Iranian Cinema, beside the aforementioned fact that many of the émigré filmmakers in question were important figures in pre-revolutionary Iran? Indeed what are the connections between all of these filmmakers themselves? Although many of them originally hail from Iran, their films display many thematic and stylistic differences, as well as contrasting visions of the experience of displacement. In what ways is it possible, therefore, and more importantly how useful is it, to conceive of all their films as a larger, collective body of work, one that is undoubtedly riddled with contradictions? Finally, what becomes of the concept of the New Iranian Cinema as a national cinema, and the concept of national cinema itself, when we begin to conceive of Iranian *filmmaking* in such a geographically dispersed manner?

Chapters 3 and 4, once again by contrast, are largely auteurist in nature, focusing on the films of Amir Naderi and Sohrab Shahid Saless respectively. These chapters are intended to provide a counterpoint to the methodological approach adopted in chapters 1 and 2. In what ways do the individual *oeuvres* of these two filmmakers, the former based in Germany and the latter in New York, resist a purely or straightforwardly exilic and/or diasporic reading? How and to what extent is the concept of authorship conducive to a better understanding of the films of Naderi and Saless, in contrast to the ways in which it is not necessarily conducive to a better understanding of the films of a director such as Kiarostami? By posing such questions I hope to guard against accusations of homogenization and essentialization, of reducing the sheer wealth of Iranian émigré filmmaking to one level of meaning, while further exploring the links between the New Iranian Cinema and Iran's most influential pre-revolutionary filmmakers.

This book, therefore, attempts to bring together the New Iranian Cinema and Iranian émigré cinema, or at the very least to shed light on some of the links between these two cinemas – to consider briefly what a view of Iranian cinema in long shot might actually look like. Eleven years have passed after all, since my initial viewing of *Through the Olive Trees*, and my knowledge of Iranian cinema is still growing and will continue to grow in the future. There will always be some films waiting to be discovered, or some aspect of Iranian cinema's neglected history waiting to unearthed. This book, therefore, represents something of a work in progress, a momentary (albeit wordy) snapshot of my constantly evolving understanding of Iranian cinema, in all its various manifestations.

1

Putting the 'New' in the New Iranian Cinema: Post-Revolutionary Iranian Cinema as Art Cinema

> In art-cinema terms (though Americans don't know it yet), we are living in the Age of Kiarostami, as we once did in the Age of Godard[1]
>
> (Philip Lopate)

> In *Through the Olive Trees*, the Iranian director [Abbas Kiarostami] has some serious cinematic fun in the manner of Truffaut's *Day for Night*.[2]
>
> (Stephen Holden)

> Kiarostami, le Magnifique![3]
>
> (*Cahiers du Cinéma*)

There is a scene at the beginning of *The Wind Will Carry Us* (Abbas Kiarostami, 1999), when the members of the film crew that is travelling to the Kurdish village of Siah Darreh – for the purpose of recording an elderly woman's impending funeral – remark to their young guide, the village schoolboy Farzad, as they approach the mountainside village for the first time: 'What a beautiful village! ... Yes, it's very beautiful ... You've hidden it well.'

'We haven't hidden it!' exclaims Farzad in reply, somewhat defensively. 'The ancestors built it here.'

This exchange between the members of the Tehran-based film crew and Farzad, as brief as it is, in certain respects serves as a metaphor for the reception of post-revolutionary Iranian cinema in Europe and North America. For instance, the film crew initially comment upon the picturesqueness and secludedness of Siah Darreh. In a similar fashion, post-revolutionary Iranian cinema has garnered much praise for its visually pleasing and exotic portrayals of Iran and its people and has been met with great interest due to its unfamiliarity and apparent esotericism. As Farzad's response indicates, however, Siah Darreh and its inhabitants possess a sense of history and centredness that exposes the presumptuous and decidedly metropolitan attitude of the film crew. Likewise, Iranian cinema has a rich pre-revolutionary tradition that is often overlooked in the 'West', belying the simplicity and predictability of the label *New* Iranian Cinema'.

It is no accident that such an interpretation may be drawn from *The Wind Will Carry Us*, a film that examines the ethical complexities of a Tehran film crew's decision to document a mourning ritual practised by Iran's minority Kurdish population. Indeed it seems particularly appropriate, given that the growing international profile of its director, Abbas Kiarostami, has been so inextricably bound up with the success of the New Iranian Cinema. Since its gradual rise to worldwide prominence following the success of *Where Is the Friend's House?* at the 1989 Locarno Film Festival, the New Iranian Cinema has been regarded and portrayed overwhelmingly as a 'minor' national art cinema, in the sense that it has been consistently championed as an alternative to mainstream Hollywood cinema. Indeed, as the epigraphs that open this chapter are intended to illustrate, since its emergence on the international film scene the New Iranian Cinema has been written about and celebrated in a way that explicitly ties it to European art cinemas, most notably the French New Wave. Since the emergence of the Italian neo-realist movement of the 1940s indigenous European art cinema has constantly been viewed as a way of countering the cultural and economic dominance of Hollywood cinema. The New Iranian Cinema, therefore, finds itself in a somewhat anomalous position previously occupied by the likes of Italian neo-realism, the French New Wave and the New German Cinema.

Analogies between the New Iranian Cinema and European art cinema, as this chapter contends, are by no means unfounded; in fact, they are frequently enlightening. They are nevertheless reflective of a wider, more questionable tendency on the part of audiences, critics and academics in Europe and North America alike, to appropriate the New Iranian Cinema almost as if it was their own and hold it up as an exemplary art cinema alternative to mainstream Hollywood. Indeed, as Laura Mulvey has observed with reference to the increasing popularity of Kiarostami's films, 'As Kiarostami's movies have appeared, foreign art-film critics and audiences have responded to them as though to a lost, no-longer-to-be-hoped-for object of desire.'[4]

This is not an example of what Paul Willemen, referring to the theoretical and ethical problems inherent in applying European and North American film theory to the study of non-Western cinemas, has described as 'a cultural cross-border raid, or worse, an attempt to annex another culture in a subordinate position by requiring it to conform to the raider's cultural practices'.[5] It is rather one particular view of the New Iranian Cinema, and a perfectly valid one at that. It is only natural, after all, for audiences to seek to engage with a foreign cinema by comparing it to other cinemas that they are more familiar with. Nevertheless, it is a view that, by the very frequency and authority with which it is proffered, has almost completely squeezed out alternative views of the New Iranian Cinema, obscuring its origins and how it has evolved over the years, overlooking the broader context in which it operates.

The extent to which it is appropriate to define the New Iranian Cinema in opposition to Hollywood cinema is open to question. Eric Egan and Ali Mohammadi, for instance, have argued that opposing the economic and cultural dominance of Hollywood cinema has little meaning for Iranian filmmakers, who are often far more concerned with their own responsibility *as* filmmakers to examine and depict the complexities of Iranian society, and who are frequently caught up in their own complex and antagonistic relationship of negotiation and compromise with Iran's film censors:

> The importance of the national is emphasized with Iranian cinema engaged in an attempt to reflect and question the multi-faceted nature of Iran, its people and their problems, while simultaneously engaged in a dialectical debate with the multi-faceted complexity of Iranian cinema itself. In this respect Iranian cinema is a national cinema not as a bulwark

against Hollywood. Its adversary is indigenous cinema and those who seek to control the medium, which sees it firmly located in the socio-political formation of the modern state, with its internal structure as a determining factor in cultural production. Whereas the third cinema had originally identified Hollywood as the enemy, for Iranian cinema, it is merely a non-entity.[6]

These two contrasting visions of the New Iranian Cinema – one, as a 'minor' national art cinema resisting the global influence of Hollywood and, two, as a more inward-looking, socially conscious cinema – are opposing ends of the same ideological spectrum. Somewhere in-between these two extremes lies not necessarily a more 'truthful' or definitive vision of the New Iranian Cinema, but perhaps an altogether less polarized understanding of what position the New Iranian Cinema occupies in today's world, straddling as it does national and international boundaries, foreign and domestic film markets, and both sides of the debate concerning the globalization of Hollywood cinema. This is not to endorse the worst excesses of theoretical or moral relativism, but rather to advocate a more nuanced appreciation of what the New Iranian Cinema might mean to different people, in different places, and at different times.

Indeed the more socially conscious view of the New Iranian Cinema outlined by Egan and Mohammadi above is far from being incompatible with an understanding of this cinema as a 'minor' cinema. As Willemen has claimed, any cinema which 'seeks to engage with the questions of national specificity from a critical, non- or counter-hegemonic position is by definition a minority and poor cinema, dependant on the existence of a larger multinational or nationalised industrial sector'.[7] According to Willemen's definition, therefore, a 'minor' cinema is characterized as much by its cultural particularity as it is by its economic, aesthetic and industrial 'inferiority' to, and difference from, dominant cinema, whether the latter be international (Hollywood) or domestic (popular indigenous cinema) in scope. The two qualities are not always mutually exclusive.

Although Egan and Mohammadi may thus understate the insignificance of Hollywood cinema for Iranian filmmakers, their argument highlights the dangers of defining Iranian cinema purely in terms of its *difference* from Hollywood cinema. For although such a comparative approach is undoubtedly useful, insofar as it provides an effective means of distinguishing and understanding the (dis)similarities between one 'foreign' cinema and another, it also risks reducing the complex social, political and economic dynamics that have contributed to the development of the New Iranian Cinema to a critically reductive binary opposition.

After briefly outlining the historical context out of which the New Iranian Cinema started to emerge – or rather re-emerge – within post-revolutionary Iran, this chapter examines how this cinema has been received as a quintessential art cinema in Europe and North America. It then goes on to consider, by way of an analysis of Kiarostami's *oeuvre*, the extent to which this reception is justified by the formal and aesthetic qualities of the films themselves, as well as how this reception is at odds with the Iranian government's own attempt to define post-revolutionary Iranian cinema as an inherently 'Islamic' cinema, and the considerable difficulties involved in such an attempt. Finally, this chapter analyses how post-revolutionary Iranian filmmakers, assailed at home and overseas, have striven to *define themselves* through their films, resisting both individually and collectively the attempt to reduce the New Iranian Cinema to just another fad in a long line of 'new wave' cinemas, and to dictate ideologically to this cinema at home. The purpose of this analysis is to begin to problematize or open up the concept of the New Iranian Cinema to new and sometimes contradictory views. This commitment is then carried a step further in chapter 2, which considers what happens to the concept of the New Iranian Cinema as a national cinema, and the concept of national cinema itself more generally, when it is viewed in relation to Iranian émigré filmmaking.

Iranian cinema after 1979

The parallels between the New Iranian Cinema and European art cinema begin with the historical contexts out of which both emerged. The Second World War had a devastating impact upon the film industries of many countries across continental Europe. It was out of this devastation, nonetheless, that many of the world's most important and influential cinematic movements arose. Similarly, the 1978–79

Iranian Revolution witnessed the upheaval of what had previously been a relatively healthy film industry within Iran. The infamous burning of the Rex Cinema in Abadan in August 1978, carried out by religious fundamentalists who objected to the theatre screening the Behrouz Vossoughi film *The Deer* (Massoud Kimia'i, 1976), and which killed hundreds of audience members inside the cinema, was an exceptionally bloody example of many similar acts of destruction perpetrated during the revolutionary period. Iran, therefore, lacked a strong cinematic infrastructure designed to support the growth and expansion of a national film industry following the Revolution. Indeed this is still a considerable problem in Iran's current film industry, the great majority of cinemas being concentrated in the capital city of Tehran. Naficy has outlined authoritatively the many other practical problems hindering the regeneration and growth of a national Iranian cinema and film culture in the immediate aftermath of the Revolution. These included

> the financial damage the industry suffered during the Revolution, a lack of government interest in cinema during the transitional period (for example, the first five-year budget plan in 1983 ignored cinema altogether), the absence of centralized authority and thus antagonistic competition over cinema between various factions (for example, MCIG [the Ministry of Culture and Islamic Guidance], the Foundation of the Disinherited, and the Revolutionary Committees), a lack of an appropriate cinematic model (there was no 'Islamic' film genre), heavy competition from imports, a drastic deterioration in the public image of the industry as a whole, the haphazard application of censorship, and the flight of many film professionals into exile.[8]

The increasing popularity of home video or VCD as well as satellite television (despite the issuing of a fatwa in 1994 outlawing the latter) has also had a detrimental impact on the Iranian film industry. Despite the specificity of these problems to post-revolutionary Iranian society, there was nothing uniquely 'Iranian' about the ensuing measures taken by the government, under pressure as they were from cinema owners and filmmakers alike, to address this crisis and deal with the impoverished state of the film industry. Like many postwar European governments that strove as much as they could to insulate their local film industries from the cultural and economic imperialism of Hollywood cinema, the Iranian government introduced a range of taxes, subsidies and quotas designed to revive and foster a national film culture. The types of financial support that were introduced included a reduction in the municipal tax on Iranian films (and an increase in the same tax on foreign imports); an increase in ticket prices; the purchase of more up-to-date technical equipment, which was sorely needed; and the exemption of institutions such as the Farabi Cinema Foundation from paying any customs duty on its imports.

These rudimentary yet vital measures were followed by more extensive policies, such as the introduction of a tax on the box-office receipts of every cinema in the country, to raise money for 'health, social security and injury insurance' for entertainers and filmmakers. A few years later, banks were permitted to offer long-term loans to support local film production. A ratings system was also established, whereby 'producers of highly rated films would earn increased revenues by exhibiting their films in higher-class theatres', entitling them to greater publicity and TV advertising. This system was eventually revised to introduce a ratings system, entitling Grade A filmmakers, for instance, to show their films at the best theatres and for longer periods of time, providing them with significant funding for their next project, and allowing them to bypass certain phases of the restrictive five-stage approval process operated by the Ministry for Culture and Islamic Guidance, which oversees the production of all films in Iran.[9] Although the system encouraged and rewarded quality film production, it also crudely equated quality with bankability, making it particularly difficult for Grade C filmmakers to further their careers financially and to shake off the stigma of their third-rate status. The increasing privatization of the Iranian economy, first under the government of Ali Akbar Hashemi Rafsanjani and then under that of Seyyed Mohammad Khatami, resulted in the reduction of subsidies for the local film industry as a whole. The results for Iran's film industry, however, were not quite as devastating as were initially envisaged. The predicted collapse of the industry has been offset to a large extent by the huge international success of Iranian cinema, and the significant amounts of foreign investment this recognition has entailed. As Naficy states, 'Iranian cinema will not be able to flourish as a viable, non-governmental, commercial industry without foreign markets.'[10]

Despite its draconian censorship laws, its continued intimidation and suppression of many filmmakers, and the often contradictory signals it sends out regarding home-grown cinema – as was demonstrated by the fate of *The Lizard*[11] (Kamal Tabrizi, 2004) – the Iranian government has overall played a significant role in resuscitating the country's film industry after the Revolution. In many ways the government has responded very shrewdly to the exigencies of the international film market, and of its own domestic film industry. It has provided space for a national art cinema to flourish, albeit one that is funded primarily by foreign investment, and whatever its motives for doing so may be. The steady increase in the number of films made annually over the past three decades, rising from a mere fifteen in 1982 to eighty-seven in 2001,[12] illustrates the effectiveness of their policies, though foreign investment has also contributed significantly to this proliferation. As Naficy acknowledges,

> Political consolidation, the centralization of imports and the passing of regulations concerning production and exhibition enhanced co-ordination and cohesiveness within the industry, brought cinema into line with Islamic values and criteria and improved overall film quality... throughout its existence, the Islamist regime has shown a surprising degree of flexibility and a great capacity for learning from its own mistakes... the internationalization and commercialization of the film industry has made possible the emergence of an inchoate, independent, auteurist cinema that is independent from Iranian tastes, commercial concerns and governmental control.[13]

It is perhaps this very independence from 'Iranian tastes, commercial concerns and governmental control' that has made the New Iranian Cinema so easily appropriable by foreign audiences. It is not merely this cinema's apparent cultural anonymity, however, that has contributed to its success overseas, and to it being celebrated as one of the world's foremost art cinemas. In what other ways, therefore, does the New Iranian Cinema lend itself to its relocation within the tradition of European art cinema?

The New Iranian Cinema as art cinema

On the one hand, 'art cinema' may appear to be a redundant concept. One has to go back nearly thirty years after all, to Steve Neale and David Bordwell's influential writings on the topic, to find any material that makes a serious attempt to tackle the idea and to explain what actually makes a film an 'art' film. On the other hand, there is still a great deal invested in the concept of art cinema (just as there is in the concept of the auteur) in the current international film market, even if it is often misused as a term of reference for any half-decent, non-English language, apparently non-commercial movie. Local arthouse cinema screens continue to provide valuable alternatives to the standardized, predominantly Anglophone fare found at faceless multiplex cinemas, while an internationally acclaimed director's name remains as strong a marketing tool as ever for their latest cinematic offerings.

Traditional notions of the monolithic and homogenizing impact of Hollywood's global reach have been replaced gradually by more subtle understandings of the heavily differentiated and diverse nature of most film reception. It is perhaps unsurprising, nonetheless, that the New Iranian Cinema found itself championed as a quintessential alternative 'art cinema', at a time when the increasing monopolization of the US film industry by several major Hollywood film studios blurred (and continues to do so) the lines separating US independent cinema from its commercial counterpart, and when most European film industries were perceived to be not only coming under serious threat from the encroachment of Hollywood cinema, but also imitating Hollywood stylistically in their own cinematic fare.

Neale ironically observes that as an institution art cinema relies just as heavily upon the notion of film as commodity as does so-called commercial cinema, catering as it does to a particular 'niche' within the international film market. Art cinema, maintains Neale, is, among many other things, a 'mechanism of discrimination'.

> Art Cinema has rarely disturbed or altered fundamentally the commodity-based structures, relations and practices

of what it likes nevertheless to label the 'commercial' film industry. It has merely modified them slightly. Certainly, radically avant-garde and insistently political practices have been persistently relegated either to its margins or else to a different social and cinematic space altogether.[14]

It is interesting, taking Neale's comments into account, to consider to what extent Kiarostami's standing on the international film scene as one of the most prominent art cinema auteurs is justified, especially in light of Mulvey's description of Kiarostami's films as having more in common with 'the avant-garde than art cinema'.[15] By turning to Bordwell's seminal essay on art cinema and the three main characteristics of art cinema that he identifies, we can begin to examine how Kiarostami has come to be held in such high regard, and the degree to which Kiarostami's films, and by extension the New Iranian Cinema itself, adhere to the paradigm of art cinema that Bordwell proposes. Which is not to suggest that Bordwell's understanding of art cinema is in any way definitive, or that it sufficiently identifies or catalogues all of the features of art cinema, textual and otherwise. Rather it is to acknowledge that Bordwell's essay remains the most significant and compelling exposition thus far on the term 'art cinema' and on the kinds of films that can be regarded as falling under its rubric. It provides one of the soundest bases upon which to consider how and to what extent Kiarostami's cinema can accurately be described as 'art cinema'.

Realism

Art cinema, which 'defines itself explicitly against the classical narrative mode, and especially against the cause–effect linkage of events', is 'realistic', claims Bordwell, not only because it shows us 'real locations', but also because it uses 'psychologically-complex' characters.[16] In contrast to the two-dimensional, objective-driven protagonists of Hollywood cinema, the characters found in art films 'lack defined desires and goals...[sliding] passively from one situation to another'. This does not mean, however, explains Bordwell, that the journeys these characters undertake, be they physical or otherwise, are always completely arbitrary. There is typically some underlying reason or motivation for their actions (or lack thereof rather), usually some 'rough shape' to their movements.

The importance of the 'realistic' qualities of art cinema that Bordwell identifies in the case of Kiarostami's cinema will be clear enough to anyone who has seen a Kiarostami film. Whether it is the film director from *And Life Goes On…*, Mr Badi from *Taste of Cherry*, or Behzad, the leader of the Tehran film crew from *The Wind Will Carry Us*, each character is distinguished by their seemingly endless wanderings through the landscapes they inhabit, and by their chance meetings with the people they encounter. In every instance, however, each character is in search of some elusive object of desire. In the film director's case it is the two child actors in *Where Is the Friend's House?* who are feared dead following the earthquake that devastated northern Iran in 1991. In Mr Badi's case it is a willing assistant in his quest to commit suicide, and by extension death itself. In Behzad's case it is milk, the village girl Zeynab and, more apparently, the documentary footage of the mourning ritual he and his film crew travel to Siah Darreh to record. In certain respects, these characters' desires are satisfied; in other respects they are not.

The circuitous paths along which these characters venture provides them with sufficient space 'to express and explain their psychological states',[17] another essential feature of Bordwell's understanding of art cinema's 'realism'. In Kiarostami's films this 'space' is typically the inside of a moving vehicle, within which the central characters engage in lengthy, meandering conversations with fellow travellers and momentary acquaintances they pick up along the way. In Kiarostami's films, however, very rarely do these conversations, these opportunities for the characters to 'express and explain' themselves, ever truly lead to a fuller understanding of the character's state of mind. Neither do they provide any form of 'therapy' or 'cure', or any kind of emotional or psychological catharsis for Kiarostami's characters. In *Taste of Cherry*, for instance, Mr Badi never reveals to any of his passengers why he seeks to kill himself, despite their persistent supplications. Indeed, if the lost souls of art cinema that Bordwell describes are 'slow to act…[yet] tell all',[18] then Kiarostami's characters are equally, if not more, slow to act and yet by contrast refuse to tell all. As Alberto Elena remarks of *Taste of Cherry*, 'Kiarostami completely rejects any psychological approach', although the landscapes

Mr Badi drives through would appear to reflect his changing outlook on life throughout the film.[19]

Kiarostami, furthermore, has displayed a consistently and, I would argue, deliberately equivocal attitude towards the merits of cinematic 'realism'. In 1993, in an interview with Farah Nayeri, he stated that his 'only inspiration is reality' and insisted that he has 'done nothing but depict reality.'[20] A mere four years later, however, in an interview conducted in 1997 with Nassia Hamid, he expresses a completely opposite view, declaring that 'reality cannot be encompassed. In my opinion the camera cannot register it.'[21]

Mulvey, in her appropriately entitled essay *Kiarostami's Uncertainty Principle*, has described Kiarostami's version of cinematic realism as defying any 'expected aesthetic and analytic framework'[22] (at least from a wholly 'Western' perspective). She highlights one moment from *And Life Goes On...* when a member of the film crew, the script girl, briefly enters the frame. The script girl's sudden presence within the frame is a clear visual paradox, disrupting the film's spatial and temporal verisimilitude, revealing the film to be a reconstruction of reality, shot not in the immediate aftermath of the earthquake but in some unspecified time following the disaster.[23] The effect is dislocating in a manner not entirely dissimilar to that experienced when a boom microphone accidentally protrudes into the frame in any number of poorly made Hollywood B movies, momentarily shattering the illusion of reality constructed on screen. Whereas in the latter the effect is usually unintentional (not to mention amusing), in Kiarostami's case it is wholly deliberate, a calculated attempt to distinguish between the reality in front of the camera and the reality behind the camera, what Mulvey calls 'the reality of the cinema, always a construction, and the reality that happens essentially elsewhere'.[24]

This distinction between reality and cinematic 'realism' is taken to extremes in Kiarostami's Koker and Poshteh trilogy, with each successive film in the cycle exposing the artificiality of its predecessor. It has already been noted, for instance, that the search for the two child actors from *Where Is the Friend's House?* provides the narrative pretence for *And Life Goes On...*. Similarly, *Through the Olive Trees* opens with a Brechtian scene, in which the actor Mohammad Ali Keshavarz directly addresses the camera, informing the viewer that in the film they are about to watch he will portray the filmmaker Abbas

Kiarostami, directing a scene from *And Life Goes On…*. In many of Kiarostami's films, therefore, there is a deliberate, concentrated effort to remind the viewers time and again that they are watching a movie, denying them the opportunity to lose themselves in the 'world of the film'. In this respect Kiarostami's self-reflexive brand of cinematic 'realism' seems a thoroughly postmodern construct, a brand which stands in stark contrast to the psychological realism of modernist art cinema (Bordwell does distinguish, though somewhat unsatisfactorily, between 'art cinema' and 'modernist cinema', describing the latter as less ambiguous than the former and more concerned with the 'split of narrative structure from cinematic style').[25]

Although Kiarostami invites clear parallels with French New Wave directors such as Jean-Luc Godard and François Truffaut, in his preference for character-based (rather than plot-driven) narratives and in his efforts to expose the inherent dishonesty of the filmmaking process, in other respects his films move beyond the clear-cut anti-Hollywood binarism of so-called modernist art cinema. Defying easy categorization or clear-cut definitions, many of Kiarostami's films present a disorienting blend of reality and fiction, intimating the existence of other realities beyond the frame of the camera.

Authorship

Art cinema 'foregrounds the author as a structure in the film's system', argues Bordwell, emphasizing the director's role as a 'formal component, the overriding intelligence organizing the film for our comprehension'. The authorial expressiveness found in art cinema is ostensibly in marked contrast to the institutionalized anonymity and narrative accessibility of Hollywood cinema. 'Within this frame of reference,' continues Bordwell, 'the author is the textual force "who" communicates (what the film is *saying*?) and "who" expresses (what is the artist's *personal vision*?).'[26]

Many analyses of Kiarostami's cinema thus far have themselves taken the form of classic auteur studies, in the mould that Bordwell proposes, viewing Kiarostami himself as *the* defining influence, the primary creative force that provides shape and uniformity to this eclectic yet remarkably consistent body of work. There are certainly enough stylistic and thematic similarities running throughout

Kiarostami's *oeuvre* (with the notable exception of *The Report* [1978]) to support such a reading. Indeed the degree to which Kiarostami explicitly inscribes *himself* (or an actor portraying himself) into his films (specifically, *And Life Goes On...* and *Through the Olive Trees*) makes them doubly receptive to such an interpretation.

The following quote from Bordwell's essay, with a few minor additions of my own, hopefully illustrates the extent to which Kiarostami's films conform to and reinforce the authorial conventions expected of 'art cinema':

> The competent viewer watches the film expecting not order in the narrative but stylistic signatures in narration: technical touches (Truffaut's freeze frames, Antonioni's pans, [Kiarostami's long takes]) and obsessive motifs (Bunuel's anticlericalism, Fellini's shows, Bergman's character names, [Kiarostami's vistas, see figures 1–4]). The film also offers itself as a chapter in an *oeuvre*. This strategy becomes especially apparent in the convention of the multi-film work (*The Apu Trilogy*, Bergman's two trilogies, Rohmer's 'Moral Tales,' and Truffaut's Doinel series [and Kiarostami's 'Koker and Poshteh' trilogy, or Makhmalbaf's 'Cinema' trilogy]. The

Figure 1 Stylistic signatures and obsessive motifs; from *Where Is the Friend's House?*

Figure 2 Stylistic signatures and obsessive motifs; from *Through the Olive Trees*

Figure 3 Stylistic signatures and obsessive motifs; from *Taste of Cherry*

Figure 4 Stylistic signatures and obsessive motifs; from *The Wind Will Carry Us*

initiated catch citations: references to previous films by the director [e.g., *And Life Goes On...* and *Through the Olive Trees*] or to works by others (e.g., the New Wave homages) [e.g., the appearance of Makhmalbaf in *Close Up* (1989)].[27]

Kiarostami himself, however, echoing his contradictory views on cinematic realism, has expressed equally contradictory opinions on his own role as a director. In the Hamid interview mentioned above, on the one hand, he asserts that 'in cinema it's the message of the filmmaker that is important, not how close to reality the film is'; on the other hand, he significantly downplays his role as a 'textual force' that attempts to either convey a message or express his own personal views to the audience through his films. On the contrary, it is rather the audience that bears the responsibility of making sense of his films. 'The film-maker can only raise questions,' states Kiarostami, 'and it is the audience who should seek the answer, who should have the opportunity for reflection to find questions in their own mind to complete the unfinished part of a work. So there are as many different versions of the same film as there are members of the audience.' From this statement it would appear that Kiarostami places a far greater emphasis upon the ability of the audience themselves to construe meanings from his films, than he does upon his own ability to express his particular artistic vision to the audience.

The statement recalls the comments made by Kiarostami some four years earlier in the aforementioned Nayeri interview, when discussing the film *And Life Goes On...* and its consideration of the significance of mourning. Once again, Kiarostami emphasizes the importance of the role the audience play in interpreting his films. What is interesting to note, however, is that although Kiarostami characteristically dismisses the desirability, and indeed even the possibility, of attempting to communicate a clear message to the audience, his reasoning on this occasion does allow for the notion that the film, and hence its director, possesses its own opinions on the issues it is addressing, and its own answers to the questions it is raising, while at the same encouraging the audience to think for themselves.

> As François Truffaut once said, 'If you have a message for the spectator, go to the post office and send him a telegram.' The only thing art can do is encourage the audience to think, in this case, to ponder the meaning of mourning. I hope the audience will wonder why, for example, a person who is mourning a beloved has to wait a whole year to marry? Perhaps the audience will come to *the conclusion the film wished them to reach*; alternatively, they may conclude that it is good to mourn, weep and wear black. As directors, we have no right to pronounce judgements. Our mission is to raise issues.[28] (my emphasis)

The above quote reveals a far more nuanced understanding of the film-viewing experience, one that recognizes the audience as capable of thinking on two levels, *taking* meaning from the images unfolding before their eyes, at the very same time as they *give* meaning to these images. In this respect Kiarostami's cinema represents an interesting reconceptualization of the role of the director. Rather than proclaim the death of the author or overstate the complete autonomy of the viewer, Kiarostami aims to place himself and his audience on an equal footing with each other, envisioning the film-viewing experience as a two-way process, the film becoming a meeting ground between two empirical subjects, a site of interpolation and negotiation. In this sense, without wishing to imply that Kiarostami's films are somehow fundamentally secular in nature, his cinema is a thoroughly *democratic* cinema.

In Kiarostami's cinema this resistance to definitiveness – or to 'certainty', as Mulvey might put it – manifests itself in the polysemous nature of the films themselves, in particular in their lack of a clear-cut resolution, what Bordwell might call their 'ambiguity', the third defining trait of art cinema he identifies. The 'ambiguity' of Kiarostami's cinema shall be considered shortly. What is important to note at this point, in relation to how the concept of authorship inflects our understanding of Kiarostami's cinema as art cinema, is that in Kiarostami's case this polysemy or ambiguity becomes so frequent, and hence so expected on the part of his viewing audience, that it eventually becomes the authorial signature in itself, the directorial motif that comes to encapsulate and, therefore, essentialize Kiarostami's diverse and frequently indefinable filmmaking style.

Kiarostami's desire to diminish his own 'presence' within the films he makes is displayed most starkly in his more recent cinematic offerings such as *10* (2002) and *Five* (2005), both of which, composed as they are of several series of extremely lengthy static shots, seemingly reduce the degree of directorial control to an absolute minimum, although *10* in particular is deceptively complex in its structural organization. There is a sense, however, in which Kiarostami cannot escape the malleability of auteur theory as it is typically practised in Film Studies, seeming as it does to anticipate and preclude his attempts to curtail his own creative autonomy and impart more interpretative freedom to the viewer. Indeed, despite these attempts, auteur-based studies of his cinema continue to be informed by an understanding of authorship similar, if not identical, to the idea outlined by Bordwell above.

Such readings of Kiarostami's films have their merits. Many of Kiarostami's films *are* after all very similar in their methodically and deliberately considered open-endedness. Nevertheless, these readings do serve, somewhat ironically, to integrate Kiarostami's films into a European tradition of a fundamentally auteur-based notion of 'art cinema', closing Kiarostami's films off to the kind of interpretative openness to which he so strongly aspires. However, as the chapter on the films of Sohrab Shahid Saless will hopefully illustrate, auteur theory can be a valuable tool. By identifying certain thematic and stylistic traits running throughout a director's body of work, and viewing them as a consistent reflection of their personal artistic vision, the concept of authorship can help to enrich our understanding of a director's *oeuvre* and guard against overly reductive interpretations, such as, in Saless's case, for instance, that his German films can be defined almost exclusively by an overriding, allegorical concern with the experience of exile. Moreover, chapter 4 is intended to demonstrate the connections between the films of Saless and those of Kiarostami, bringing this overview of post-revolutionary Iranian filmmaking in a sense full circle, highlighting the physical and artistic links between the New Iranian Cinema and Iranian émigré filmmaking.

Ambiguity

The open-endedness of many of Kiarostami's films, and hence their ambiguity, is where he most clearly invites comparisons with the directors of European art cinema. 'The art film is nonclassical in that it foregrounds deviations from the classical norm – there are certain gaps and problems,' explains Bordwell. 'But these very deviations are *placed*, resituated as realism (in life things happen this way) or authorial commentary (the ambiguity is symbolic).' This measured ambiguity ideally provokes questions in the minds of the audience, questions that the film does not try to answer as such. Rather the film offers a number of possibilities, a degree of uncertainty that the informed viewer enjoys and acknowledges as deliberate. However, 'if the organizational scheme of the art film creates the occasion for maximizing ambiguity,' continues Bordwell, 'how to conclude the film? The solution is the open-ended narrative. Given the film's episodic structure and the minimization of character goals, the story will often lack a clear-cut resolution.'[29]

Such a strategy certainly seems to inform some of Kiarostami's most famous films. By the end of *And Life Goes On...*, for instance, we are none the wiser as to whether the two child actors from *Where Is the Friend's House?* survived the earthquake. Likewise, by the end of *Taste of Cherry* it is by no means clear whether Mr Badi has successfully committed suicide. Both films instead conclude before their central characters reach the end of their respective journeys, or in Mr Badi's case, before he reaches the point of death (though the closing sequence of *Taste of Cherry* does show the actor who portrays Mr Badi alive and well, conversing with the director and other actors who appeared earlier in the film, revealing everything that has come before it to be a construct). Such conclusions direct the viewer to what Mulvey has described as 'a level of perception and understanding beyond the desire to 'what know happens in the end'.[30]

This strategy extends to Kiarostami's earlier films also. As Geoff Andrew has noted, with reference to Kiarostami's first short film, *Bread and Alley* (1970), as well as his later films for Kanun (Centre for the Intellectual Development of Children and Young Adults), although it is 'faintly didactic ... it is never remotely 'preachy', and it's difficult to say with any certainty just what lesson we are supposed to take away from it'.[31]

There exist some notable exceptions to this rule, however. *Where Is the Friend's House?*, for example, concludes with the safe return of Mohammad's homework book, although it is a visibly winding and indirect path by which this resolution is eventually reached. Similarly, though the severely minimalist quality of the concluding shot of *Through the Olive Trees* would perhaps suggest a more openly interpretative framework, the film leaves the audience in little doubt as to the reciprocal nature of Tahereh's response to Hossein's constant confessions of love.

Hamid Dabashi takes a somewhat similar view of this shot in his 1995 *Critique* essay on the film, insofar as he argues that the shot is far from ambiguous. Where I take issue with Dabashi's argument, however, is in his contention that the final shot of *Through the Olive Trees*, and indeed Kiarostami's cinema as a whole, rather than being enigmatic or open to interpretation, is innately resistant to interpretation altogether. Instead, by recognizing the sheer materiality of the physical world through the unrelenting gaze of Kiarostami's camera, the final shot of *Through the Olive Trees* defies any tenuously symbolic or metaphorical readings, allowing the images to speak for themselves as it were.

> [Kiarostami] dwells comfortably, deliberately, and with an ease that disarms all concocted readings, in that ironic

space he crafts for his camera between fact and fantasy. One should not see this film with any set expectation of where the lines of demarcation are drawn between fact and fantasy, between the real and the concocted, between the received and the staged, between location and studio, living and acting. One has to let oneself loose and permit Kiarostami's camera work its magic and reveal a mode of being carved between any dual set of binary opposition... Under Kiarostami's gaze, reality is reread backward to a material irreducibility. At the moment of that material recognition, Kiarostami holds his camera constant and tries to negotiate a new definition of reality.[32]

However, as I have proposed above, Kiarostami tries not so much to *define* a new reality as he does to *imply* the existence of other realities beyond the diegetic world of the film. Dabashi takes his line of argument considerably further in his subsequent work, *Close Up*, in which he argues that all of Kiarostami's films prior to *The Wind Will Carry Us* are manifestly 'launched against interpretation'.[33] According to Dabashi, Kiarostami's early cinema represents not only the triumphant culmination of a particularly Iranian tradition of artistic resistance to metaphysical tyranny and essentialization, but also a victory against the totalizing power of hermeneutics in general.

> Kiarostami's career has been constitutional to a visual modulation of *sign* as hermeneutically resistant to cultural *signification*. This is the singular achievement of Iranian cultural modernity that has come to full creative fruition in Kiarostami's films. If, before, Kiarostami, we had poetically shattered the word to dislodge the metaphysical claim of signification to it, with Kiarostami, we have visually mutated the very contention of signification back to its glorious stage of *signation*, sensual *sign* before any metaphysical insistence on it to *significate*. The reason that Muslim ideologues in Iran have so violently attacked Kiarostami's film is precisely this disturbing stripping of the real from all its violent metaphysical claimants, which has visually allowed the *sign*

simply to *signate*, palpitate with semiotic sensuality, without ever lapsing into habitual modes of *signification*.[34]

There are clear echoes here of Susan Sontag's call for an 'erotics of art' in her essay *Against Interpretation*. As Donato Totaro has pointed out, however, Sontag is 'not against interpretation per se, but rules of interpretation', the systematic use of all-embracing, rigid theoretical paradigms, such as Freudianism, as a means of repetitively and redundantly *imposing* meaning upon works of art, rather than *revealing* meaning.

> [Sontag] is against the practise of using an interpretative grid over and over to "decode" disparate works of art. When done indiscriminately the films in question begin to look alike, and the process reveals more about the critic than the film. These type of interpretations are reductive (reducing the film to a preconceived model) and prescriptive rather than descriptive (based on sensual surface properties of the art).[35]

By contrast Dabashi's call, for viewers of Kiarostami's cinema to immerse themselves in the sheer sensuousness of his images rather than to interpret them, seems ideologically opposed not only to the metaphysical violence and 'hermeneutic paralysis' he so rightly critiques, but also to the act of interpretation on a more individualized, personal level, a viewpoint that is clearly at odds with Kiarostami's insistence on the role of the audience as an equal participant in deciphering and making meaning of his films, an insistence that Dabashi describes as disingenuous, a 'refusal to engage in a critical reading of his own cinema', a 'bogus democratic gesture, because who else is to decide other than the audience?'[36]

With *The Wind Will Carry Us*, argues Dabashi, Kiarostami has allowed his global success as a filmmaker to go to his head, pandering to Western audiences' Orientalist tastes for the 'exotic' and fascination with the 'Other', by creating what is essentially an ethnographic study of an Iranian-Kurdish village, if not from a 'Western' or First World perspective, then from a decidedly middle-class and urban viewpoint. One scene in particular bears the full brunt of

Dabashi's criticism, one in which the filmmaker Behzad, in search of some milk, follows a local peasant girl called Zeynab into the dark underground stable beneath her house, in order to try to seduce her. Composed almost entirely of one long, protracted, immobile single take, much like the final shot of *Through the Olive Trees*, the scene shows Zeynab sitting in the shadows of the stable milking her cow, as Behzad tries in vain to coax a reaction from her from off-screen, even going so far as to recite a Farough Farrokhzad poem, from which the film takes its title. Dabashi's polemic against this scene lambastes Kiarostami for ceasing to universalize Iranian dignity; though lengthy, the comment bears quotation in full and provides a sense of the vitriolic language Dabashi employs to critique this scene:

> From the moment that Kiarostami's camera leads us into the dark, dungeon-like stable where the girl is milking a cow until the moment the protagonist leaves with a bucketful of milk and a satisfied grin on his face, we pay through the nose for every pleasure we took in Kiarostami's not showing the private moments of souls exposed in his previous films, for every ounce of joy in not hearing Tahereh and Hossein converse at the end of *Through the Olive Trees*... We are punished for all these past delights and uplifting moments by having to watch this ghastly sequence of Kiarostami's camera seducing the mutely innocent peasant girl ... Kiarostami's mise-en-scène is a brutally accurate picture of dehumanization. From the vantage of Kiarostami's voyeuristic camera, all we see is the backside of the cow, with the girl squatting to milk her in the dim, dungeon-like depths of an ocular masturbation... Betraying every principle of visual decency that Kiarostami had honoured in all his previous films, the stable sequence in *The Wind Will Carry Us Away* is the nightmarish negation of every film he ever made, the return of all that his cinema had repressed, negated, and defied... What is particularly disturbing about the stable sequence is that Kiarostami's camera is so overwhelmingly powerful that it is not even aware of its power, and in this oblivion he exerts this power against the

weakest, most vulnerable, and mutest subject. The stable sequence is one of the most violent rape scenes in all cinema. Kiarostami fails in this film because he ceases to universalize this particular Iranian village ... he begins to particularize a universal indignity.[37]

What Dabashi overlooks in his analyses of these two scenes from *Through the Olive Trees* and *The Wind Will Carry Us*, however, is the relative simplicity of the former and the deceptive complexity of the latter. The problem with Dabashi's analysis of the stable scene, for instance, is the absolute intolerance it seems to show toward any other possible interpretations or alternative readings of this scene – in other words, its failure to recognize the scene's strongly polysemous nature. On the one hand, Behzad is very clearly trying to violate Zeynab, metaphorically speaking, by persistently asking her to reveal her face, while the camera similarly subjects Zeynab to its cold, impassive, unrelenting gaze. But on the other hand – as Jonathon Rosenbaum has observed in his book on Abbas Kiarostami, co-authored with Mehrnaz Saeed-Vafa – despite Behzad's repeated supplications, Zeynab *does not show her face*,[38] barely even acknowledging Behzad's presence throughout the scene (note also that for some reason Dabashi never refers to Zeynab by her actual name, despite it being clearly mentioned several times throughout the film). Seen in this light, Behzad's attempt to charm Zeynab, by loftily reciting a poem to her, appears to be as much a sign of desperation as it is one of patronizing condescension. What is also particularly amusing about the scene is the way in which Zeynab herself actually undercuts the romantic mood that Behzad is trying to create, by interrupting him before he manages to finish the poem, bluntly informing Behzad that the bucket is full of milk just as he is about to utter the poem's final lines.

Zeynab, moreover, is clearly much more in control of the space around her within this scene than Behzad. For instance, she has to guide Behzad in and out of the stable, to save him from tripping over or bumping into objects. Unlike Zeynab, Behzad is clearly out of his element. He emerges from the stable looking more like a fool for attempting to woo Zeynab than a contented lecher who has successfully seduced his prey. Moreover, Zeynab actually makes her mother return the money that Behzad offers them for the milk, as accepting it would be to allow Behzad to 'possess' her, symbolically speaking, to pay for the time they spent together, suggesting that Kiarostami is fully aware of the moral ambiguities of this scene and the dubious nature of the relationship between the filmmaker and his subject.

Zeynab also uses the darkness within the cave to her advantage, to better conceal herself from Behzad's prying eyes, as well as from the gaze of Kiarostami's camera. Indeed if the unrelenting gaze of Kiarostami's camera in *The Wind Will Carry Us* ultimately fails to rescue these particular signs of Iranian life from the hermeneutic paralysis of interpretation – and to be honest, symbolically heavy-handed as it undoubtedly is, this is not one of the most subtle scenes in Kiarostami's cinema – then it equally fails to force its own kind of voyeuristic paralysis upon Zeynab. Through her language, through her silence, through her movements and behaviour, Zeynab retains a great deal of agency and autonomy, not only from Behzad, but also from Kiarostami's camera itself.

Rather than constituting a lurid ethnographic study, therefore, *The Wind Will Carry Us* seems to be a meditation on the impossibility of capturing on film the essence of this particular Iranian village, and the ethical problems involved in attempting to do so. Dabashi, for instance, notes with great insight the way in which the unequal domestic power relations between Iran (represented by Behzad and the city of Tehran from which he comes) and its ethnic minorities such as the Kurds (represented by the villagers of Siah Darreh) mirror the unequal global power relations between the 'West', represented by metropolitan centres such as London and Washington, and what Dabashi calls their 'satellite peripheries', those countries which have been culturally colonized and exoticized by Western media and so-called nativist filmmakers such as Kiarostami.[39]

What Dabashi's observation fails to take into account, however, is the extent to which the character of Behzad, aside from his physical resemblance to Kiarostami, represents a critical self-portrait on the part of the director, a highly unsympathetic portrayal of the kind of nativist filmmaker which critics such as Dabashi have accused Kiarostami himself of becoming. Indeed, Behzad actually fails in everything he sets out to do in the film. As pointed out above, he fails miserably in his efforts to seduce Zeynab. He also fails to record the mourning ritual following the elderly woman's funeral, the very purpose for which he and his film crew travel to Siah Darreh in the first place, as she stubbornly refuses to die during the course of their stay. It is also important to note that Behzad never even sees this old woman in the flesh – just as he never really 'sees' Zeynab – but rather receives constant updates about her faltering health from the young schoolboy Farzad.

This play on being *seen* and *unseen*, which is illustrated vividly by the aforementioned stable sequence, constitutes a major theme running throughout the entire film, especially in respect to those characters who remain unseen or, perhaps more significantly, gradually *disappear* from view as the film progresses. It is, moreover, intimately linked with the film's unflattering depiction of Behzad as incapable of establishing any meaningful connections with any of the inhabitants of Siah Darreh, in particular Farzad, who acts as Behzad's guide about the village for the majority of the film. Farzad represents the best opportunity for Behzad to form a firm friendship. Behzad, however, hurts Farzad's feelings when he lashes out at the boy for revealing to his film crew that the old woman's condition is actually improving. The boy ostensibly rejects Behzad's subsequent attempt at an apology, refusing to shake his hand and – in a later scene during which Behzad drives about Siah Darreh desperately searching for help to rescue Zeynab's lover Youssef, who has been buried alive – declining Behzad's offer of a lift in his car. In contrast to previous scenes in the film in which Behzad and Farzad converse with each other, which employ a traditional-shot/reverse-shot pattern, in this scene the camera remains firmly fixed on Behzad sitting in the driver's seat of his car, as he looks out of the window addressing Farzad, who remains off-screen. The viewer continues to hear Farzad but never sees him again after his falling out with Behzad. In a similar fashion, we never see Zeynab again after the stable sequence, after Behzad's failed attempt to seduce her. His film crew also desert him, mysteriously disappearing midway through the film (it is unlikely they returned to Tehran, for they leave behind the car in which they came to Siah Darreh). As the film progresses, as Behzad becomes gradually more and more alienated from his surroundings and the people around him, our view of Siah Darreh becomes increasingly restricted and its inhabitants ever more elusive.

This tension between being seen and unseen is suggested very early in the film, when Behzad tries to take some photos of the woman working in the local teahouse. As the woman and her husband argue, Behzad surreptitiously tries to take some photos of their quarrel but is forbidden from doing so by the wife. For the majority of this scene, the camera lingers on Behzad as he watches the couple argue off-screen. This is significant because it demonstrates how the audience's point of view is not constantly filtered through Behzad's perspective. The audience rather spends as much time watching Behzad observing the world around him, and his reactions to what he sees, as they do actually 'seeing' Siah Darreh through Behzad's eyes.

We are reminded of this scene later in the film when Behzad passes through the teahouse once again and, in contrast to his previously inquisitive behaviour, expresses no interest in the fact that a major quarrel has obviously occurred between the wife and her husband. The awkward silence between the two, as well as the stern looks on both of their faces, betrays as much information. Preoccupied with the making (or rather non-making) of his documentary, however, Behzad becomes increasingly detached from and disinterested in the world around him, while the viewer is invited to observe details Behzad fails to notice.

The film's penultimate scene provides a suitably ironic denouement to the film's meditation on the theme of 'looking'. As Behzad leaves Siah Darreh at dawn empty-handed, with no film crew or documentary to speak of, he manages to take some quick photos of a procession of women passing through the village. This march may or may not be the old woman's funeral procession. Although they are all wearing the same clothes, the women certainly do not appear to be in mourning as such. Indeed their calm and orderly behaviour contrasts starkly with the more dramatic description of the mourning ritual Behzad received earlier in the film from a local schoolteacher, who informed Behzad that the female mourners performed acts of self-mutilation, scarring their own faces. Nevertheless, these photos, taken fleetingly from the window of Behzad's car just before his departure, these stolen images as it were, are the only physical proof by the end of the film that he was ever in Siah Darreh. The village, and perhaps by extension Iran, and even reality itself, the film would seem to suggest, are things that can be seen or captured only in brief glimpses and snapshots and can never be comprehended fully or in their entirety.

One of the problems with this hypothesis, and with *The Wind Will Carry Us* in general, is the way in which it suggests that the myth of an underlying Iranian reality is somehow impenetrable or unknowable and, therefore, somehow more 'authentic' and/or 'real'. Indeed the way the narrative of the film is structured itself contributes to this sense of mythic time slowly unfolding, with one day seamlessly blending into another, until it is eventually revealed a little over an hour into the film that Behzad and his film crew have been in the village for over two weeks. The fact that *The Wind Will Carry Us* is one of Kiarostami's rarer works, insofar as it is not overtly self-reflexive, and that it does attempt to expose the artificiality (or disrupt the verisimilitude) of the diegetic world portrayed on screen adds to this sense of languor. In constructing a completely insulated cinematic world for the first time since *Where Is the Friend's House?* in 1987, Kiarostami defied the expectations of audiences in the 'West', who no doubt expected another self-reflexive tour de force. It is arguably this complete absence of self-reflexivity that garnered the film such a hostile response from various quarters.

The Wind Will Carry Us nevertheless remains a rigorous interrogation of the filmmaking ethic, or rather of lack thereof, behind the very kinds of works upon which Kiarostami's reputation as a renowned international auteur is based. In this respect, it is significant that *The Wind Will Carry Us*, made in 1999, falls in-between Kiarostami's other films *Taste of Cherry* and *10*, made in 1997 and 2002 respectively, because in many ways it appears to be a transitional film for Kiarostami, an exorcism of sorts, of all of the thematic concerns, aesthetic features and directorial signatures that had come to epitomize his cinema, before he embarked upon the bold stylistic experiment that was *10*.

To return to the closing shot of *Through the Olive Trees*, Dabashi is correct to observe that there is nothing inherently ambiguous or 'enigmatic' about this shot. But this is not because the shot itself is innately opposed to interpretation. Rather it is because the resolution that Kiarostami provides on this occasion is so simple and so *unambiguous* in its meaning, that it defies any *misinterpretation*. Indeed the conclusion of *Through the Olive Trees* is quintessentially a 'happy ending', in the strictest Hollywood sense of the term. Although there is no romantic kiss or lasting embrace, the boy (Hossein) clearly 'gets the girl' (Tahereh). Which is not to say that the shot completely defies analysis or is closed off to other possible forms of interpretation. There still remain the obvious questions of 'What exactly did Tahereh say?' and 'How did she say it?' It is certainly significant that the shift in the film's score, from pensive to joyful, is timed to coincide exactly, and moreover *ambiguously*, with the cessation of Hossein's pursuit of Tahereh. For as Tahereh finally turns to Hossein and acknowledges his presence, the music stops as she utters her reply. Despite the momentary silence on the soundtrack, the audience cannot hear Tahereh, because of her physical distance from the camera. This momentary silence is a blank space, the missing piece in a cinematic jigsaw puzzle that is left empty to be filled in by the viewer. As Elena argues, although the final shot of *Through the Olive Trees* is decidedly unambiguous, Kiarostami continues to encourage the audience to play an active part in completing the film, in making meaning of what they see and hear or, as in this instance, of what they *do not* see and hear.

> The audience is made to flounder straight away among the various planes and levels through which the film moves, invited to let themselves be carried away by this tide of confusion and occasional narrative obscurity, a closely woven web that Kiarostami unmistakably delights in weaving. But suppressing the audience's participation could not be further from the director's intentions. Instead, by these means he invites us to play an active part in the story (which despite everything does exist in the film); he demands we take up a stance with regard to what we are seeing... The ethos of Kiarostami's view of the world lies in this inherent and fundamental ambiguity.[40]

As Tahereh turns away from Hossein and continues on her way, the music recommences, and Hossein runs back along the path whence they came, visibly skipping and jumping with joy. The shift in musical mood thus also functions *meaningfully*, to reflect Hossein's inner emotions. Although Dabashi's emphasis on the physicality or sensual quality of this shot is certainly helpful in outlining the elusively erotic quality of many of Kiarostami's images, his argument is fundamentally compromised, somewhat paradoxically, by the prescriptive interpretative paradigm of *anti-interpretation* via which he understands Kiarostami's cinema overall, and to which he demands all of Kiarostami's film adhere. Or to put it more simply, Dabashi's argument that the shot in question is inherently opposed or resistant to interpretation is *itself* inevitably an interpretation, an opinion that has been reached by way of an analysis of the formal properties and the aesthetic qualities of the shot. It is, therefore, a contradictory and unsustainable position. Kiarostami himself has spoken of his original intention to end the film on a far more inconclusive note, which would have seen Hossein and Tahereh gradually disappear from view, Hossein's love perhaps forever unrequited. What eventually changed his mind, explains Kiarostami, was his desire to depart briefly from reality, to break down the class barriers separating Hossein and Tahereh, and to fantasize momentarily:

> At first I thought of leaving the couple to walk slowly away into the distance until they could no longer be seen. I thought there would always be an insuperable class barrier between them and that there was therefore no reason why the girl would consent... [Later] I said to myself, though, that I could leave tradition to one side and dream a little in this sequence, wishing and suggesting that she finally gives him a positive answer... Film-making gives me this opportunity: to forget about reality sometimes, to break away from it and dream from time to time. And in my opinion, the audience has the same feelings at that moment, because they share the same desire to change reality.[41]

Therefore, as noted above, in his analyses of the stable sequence from *The Wind Will Carry Us* and the closing shot of *Through the Olive Trees*, Dabashi underestimates the complexity of the former and overestimates the simplicity of the latter. Like most of Kiarostami's cinema, the final shot of *Through the Olive Trees* is ambiguous in certain respects, and unambiguous in others, walking a fine line between certainty and uncertainty, just as Kiarostami himself performs a subtle balancing act between addressing issues of particular importance to Iranian society, and appealing to the tastes of the international art cinema audiences upon whose continued interest and patronage his career as a filmmaker so vitally depends.

The ambiguity of Kiarostami's cinema nevertheless has its roots more in the traditions of pre-revolutionary Iranian filmmaking than in the conventions of European art cinema. Indeed the closing shot of *Through the Olive Trees* reveals not so much a penchant for ambiguity, considered or otherwise, as it does a preference for an indirect, understated mode of narration that is reminiscent of the films of Sohrab Shahid Saless. The connections between the films of Saless and Kiarostami will be considered at greater length in chapter 4. It is regrettable to observe at this point, however, that Dabashi, who has in the past rightly challenged accusations levelled at Kiarostami, that the director is guilty of 'self-hatred, of being incapable of anything but disgust and denigration for his actors, audience, and ultimately himself and his national and cultural identity',[42] has eventually come to reiterate these very same indictments.

At the crossroads

There are clear limitations, therefore, to viewing Kiarostami's films constantly through the prism of European art cinema. As noted previously, however, such an approach is not without merit. At best, it can serve as a means of introducing us to the more culturally specific aspects of contemporary filmmaking in Iran; take, for example, Godfrey Cheshire's 1993 article *Where Iranian Cinema Is*, where we are introduced to both Kiarostami and Makhmalbaf as latter-day versions of Godard and Truffaut respectively.[43]

In this vein, Devin Orgeron's 2002 *Cineaction* essay remains one of the most insightful and well-considered analyses of the intimate links between Kiarostami's cinema and the traditions of European art cinema. It thus provides a useful counterpoint to the blanket application of Bordwell's model of 'art cinema' to Kiarostami's cinema, an application which, despite the arguments made above, this chapter might otherwise be construed as endorsing. In brief, Orgeron focuses primarily on each cinema's shared use of the road, an image running through nearly all of Kiarostami's works, as a symbol 'to comment critically upon international and particularly non-Western cinema's longstanding and conflicted relationships with the image-machines of America and Hollywood in particular'.⁴⁴ This symbolism, argues Orgeron, explicitly ties Kiarostami to other prominent European art cinema directors such as Godard, Vittorio De Sica, and Wim Wenders, all of whom use the motif of the road in their films in a similarly metaphorical and critical manner. Orgeron provides one particularly illuminating and compelling comparison between Godard and Kiarostami's critical employment of US (in Kiarostami's case, also European) iconography, demonstrating equally dubious attitudes towards American (and once again in Kiarostami's case, more generally, 'Western') cultural imperialism.

> Godard's fascination with the automobile and the road is rooted in his fascination with (and skepticism of) all things 'American.' The automobile is an inarguably American item, and Godard enhances and highlights its Americanness by frequently using American cars in his films. The automobile, however, is also metaphorically important to Godard's cinema. It is the embodiment of transportability and signifies the global movement of American culture... Kiarostami's films are similarly self-reflexive, similarly skeptical of the curious mobility of Western culture. One of Kiarostami's earliest Godardian experiments is explicitly concerned with highways. *The Solution* (1978) is a highly formal, eleven-minute film following a man on an isolated mountain road as he rolls a newly repaired tire to his stranded automobile... The film's protagonist drives a French Citroën, wears a Vietnam-era American flak jacket, and his actions are set to Western classical music. Like his Italian and French narrative predecessors, the protagonist in this short film is surrounded by signifiers of cultural mobility at the moment of his own problematic stasis.⁴⁵

Orgeron also draws the reader's attention to one particularly telling moment in *Taste of Cherry*, when Mr Badi encounters a young man wearing a UCLA t-shirt, which Orgeron interprets as a wry commentary, a 'not-so-subtle joke about the reach of American culture' as well as about the 'film-school culture that has deemed Kiarostami the auteur of the moment'.⁴⁶ Orgeron, however, acknowledging the importance of Cheshire's efforts to place the New Iranian Cinema within its particular historical and cultural contexts, also notes how Kiarostami's cinema is equally indebted to a 'tradition of Persian philosophy and literature ... [that has] used the form of the journey to comment upon the contemporary condition'.[47]

It is hopefully evident by this point how often Kiarostami's characters embark upon journeys, spiritual as well as physical, although they are often apparently ignorant of the potentially transformative aspects of their travels. Though, as has been noted already, very rarely do Kiarostami's characters ever reach the end of their journeys. Their return home or their arrival at some new destination is frequently suspended, their attainment of another level of self-awareness and understanding eternally delayed or left in doubt.

The more comprehensive and nuanced view of Kiarostami's cinema, and of the New Iranian Cinema in general, found in Orgeron's essay is infinitely more conducive not only to a better understanding of its more esoteric aspects, but also to a deeper appreciation of its very real links to Italian neo-realism, the French New Wave, and the New German Cinema. It also sheds light on the means by which Iranian filmmakers such as Kiarostami negotiate their own paths through the narrow and occasionally conflicting channels of the international film industry.

Other factors, of course, have also clearly contributed to the increased popularity of the New Iranian Cinema in Europe and North America. The largely progressive image of Iran that emerges from these films, for instance, significantly undermines the demonization of the country by Western media following the Revolution (and, more recently, following 9/11). Besides Edward Said, known for his powerful critique of US media coverage of the Iranian Revolution and the ensuing hostage crisis,[48] Naficy has also written eloquently on the types of images and stereotypes that were endlessly recycled and circulated throughout the public domain by the media:

> Iran was converted to a sign system, consisting of a limited repertoire of discrete and disembodied signs often repeated ad nauseum: bearded and turbaned mullahs, thick from Khomeini, veiled women, raised fists, unruly and frantic mobs shouting 'Death to America', 'Death to Carter', and finally the image of the blindfolded American hostage which

opened the ABC's Nightline programme throughout the so-called 'hostage crisis'.[49]

Not only for European and US audiences, but also for Iranian audiences living overseas, the New Iranian Cinema provided a much needed contrast to this media onslaught. As Michael M. J. Fischer notes, 'At the first North American film festival where it was shown, *Bashu* elicited tears and cheers from a staunchly anti-revolutionary Iranian audience, which suddenly found itself confronted with evidence that not all that was happening in Iran was bad.'[50]

Admiration for the New Iranian Cinema, therefore, was not simply a matter of discovering an alternative cinema to oppose the dominance of Hollywood. For many of its advocates at home and abroad it was also an effective method of resisting the vilification of the Iranian people by the Western media, while for many Iranians living overseas it was clearly a cathartic process of sorts, a means of rediscovering and experiencing their country vicariously through the medium of film.

The sympathetic image of Iran that came to be associated with the New Iranian Cinema, however, was to a certain extent also complicit with the perpetuation of what Bill Nichols describes as the 'humanist framework' promoted by international film festivals. Nichols comments insightfully on how the film festival experience 'inflects and constructs the meanings we ascribe' to newly 'discovered cinemas', and on how the 'humanist framework' encouraged by festivals predisposes audiences to interpret a sometimes extremely diverse and contradictory body of films in a very one-dimensional and uniform way:

> The usual opening gambit in the discovery of new cinemas is the claim that these works deserve international attention because of their discovery by a festival... Films from nations not previously regarded as prominent film-producing countries [such as Iran in 1989] receive praise for their ability to transcend local issues and provincial tastes while simultaneously providing a window onto a different culture. We are invited to receive such films as evidence of artistic maturity – the work of directors ready to take their place

within an international fraternity of auteurs – and of a distinctive national culture – work that remains distinct from Hollywood-based norms in both style and theme ... To what extent does the humanist framework encouraged by film festivals and the popular press not only steer our readings in selected directions but also obscure alternative readings or discourage their active pursuit?[51]

The perhaps unexpected 'humanism' of the New Iranian Cinema has supplied a necessary counterpoint to the overwhelmingly negative media portrayal of Iran over the past three decades. Ironically, this 'humanism' has also helped to reinforce the legitimacy of the very institutions that, though often the only available outlets for such non-English language fare, arguably do just as much to misrepresent the sum total of a country's cinematic output, as they do to widen the knowledge of international film audiences.

Kiarostami is clearly foremost among the group of Iranian auteurs who, like other non-Western directors before them, such as Akira Kurosawa and Satyajit Ray, were 'discovered' by Western audiences via international film festivals. As if to bear out the continuing validity of Nichols's remarks, as the popularity of the New Iranian Cinema gained further momentum, many more directors were quickly 'discovered' and portrayed as being somehow representative of the entire spectrum of film production inside Iran. There is nothing particularly 'Iranian', however, about this process of constructing and defining a foreign national 'art cinema'. Just as a mere handful of European directors – such as Godard and Truffaut in the French New Wave, and Wenders, Werner Herzog and Rainer Werner Fassbinder in the New German Cinema – became representative of their country's cinema, so too post-revolutionary Iranian cinema has come to be typified by the works of a few internationally successful and acclaimed auteurs, most notably Kiarostami, Makhmalbaf, Dariush Mehrjui, Majid Majidi, Jafar Panahi and Bahram Beyza'i. This exclusive canon of male directors has nevertheless widened to incorporate important women directors such as Rakhshan Bani-Etemad, Tahmineh Milani and Samira Makhmalbaf.

Those who criticize the New Iranian Cinema's dependence on foreign markets often also fail to realize that there is nothing uniquely

'Iranian' about this phenomenon. Ask any self-respecting film buff who the quintessential British directors are, for instance, and they would most likely mention names such as Ken Loach, Mike Leigh, Terence Davies, and, if they were to be a bit more parochial, perhaps Lynne Ramsey or Peter Mullen in Scotland. None of these supposed ambassadors for 'British' film culture, however, much like their Iranian counterparts, enjoys substantial commercial success at the domestic box office. Like Iranian filmmakers, they rely upon an international art cinema and film festival circuit to market and distribute their films. To single out the New Iranian Cinema for its reliance on foreign markets, therefore, is particularly selective. Furthermore, in Iranian cinema there is arguably not as large a disparity between films that achieve international success and those that are successful domestically at the box office, as there is in the cinemas of other countries. Internationally acclaimed films such as *I'm Taraneh, 15* (Rassul Sadr-Ameli, 2001) and *Women's Prison* (Manijeh Hekmat, 2001), reached numbers 5 and 6 respectively in the 2002 box office top ten in Tehran. Over the past several years, many other Iranian films, praised overseas, have also enjoyed success at home, such as *The Girl in the Sneakers* (Sadr-Ameli, 1999, Iran) and *The Colour of Paradise* (Majid Majidi, 1999, Iran) and *Under the Skin of City* (Rakhshan Bani-Etemad, 2001). However, the number one box office hit of 2002, the big-screen version of the long-running and popular children's television show *Kolah, Ghermezi and Sarvenaz* (Iraj Tahmasb, 2001), named after its puppet protagonists, will probably never receive much international attention, though that should perhaps be attributed more to exclusionary practices of the international film festival circuit that Nichols so expertly examines, than to the film's quality.[52]

But if the 'humanism' of the New Iranian Cinema made it more susceptible to its appropriation and celebration in Europe and North America as an archetypal 'art cinema', then to what extent is this at odds with the Iranian government's own attempts to 'Islamize' Iranian cinema following the Revolution? In what way might a consideration of how accurately post-revolutionary Iranian cinema can be described as an 'Islamic' cinema contribute to our understanding of the New Iranian Cinema overall, or rather to the wider view of Iranian filmmaking that this book proposes?

An 'Islamic' cinema?

As Andrew Higson argues in his seminal 1989 essay *The Concept of National Cinema*, there are two primary methods of establishing 'the imaginary coherence' or 'specificity' of a national cinema. The first method is an outward-looking process, whereby the national cinema in question defines itself in opposition or contrast to other national cinemas, asserting its difference and 'otherness'. The second method is an inward-looking process, whereby the national cinema in question defines itself 'in relation to other already existing economies and cultures' within that nation-state.[53] The Iranian government appears quite clearly to have sought to define the national character of its country's cinema in a way that very strongly resembles both of the methods identified by Higson.

On the one hand, via the guidelines published in mid-1982 regulating the exhibition of films and videos within Iran, the government clearly sought to distinguish Iranian cinema from the 'morally corrupt' cinemas of Western nations (cinema itself was, after all, a Western-imported technology). Directly targeting films that – among other things – challenged the concept of monotheism, encouraged blasphemy, and compromised the political stability of the country and its government, these guidelines reflected the desire to imbue Iran's indigenous film production with specifically 'Islamic' values.[54] Despite the obvious similarities between the measures introduced by the Iranian government following the Revolution, to protect the country's domestic film industry from foreign competition, and those introduced by many post-Second World War European governments for the very same purpose, what distinguishes the Iranian case is its basis in a fear of ideological contamination.

On the other hand, the Iranian government also sought to purge the medium of the harmful influences with which it had come to be associated within Iran during the pre-revolutionary era. Indeed, if the loss of so many of its most gifted filmmakers following the Revolution represented for Iran an overwhelming physical break with its rich pre-revolutionary cinematic traditions, then the attempt to purify or 'Islamize' Iranian cinema symbolized a clear ideological break.

In 1996 the Ministry for Culture and Islamic Guidance issued a booklet further clarifying what themes were 'acceptable subject matter' for Iranian filmmakers (such as the Iran–Iraq war, the Revolution, the role of women in Iranian society).[55] The problem with such vague regulative guidelines, however, is that they are extremely open to interpretation. Furthermore, as Higson himself has elaborated more recently, despite the apparent applicability of his argument to post-revolutionary Iranian cinema, and indeed to most 'national' cinemas in general, the inadequacy of such a model, in addition to its underlying Eurocentrism and reductive binarism, is that it risks taking for granted the supposed homogeneity of the nation-state:

> There is undeniably a danger that my essay transformed a historically specific Eurocentric, even Anglocentric version of what a national cinema might be into an ideal category, a theory of national cinema in the abstract that is assumed to be applicable in all contexts...The problem with this formulation is that it tends to assume that national identity and tradition are already fully formed and fixed in place. It also tends to take borders for granted and to assume that those borders are effective in containing political and economic developments, cultural practice and identity. In fact of course, borders are always leaky and there is a considerable degree of movement across them (even in the most authoritarian states)...Seen in this light, it is difficult to see the indigenous as either pure or stable. On the contrary, the degree of cultural cross-breeding and interpenetration, not only across borders but also within them, suggests that modern cultural formations are invariably hybrid and impure. They constantly mix together different 'indigeneities' and are thus always re-fashioning themselves, as opposed to exhibiting an already fully formed identity.[56]

As if to bear out the validity of Higson's more recent observations, many post-revolutionary Iranian films have explored the diversity of post-revolutionary Iranian society. From films such as *Bashu, the Little Stranger* (Beyza'i, 1988), which focuses on the relationship between a young boy from war-torn southern Iran and a peasant woman from northern Gilan (neither can understand the other because they do not speak the same dialect, and in one scene the woman wonders at her inability to wash clean the boy's naturally darker skin); to films such as *The Wind Will Carry Us*, *A Time for Drunken Horses* (Bahman Ghobadi, 2000), *Baran* (Majidi, 2001) and *Turtles Can Fly* (Ghobadi, 2004), which examine the lives of Iran's minority Kurds; to the numerous films that hint at or confront directly the political, social and economic marginalization of Iran's minority Afghan populations (among them *The White Balloon* (Panahi, 1995, Iran), *Taste of Cherry* and *Djomeh* (Hassan Yektapaneh, 2000). All of these films examine the varied cultural make-up of contemporary Iran and its people and point to the impossibility of representing or viewing Iranian society as in any way monolithic or 'pure'.

Any attempt to impose uniformity upon the cinema of such a culturally and ethnically diverse country was perhaps doomed to failure. The hybridity of post-revolutionary Iranian society was not the only factor hindering the institutionalization of an Islamic cinema, however. Other factors included the fickle and unsystematic enforcement of the guidelines identified above. Whereas the classical Hollywood mode of production, as David Bordwell, Janet Staiger and Kristin Thompson have quite convincingly demonstrated, led to the institutionalization of a predominantly standardized aesthetic that emphasized narrative causality and psychological coherency, manifesting itself through such practices as continuity editing,[57] the *Iranian mode of production* that the Iranian government tried but failed to inculcate was an attempt to infuse Iranian cinema with a code of Islamic values that manifested itself at best at a narrative or thematic level, rather than at a stylistic one.

As Naficy also rightly points out, an 'Islamic' aesthetic can be seen to manifest itself to a certain extent through the complex representations of women in Iranian cinema, though it may be due more to legal necessity rather than an artistic impulse on the part of the filmmakers themselves. The restrictions imposed upon the depiction of women in Iranian films following the Revolution, and the predominantly formulaic but occasionally ingenious methods resorted to in order to portray female characters in a manner conforming to censorship laws, have directly affected the 'look' of post-revolutionary Iranian cinema:

> It is in the portrayal and treatment of women that the tensions surrounding the Islamization of cinema crystallize...

> Muslim women must be shown to be chaste and to have an important role in society as well as in raising God-fearing and responsible children. In addition, women were not to be treated like commodities or used to arouse sexual desires...To use women, a new grammar of film evolved, which included the following features: women actors being given static parts or filmed in such a way as to avoid showing their bodies...In addition, eye contact, especially when expressing 'desire', and touching between men and women were discouraged. All this meant that until recently women were often filmed in long-shot, with few close-ups or facial expressions.[58]

There is insufficient space here to do justice to the sheer variety of stylistic techniques that are employed to depict women in post-revolutionary Iranian cinema, such as the precise choice of shots, methods of framing and modes of performance. It hopefully suffices to observe that the restrained and desexualized portrayals of women in post-revolutionary Iranian cinema are a far cry from the decidedly more risqué depictions of women in pre-revolutionary Iranian cinema, although there are some exceptions on both sides. Films such as *Dash Akol* (Kimia'i, 1974) and *Prince Etehjab* (Bahman Farmanara, 1974) both contain female nudity (the latter even featuring a brief scene of nude female torture). Indeed one of the reasons why the representation of women has become such an enduring subject in discussions about the New Iranian Cinema (to the neglect of other important issues I would contend) is that it is one of the few easily discernible cornerstones which identify these films as uniquely 'Iranian' and upon which a specifically Islamic cinematic aesthetic can be seen to base itself.

Foremost among the problems hindering the institutionalization of an Islamic cinema was the inability to define clearly what exactly constituted an Islamic film aesthetic. This is not to suggest or maintain that any viable national cinema must pioneer or be tied to a distinctive film style, but rather to point to the difficulties of representing Islam aesthetically via the medium of cinema. As Oleg Grabar observes in his book *The Formation of Islamic Art*, though not with specific reference to cinema, the precise meanings attached to the word 'Islamic' when used to describe anything outside the rubric of Islam are decidedly vague.

> What does the word 'Islamic' mean when used as an adjective modifying the noun 'art'? What is the range of works of art that are presumably endowed with unique features? Is it comparable in kind to other artistic entities? 'Islamic' does not refer to the art of a particular region, for a vast proportion of the monuments have little if anything to do with the faith of Islam. Works of art demonstrably made by and for non-Muslims can appropriately be studied as works of Islamic art...[W]e are not very clear on what is really meant by 'Islamic' except insofar as it pertains to many of the usual categories – ethnic, cultural, temporal, geographic, religious – by which artistic creations and material culture in general are classified, without corresponding precisely to any of them. There is thus something elusively peculiar and apparently unique about the adjective 'Islamic' when it is applied to any aspect of culture other than the faith itself.[59]

Some commentators have gone so far as to argue that the Iranian government's attempt to 'Islamize' the country's cinema has ironically produced a cinema that is decidedly secularist in its overall outlook and, in fact, 'bereft of Islam'.[60] Such arguments have been made with particular reference to the depiction of children in post-revolutionary Iranian cinema. On the one hand, Azadeh Farahmand, for example, has argued that representations of children in recent Iranian cinema are 'informed by sentimentality and an obsessive romance with children's supposed innocence, purity and beauty', in a way that clearly panders to the 'humanist framework' promoted by the international film festivals described above by Nichols. The child as a symbol of humanism indeed has a long history in international art cinema, from films such as *The 400 Blows* (Truffaut, 1959) to Ray's 'Apu' trilogy (1955–59). Such representations in Iranian cinema, asserts Farahmand, are symptomatic of films made following the international success of *Where Is the Friend's House?* and differs markedly from the less idealized, grittier portrayals of children in Iranian films of the 1970s and 80s, such as *A Simple Event* (Saless,

1973), *Harmonica* (Naderi, 1974), *The Runner* (Naderi, 1985), *Water, Wind and Dust* (Naderi, 1988) and *Bashu, the Little Stranger*.[61]

Some of the concerns Farahmand expresses regarding this shift – that it is motivated by a 'desire to renegotiate an image of Iranian society and to counter militant revolutionary stereotypes of Iranians through representations of children' – definitely ring true. There certainly appears to be a disturbing trend in Iranian cinema where certain films, such as *The Colour of Paradise*, *The Silence* (Mohsen Makhmalbaf, 1998) and *A Time for Drunken Horses*, explicitly link childhood with a physical disability (e.g., blindness), leaving these films open to accusations of manipulating the audiences' emotions via their particularly vulnerable child protagonists. However, certain commentators have pointed to the way in which children in Iranian cinema typically represent a distinctly secularist outlook, one that defies the official state-sanctioned version of Islam. An outlook that, as Egan and Mohammadi might put it, in stressing man's responsibility 'for his own actions, life, and destiny, serves as a huge affront and challenge to the Islamic government's belief system, legitimacy and concept of freedom'.[62] (Mohammadi and Egan go on to examine the controversy caused by *Taste of Cherry*, in its portrayal of Mr Badi as a man intent on committing suicide, in a sense the ultimate physical expression of self-determination.) Naficy has outlined in greater detail the way in which children in Iranian 'art cinema' have come to serve as secular yet ethical substitutes for traditional religious figures in Islamic belief:

> The optimism and ethicalism of the Art Cinema films had a messianic source, which made the contemporary bad times tolerable because of the hope that a messiah will one day make them better. But this messianism was not strictly speaking religious or Islamic, for its agent was not a religious figure, a Mahdi or (for the Shi'is) the twelfth imam who is in occlusion, but often a surprising secular figure: a child. The purported innocence of children allowed revelation to be channelled through them and the messianic structure permitted hope of redemption and salvation to come through their individual actions...The radicalism of these films lies in their secular hope for the

future and in their secular but ethical construction of life's fundamentals.[63]

By contrast, Fischer's in-depth study of the influence of Iran's oral, literary and visual traditions upon the country's contemporary cinematic practices takes a somewhat different route, examining the (in)compatibility of the Islamic religion with modern media. Fischer utilizes Jacques Derrida's concept of *globalatinization*, the theory that 'teletechnological media and Christianity are currently allied and hegemonic in making all visible, incarnate', and hence knowable. This phenomenon clashes with 'Islam and Judaism, which refuse this iconicity and this presencing, insisting on infinite commentary, because God is never directly self-revealing',[64] or with what Grabar might describe as the preference in Islamic tradition in general and in Islamic art in particular for 'nonrepresentational' symbolism.[65] However, as Derrida argues, explains Fischer, such teletechnologies, by way of their very own ubiquity, ultimately exhaust their own global reach and totalizing power. Therefore, as Fischer argues, rather than regarding globalatinization as a process whereby the Western media relentlessly imposes its own Christian-cum-capitalist outlook upon the rest of the world, it should be understood as an inherently two-way process in which various competing ideologies inflect and interpolate each other at a local as well as global level:

> One needs...not to speculate not too much from afar, nor to grant too much too quickly to the forces of abstraction, capital, and specularization, but rather to engage ethnographically with the directors, producers, distributors and audiences, with their understandings, references, and allusions. It is not at all clear that globalatinization is the end of commentary or that the forces of capital and concentration of media ownership merely suck all into a Christian-defined terrain or performativity, though it may well be that the Muslim world today is a site par excellence of telecommunicative dissemination and of displacements of locality and tradition...[Globalatinization] need be neither a homogenizing process nor a wild frenzy of unstable positions driven merely by efforts to stake claims in the market. It can

also work to establish niches in diasporic and transnational circuits.⁶⁶

Fischer then goes on to demonstrate, via an analysis of four Iranian films – *Need* (Ali Reza Davoudnezad, 1992), *The Blue Scarf* (Bani-Etemad, 1995), *The Glass Agency* (Ebrahim Hatamikia, 1997) and *The Wind Will Carry Us* – that far from being 'bereft of Islam' contemporary Iranian cinema is, in fact, deeply informed by an Islamic philosophy (in some instances an explicitly *Shi'i* Islamic philosophy, one that directly explores the notion of sacrifice), even if Iranian cinema as a whole exhibits a realist aesthetic that draws on 'earlier Italian neorealist and East European absurdist styles'.⁶⁷ This (Shi'i) Islamic philosophy or code of ethics, however, is not something that has been uniformly imposed upon post-revolutionary Iranian filmmakers by the state but is rather a personalized Islamic sensibility of sorts, an outlook on life which exists to varying degrees within certain individual filmmakers, and which manifests itself in different ways in their films. In a similar vein Grabar has observed, with specific reference to the transition from pagan to Christian art in the Mediterranean, that a transformation in meaning does not always equate to a parallel transformation in form, and vice versa. Although there may be nothing particularly 'Islamic' about a long shot or a jump cut, for instance, that does not mean that the decision to employ a long shot or a jump cut is not itself informed by an Islamic sensibility. It is in this sense that the apparent platitude of describing cinema as a 'universal' language gains some considerable weight.

> Change in meaning and change in form are two separate phenomena that depend on each other but do not necessarily coincide ... [C]hange consists not only in modifications to the visually perceptible features of form and subject matter but also to an interplay between these features and a feature that is less easy to comprehend, the mind of the beholder. In other words it is likely, or at least possible, that the fact that a Muslim looked at or used a form gave a different sense to that form, and that this difference of visual understanding or of practical use is largely what affected the making of further forms.⁶⁸

Although Grabar acknowledges that it is, of course, impossible to comprehend fully the 'mind of the beholder', Lloyd Ridgeon's essay about *A Moment of Innocence* (Mohsen Makhmalbaf, 1996) remains one of the most astute analyses of the bearing that filmmakers' personal experiences and religious beliefs have upon the nature of their works. Although Makhmalbaf is a director who has found great favour with critics in the West due to the thoroughly postmodern quality of his films, which often reject a linear narrative structure and embrace an explicit self-reflexivity – perhaps none more strongly than *A Moment of Innocence* – Ridgeon argues that the film offers a 'spiritual, Islamic perspective on the apocalypse'. The film is Makhmalbaf's attempt to document the moment from his youth when he stabbed a policeman, an act for which he was imprisoned when he was a member of a pro-revolutionary group in 70s Iran. As the film reaches its climax when a young Makhmalbaf moves to stab the policeman, symbols of violence (a gun and a knife) are replaced by symbols of peace (some bread and a flower) in the film's closing freeze-frame image. Distinguishing traditional visions of the apocalypse in Shi'ite Islam as the imminent appearance of the Mahdi on the one hand from a more personal, internalized moment of self-realization (which has it roots in Sufism) on the other, Ridgeon explains how this small act of pacifist defiance of violence emphasizes the importance of individual responsibility and self-determination:

> The old generation is redeemed: The expectation of the Mahdi is to be undertaken in a more poetic fashion; the hungry should be fed and trees should be planted in Africa [presumably a reference to Makhmalbaf's earlier film *'Arusi-ye Khuban/Wedding of the Blessed* (1989, Iran), in which the protagonist, a traumatised veteran of the Iran-Iraq war, watches images of starving African children on television]. The young generation becomes the Mahdi to restore justice and order in a peaceful way to the world... This is a modern form of Shi'ism, an individualist Shi'ism that accords more with many of the forms of modernism and individualism found in the West. The apocalypse is not postponed, but is anticipated and interiorised by the individual, leaving him with the responsibility to act.[69]

Makhmalbaf's willed redemption of his younger self, therefore, reflects his disillusionment with the violent means by which he formerly sought to bring about revolutionary change in Iran, and his hope for the future of the country's contemporary youth. The film's insistence on individual responsibility, often mistaken for individualist secularism in the 'West', as Ridgeon demonstrates, is, in fact, deeply rooted in the Sufi tradition of Shi'ite Islam. Thus, if the cinema that emerged from Iran following the Revolution can in any way be accurately described as 'Islamic', it is due more to the efforts of the filmmakers themselves, than to their government's attempt to institutionalize their own official version of Islam. To what extent is it correct, however, to characterize the filmmakers of the New Iranian Cinema as *collectively* opposed to the attempt, at home *and* abroad, to dictate the nature of their cinema? In other words, what similarities exist between their films to justify such a viewpoint, aside from the distinctively personal Islamic philosophy that most exhibit to varying degrees?

A cinema of resistance

Describing any cinema as a 'cinema of resistance' is fundamentally problematic, as it implies a degree of strategic cooperation between the filmmakers in question; such an implication may not necessarily be an accurate reflection of how Iranian cinema actually operates. However, the epithet seems particularly appropriate to the New Iranian Cinema, thanks to the remarkably similar ways in which post-revolutionary Iranian filmmakers have resisted attempts by Western critics and audiences to pigeonhole their cinema as a 'new wave' quasi-European art cinema as well as fought attempts by their own government to control this cinema ideologically. As Naficy observes, international acclaim for Iranian cinema has not translated into 'political prestige for the Islamist regime, as the regime's opponents in exile had feared'. On the contrary, foreign audiences and critics have generally been sophisticated enough 'to understand the constricted political contexts in which the films were produced', praising 'the initiative and skilfulness of the filmmakers...not government largesse or manipulative capacity, for the high quality of the films'.[70]

This resistance to being perceived and treated as political pawns by their own government has manifested itself thematically and stylistically in the works of post-revolutionary Iranian filmmakers, via a preference for what Bordwell might call 'ambiguity', but what is perhaps more accurately described as polysemy. Denied the possibility of openly criticizing their own regime, and without recourse to the often equally provocative ambiguity of European art cinema, post-revolutionary Iranian filmmakers have opted instead for a mode of storytelling that is open to multiple levels of interpretation. Ironically, it is this very polysemy, based as it is in a desire that is inherently political in itself, to avoid legitimizing the Iranian regime, which has led to the accusation that post-revolutionary Iranian cinema lacks a political or social conscience. Some critics, such as Ali Reza Haghighi, have charged post-revolutionary Iranian filmmakers with the failure to reflect the complexity of the political situation inside their own country:

> Since 1983, when the administration of cinema in Iran became centralized and regulated, the Iranian film industry has been unable to reflect significant elements of realpolitik. Political themes depicted in films are either past events (such as the crimes of the previous regime) or marginal issues (such as anti-revolutionary groups) after they have been resolved and are no longer a concern of society. In other words, cinema has not reflected the contemporary Iranian political scene.[71]

As Dabashi's critique of *The Wind Will Carry Us* above also illustrates, this opinion of the New Iranian Cinema is relatively commonplace, especially among Iranian émigrés. In this respect, Chaudhuri and Howard Finn's *Screen* article represents a major step forward in thinking productively about the way in which the open-ended nature of many Iranian films encourage rather than discourage political interpretations. Utilizing Pier Paolo Pasolini's concept of poetic realism, Paul Schrader's notion of the arrested image, and Gilles Deleuze's theory of the time-image, they point to the significance of the number of freeze-frame shots which conclude so many Iranian films, such as *Close Up*, *A Moment of Innocence*, *The Apple* (Samira Makhmalbaf, 1998), and *The White Balloon*. Their analysis of the concluding shot of *The White Balloon*, one of the most internationally popular Iranian films of the 90s, illustrates the multitude of possible readings such 'open' images invite, despite their initial incomprehensibility (which film critics in the West are often too quick to describe, somewhat lazily, as 'surreal', as if the word 'surreal' is somehow capable of encompassing all the potential meanings such complex images suggest):

> The film ends with the clock ticking down to New Year, an ominous offscreen explosion, and a freeze-frame: the Afghan refugee boy with his white balloon. The Afghan boy is in every sense 'marginal' to the narrative – this is, of course, the point. He has barely figured in the film, neither has the white balloon. And, one might add, neither have the Iranian political situation nor the question of Afghan refugees in Iran. Yet *The White Balloon* is the title of the film and this is the final image – one that, by its very unexpectedness and the fact that it is a long-held freeze-frame, announces itself as the crucial image of the film, a static image we are given the necessary time to 'read'... the implication is that the Afghan refugee will not be going home to celebrate the New Year – he has no home. But the image is too ambiguous, too 'strong', to be reduced to one level of interpretation.[72]

For Chaudhuri and Finn, therefore, the closing shot of *The White Balloon* does not so much provide a sense of resolution to the narrative, insofar as the white balloon of the title is finally revealed, as it does strongly hint at the plight of Iran's Afghan refugees. Such images represent what Chaudhuri and Finn, paraphrasing Deleuze, call 'the open-ended politicization of the image',[73] a defiance of the efforts of the Iranian regime to impose their own will upon the New Iranian Cinema, to purge the medium of political and ideological discord. 'Iranian filmmakers have utilized the open image to circumvent a particularly strict form of censorship and point to the plurality of truth and experience in a political context where a repressive notion of one truth is imposed by the state.'[74]

Chaudhuri and Finn's argument is also largely applicable to many of the static long takes which conclude so many Iranian films, such as the Kiarostami films discussed above. Although they are not freeze-frame images as such, their overall stillness, combined with the lack of movement within the frame, can provoke a similar response from the viewer. The preponderance of this technique amongst such a relatively close-knit group of filmmakers (for instance, the Makhmalbaf family frequently assist on each other's films, while Panahi himself is very much a disciple of Kiarostami) amounts to what could accurately be described as a collective strategy of resistance to ideological and political determinism on the part of Iran's foremost contemporary filmmakers (rather than a resistance to interpretation altogether, as Dabashi would have it). Such a generalization, however, should not and cannot be understood as representative of the entire spectrum of filmmaking within Iran. Many other filmmakers, who do not enjoy the same automatic access to foreign markets as directors such as Kiarostami and the Makmalbafs, are frequently engaged in their own individual, antagonistic battles of negotiation and compromise with Iran's film censors.

Reframing the New Iranian Cinema

The paradoxes of the New Iranian Cinema are many: new yet old; global yet local; modernist yet postmodern; Islamic yet secular. A better understanding of these paradoxes is nevertheless crucial to the more comprehensive panorama of Iranian filmmaking that this book attempts to outline. The danger in sketching such a broad and far-reaching overview, however, is that it risks overlooking some of the finer aspects or smaller details that characterize this cinema. This chapter has tried to compensate for such oversights by way of some close analysis of several of the key films of the New Iranian Cinema, as well as by comparing the different ways in which this cinema has been constructed and imagined as a 'national cinema' within Iran and overseas in Europe and North America, teasing out and examining the contradictions between these two contrasting visions of the New Iranian Cinema wherever they may arise.

Although there are clear parallels to be drawn between European art cinema and the New Iranian Cinema, in terms of the many thematic and aesthetic devices that characterize both, in most instances there exist subtle yet significant differences between how these devices are employed. Filmmakers working in Iran are influenced as much by their country's rich literary traditions as they are by the practices of their European counterparts. At the same time, the works of contemporary Iranian filmmakers reveal the influences of their own cinematic forefathers, foremost among them being, as this book shall contend, Saless.

Likewise, the New Iranian Cinema exhibits a clear humanist sensibility that is commonly perceived as secularism in the 'West'. This has nothing to do, however, with the ostensibly non-religious outlook of many recent Iranian films, most of which, as pointed out above, are imbued with a deeply personalized sense of Islamic values. It has instead everything to do with the outdated and harmful prejudices of film critics and audiences, preconceptions which require that every version of Islam be inherently 'fundamentalist' in nature (which is not to stereotype Europe or North America, especially the latter, as secular societies). As Tariq Ali observes in his *Guardian* article on the issue of censorship in Iranian cinema, religion 'is visible in many guises in some of these films, but never centre stage and never official'.[75]

Finally, in-between these two competing visions of the New Iranian Cinema, one Eurocentric in nature and the other official, the filmmakers themselves have striven as best they can to put forward their own *personal* visions of contemporary Iran and its people. The methods by which they have sought to achieve this are by no means uniform but in some instances share enough similarities to warrant the description of the New Iranian Cinema as a 'cinema of resistance', not in a militaristic sense, but in the sense that Iranian filmmakers have consistently defied attempts on both fronts to categorize and define their works, as a model 'art cinema' on the one hand, and as a state-sanctioned 'Islamic' cinema on the other hand.

Such wariness on the part of Iran's current generation of filmmakers undermines any accusations that they are ignorant of the fraught position they occupy in the West as supposed ambassadors for contemporary Iranian culture or that they are guilty of neglecting the political and social complexities of modern Iran. This much is illustrated by the scene from *The Wind Will Carry Us* when one of the schoolteachers in Siah Darreh expresses his reservations regarding Behzad's intention to document the graphic mourning ritual that will follow the elderly woman's impending death. 'You look on it from the outside,' he says to Behzad. 'It may interest you. But personally...', he trails off, leaving his sentence unfinished. Like the schoolteacher,

Iranian filmmakers are very conscious of how they and their country are perceived. They are more than aware of who is watching them, whether the glance is cast from outside or from within their own country.

Such a wider and more nuanced understanding of the New Iranian Cinema serves to disprove the notion that this cinema is in any way homogeneous or monolithic. The existence of a prolific and widespread Iranian émigré cinema, by contrast, begins to call into question the very geographical integrity of Iranian cinema itself, and the whole concept of 'national cinema' in general. What is the nature of this other side to Iranian cinema, produced by émigré filmmakers working *outside* of their (ancestral) homeland? What are its links to the New Iranian Cinema? It is these questions which this book now goes on to consider, in effect taking a step backwards in order to move closer to a fuller understanding, or to gain an even broader perspective, of the multifaceted nature of contemporary Iranian filmmaking.

2

From Iran to Hollywood and Some Places In-Between: Iranian Émigré Filmmaking

In her book *Exiled Memories: Stories of the Iranian Diaspora*, a collection of personal narratives by Iranian Americans living in the United States, Zohreh C. Sullivan explains how, on those occasions when she was confronted with silence from the interviewees whose stories comprise her book, she would ask them the following question: 'If you were to make a film of your life, what moment or image would you choose to start with? How would you shape your story?'[1]

I remember being similarly struck while reading Antonio Gramsci's *Letters from Prison*, when, in a letter dated 12 February 1927, the author describes his transfer from the island of Ustica to the San Vittore prison in Milan as one very long 'cinematic event'.[2] During this journey, Gramsci was, of course, going into exile, an *internal* exile, imprisoned within his own country.

Gramsci may simply have been referring to the picturesque vistas of the Italian landscape he encountered during his journey. But his remark, as does Sullivan's, begs the question of what it is about cinema that makes it such an appropriate and effective means of depicting the experience of displacement. Is it the ability to visualize this experience, to give shape, colour and movement to one's memories, traumatic or otherwise? Is it the ability to combine this visualization with sound, either the strange noises encountered upon entering a foreign country or alien environment, or the familiar, evocative noises of one's homeland? Is it the ability to overlay all of this with a voiceover narration, thereby personalizing the story of displacement in a way that is not possible in other, single-sensory mediums?

In his essay on the mixed aesthetics of Third World cinema as well as émigré filmmaking, Robert Stam argues that it is the unique ability of cinema to combine image and sound, and to cross a variety of different times and places, that accounts for its capacity to represent cultural hybridity and the sense of spatiotemporal dislocation. Utilizing Mikhail Bakhtin's influential concept of the chronotope, which Naficy neatly summarizes as 'literally, "time-space"... a "unit of analysis" for studying texts in terms of their representation of spatial and temporal configurations',[3] Stam offers an eloquent and compelling exposition of cinema's unique ability to 'express cultural and temporal hybridity'.

> As a technology of representation, the cinema mingles diverse times and spaces; it is produced in one constellation of times and spaces, it represents still another (diegetic) constellation of times and places, and it is received in still another time and space (theatre, home, classroom). Film's conjunction of sound and image means that each track not only represents two kinds of time, but also that they mutually inflect one another in a form of synchresis. Atemporal static shots can be inscribed with temporality through sound. The panoply of available cinematic techniques further multiplies these already multiple times and spaces. Superimposition redoubles the time and space, as do montage and multiple frames within the image. The capacity for palimpsestic overlays of images and sounds facilitated by the new computer and video technologies further amplify possibilities for fracture, rupture and polyphony. An electronic 'quilting' can weave together sounds and images in ways that break with linear single-line narrative, opening up utopias (and dystopias) of infinite manipulability. The 'normal' sequential flow can be disrupted and sidetracked to take account of simultaneity and parallelism. Rather than an Aristotelian sequence of exposition, identification, suspense, pathos and catharsis, the audio-visual text becomes a tapestry... cinema embodies the inherent relationality of

time (chronos) and space (topos); it is space temporalized and time spatialized , the site where time takes place and place takes time.[4]

For Stam, therefore, it is the 'chronotopic multiplicity' of cinema that makes it such a suitable medium for expressing the spatial, temporal and cultural instability of exilic and diasporic identities and the increasing overlap between the First and Third Worlds.

It is perhaps this 'chronotopic instability' that has enabled the many filmmakers who left Iran, in the period leading up to and following the Revolution, to tell their own stories, many of them autobiographical in nature, of physical, cultural and psychological displacement. Over the past thirty years these filmmakers have produced a varied and diffuse Iranian émigré cinema which, as Naficy explains, has only begun to acquire a collective dimension in recent years, with numerous film festivals across Europe and North America showcasing their works.[5]

The existence of such a cinema, like all émigré cinemas, directly calls into question traditional understandings of the New Iranian Cinema and all national cinemas in general as geographically insulated phenomena. As Naficy has observed in a recent essay on Iranian émigré cinema,

> These exile films are also part of what might be called the Iranian 'national cinema,' for in our current age of globalization and dispersion national cinemas can no longer be limited to only the films made within the bounded geographic borders of nation-states. Since not only movies travel across borders, as they have from the start of the industry, but also moviemakers and movie audiences, the static and bounded concepts of national cinema, or nation-state, need elasticity of their own.[6]

On the one hand, the logic informing such an argument may seem very straightforward: there are many Iranian filmmakers working outside of their homeland (ancestral or otherwise), ergo, Iranian cinema, and by extension all national cinemas, can no longer be conceived of as running purely along geographical lines. On the other hand, there are a number of assumptions underlying this argument, not least of which is the belief that the nationality or heritage of a filmmaker is in itself enough to determine the national identity or belonging of their works. However, films are usually made by a number of different people from a variety of cultural backgrounds, all working at different levels in the filmmaking process. This is not to argue that a film made in Germany, for example, cannot be regarded as an 'Iranian' film simply because an Iranian does not occupy the primary creative role of director. Rather it is to argue that, even though the majority of the films considered in this chapter are directed by Iranians, any claims for national belonging by or on behalf of the filmmaker(s) in question must be tempered by the knowledge that, typically, their work 'belongs' to more than one person and is contingent upon other factors, such as where the film was shot and who financed it. A film such as *Nightsongs* (1984), for instance, directed by Iranian émigré filmmaker Marva Nabili, by virtue of its predominantly Chinese-American cast, not to mention its subject matter, is an example of émigré cinema that is as much Chinese as it is Iranian.

Moreover, there is a clear theoretical contradiction between positing the existence of a boundless national cinema and arguing that any film can potentially be considered 'Iranian', provided the origins of its maker(s) can be traced back to the precise geographical location currently known as 'Iran'. The former is predicated on the notion that all national borders are infinitely amorphous and flexible, while the latter is predicated on the notion that fundamentally there is a degree of fixity to these same borders, such that we can safely speak of the country Iran as if it is a perfectly knowable, geographically bounded entity, at the same time as we contend that any film made anywhere in the world is potentially an 'Iranian' film. It is the theoretical equivalent of having your cake and eating it. But if Iran can be everywhere, then ultimately Iran is nowhere.

Indeed, rather than putting forward some metaphysical, all-encompassing notion of Iranian ethnicity and thereby proclaiming their affinity with the directors of the New Iranian Cinema, many Iranian émigré filmmakers are explicitly concerned with problematizing the concept of fixed identities.

It would, of course, be presumptuous to think that all émigré filmmakers feel it incumbent upon themselves to make films exploring their own hybrid sense of identity, if only because it overlooks the degree to which they may have assimilated into the society of their host country, a host country that many second and third-generation filmmakers will consider their home. Nevertheless, as the films considered in this chapter demonstrate, the question of one's national, cultural and personal identity is understandably a pressing issue for many émigré filmmakers.

Thus, rather than positing the existence of an all-encompassing – albeit multi-sited – extra-national Iranian cinema, it is perhaps more useful to consider how and to what extent these films are concerned, on an individual level, with the experience of displacement and the ways in which it affects a stable and/or complete sense of selfhood, to arrive at an understanding of the degree to which these films constitute an extra-national Iranian cinema by the ways that they engage with their own sense of *Iranian-ness* and, somewhat paradoxically, challenge a fixed, homogeneous notion of Iranian identity.

Another assumption implicit in the argument that émigré filmmaking constitutes a major challenge to how we have traditionally studied and understood national cinemas is that the concept of national cinema itself is outmoded and inflexible, ill-suited to the dominant theoretical trend in Film Studies, which is gradually recognizing the inherently transnational nature of most filmmaking. This assumption is borne out to some extent by the number of national cinema studies that have overlooked the contribution made by émigré filmmakers to the cinematic output of their host countries, as well as by the possible connections between the films produced by filmmakers working overseas and the indigenous cinemas of their homelands.

But the concept of national cinema has never merely been a question of geographical belonging or rootedness. It has also typically been, among other things, and to greater and lesser extents, a question of the thematic and stylistic cohesiveness (or indeed, lack thereof) of the films of a particular region over a given period of time; the extent to which this cohesiveness is the result of state intervention or artistic self-determination; and the ways in which films are reflective, individually and collectively, of the specific historical and cultural contexts in which they were made.

These questions are key to our understanding of any 'national' cinema and must be considered in relation to the ethnicity of the filmmakers who produce that cinema, especially when positing the existence of an extra-national cinema produced by émigré filmmakers, separated as they often are by differences in language and location, not to mention their contrasting visions of the experience of displacement. It would be somewhat premature, therefore, to declare the concept of national cinema obsolete simply because of the belated recognition that 'national' cinemas are rarely ever geographically discrete entities.

Is it not possible instead to develop a more nuanced understanding of the term 'national cinema', one that enables us to analyze and discuss the cinematic output of a country, the boundaries of which may be contested and change over time, without endorsing the geographic totality and integrity of the nation above all other considerations; an understanding that recognizes the culturally intertwined nature of the birth and development of many 'national' cinemas without indulging what Stuart Hall once astutely identified as the 'superficiality of old style pluralism where no boundaries are crossed...the trendy nomadic voyaging of the postmodern or simplistic versions of global homogenization – one damn thing after another or the difference that doesn't make a difference'?[7]

The precise implications for the concept of national cinema will be discussed more closely in the conclusion to this book. This chapter considers the degree to which the films analyzed below can be regarded as constituting a collective body of work, aside from though not independent of the fact that they are all made by Iranians. As noted above, the main theme linking nearly all of these films is their explicit concern with the experience of displacement and its effect, both positive and negative, on one's sense of identity. But does this concern allow us to conceive of these films as forming a part of the 'national' Iranian cinema that has been produced outside of Iran? Or is such a far-reaching comprehension of 'national' Iranian cinema at the expense of a more detailed, subtle understanding of what might more accurately be described as various forms of contemporary Iranian *filmmaking*?

Before discussing the films themselves, this chapter provides an analysis of Naficy's monumental work on exilic and diasporic filmmaking, entitled *An Accented Cinema*, in addition to a brief overview of the theoretical developments that have taken place in the field of exile and diaspora studies in general. Because Naficy's work has had such a large bearing upon my own research and has been so influential in studies of émigré cinema overall, it is necessary to address his theories at some length. What follows, therefore, is an analysis of how Naficy's proposed concept of 'accented cinema' is conducive to a better understanding of Iranian émigré filmmaking, as well as the limits of his methodological approach.

Thereafter follows an analysis of the works of a variety of Iranian émigré filmmakers working across Europe and North America since the Revolution. The group of films considered below are assembled into units of analysis according to such factors as temporal contiguity, geographical location and the similar attitudes they exhibit towards the experience of displacement. The overall structure of this chapter nevertheless is largely chronological in nature, intended to reflect the gradual shift from a myopic and exclusionary view of the experience of displacement, discernible in films such as *The Mission* (Parviz Sayyad, 1983), to a broader and more inclusive outlook, as displayed by the pan-diasporic quality of films such as *America So Beautiful* (Babak Shokrian, 2001), a transformation analogous to the shift in exile and diaspora theory outlined below.

It should be noted, however, that my analysis is limited to those films that, quite simply, I was able to lay my hands on. The films I consider were obtained from a variety of sources, including film archives, film museums, television stations, production companies and in some instances the filmmakers themselves, and from a variety of countries, from Iran to Sweden, Germany and Italy, to the United States and Canada. Needless to say, the difficulty I had in obtaining many of these films is itself reflective of the itinerant nature of Iranian émigré filmmaking. In the case of filmmakers such as Naderi and Saless, it is also reflective of the current critical standing (or rather lack thereof) of their films, making the acquirement of all these films a logistical, financial and practical impossibility. It needs to be stressed, therefore, that the films considered in this chapter and in this book overall are by no means representative of the entire spectrum of Iranian émigré filmmaking. Indeed no study of Iranian émigré filmmaking would be complete without a consideration of the works of other important filmmakers such as Houshang Allahyari in Austria and Parviz Kimiavi in France. The analysis undertaken in this chapter, nonetheless, amounts to a significant and wide-ranging study of the current state of Iranian émigré filmmaking. More importantly, for the specific purposes of this book, this analysis promises to expand our understanding of post-revolutionary Iranian cinema.

Naficy's 'accented cinema'

Acknowledging the influence of Bakhtin upon his own work on émigré filmmaking, Naficy proposes the term 'accented cinema', in his monumental work of the same name, as a means of theorizing and categorizing collectively the body of films made by individuals whom he describes as the many exilic, diasporic and postcolonial ethnic and identity filmmakers from all over the world, though his scope of enquiry is broadly limited to 'postcolonial, Third World' filmmakers working in the 'West'. What unites all of these 'accented' filmmakers, argues Naficy, despite their different cultural backgrounds and experiences of displacement, is their 'liminal subjectivity and interstitial location in society and the film industry'.[8] Their films also typically require on the part of the viewer a new set of viewing skills, a degree of cinematic literacy that are not demanded by the standardized film language of mainstream Hollywood cinema:

> Although there is nothing common about exile and diaspora, deterritorialized peoples and their films share certain features, which in today's climate of lethal ethnic difference need to be considered, even emphasized. ... not only watching and listening but also reading, translating and writing. ... [are] all part of the spectatorial activities and competencies that are needed for appreciating the works of these filmmakers, which I have termed 'accented cinema'.[9]

In defining 'accented cinema' mainly in opposition to Hollywood and dominant/capitalist modes of film production, exilic and diasporic films are distinguished by their 'accented', small-scale mode of production, be it individual or collective. Stylistically, 'accented cinema' is characterized by its 'smallness, imperfection, amateurishness and lack of cinematic gloss'.[10] The similarities between 'accented cinema' and Octavio Getino and Fernando Solanas's concept of Third Cinema are clear.[11] Although less polemical than Third Cinema, 'accented cinema' is 'nonetheless a political cinema that stands opposed to authoritarianism and oppression. If Third Cinema films generally advocated class struggle and armed struggle, accented films favour discursive and semiotic struggles.'[12]

Like their Third Cinema counterparts, 'accented' films directly challenge established conventions of filmmaking by mixing and confusing genres (such as fiction and documentary), by problematizing straightforward viewer identification, by fragmenting traditional narrative structure and time and by literally *looking* crude and unaccomplished (purposefully or otherwise), as if they were the work of non-professionals, which, of course, they frequently are. (Many of these features are characteristic of the New Iranian Cinema itself). 'Accented' films, moreover, share certain thematic concerns (manifested in their narratives of journeying, border crossing and identity crossing) and certain formal features (such as their epistolarity, their self-reflexivity and most significantly their chronotopic visions of the homeland or life in exile and diaspora).

Like Stam, Naficy also employs the concept of the chronotope as a means of examining how 'accented' films 'link the inherited space-time of the homeland to the constructed space-time of the exile and diaspora'.[13] Naficy illustrates how representations of the homeland and life in exile and diaspora frequently take the shape of what he describes as open-form and/or closed-form chronotopes. Open-form chronotopes, with their visual motifs of landscapes, mountains, monuments and various other national signifiers, foster a cathected and fetishized vision of the homeland. The mise-en-scène of closed-form chronotopes, by contrast, construct a synaesthetic vision of life in exile and diaspora as claustrophobic, oppressive and imprisoning. This visual style is also often combined with what Naficy calls 'narratives of panic and pursuit'.[14] The table below (which is by no means exhaustive) should provide a clearer picture of the dichotomy Naficy proposes:

Open-form	**Closed-form**
exterior locations	interior locations
mobile framing	static framing
bright, natural lighting	darkness, shadows
long shots	close ups
timelessness	temporality

As Naficy points out, however, this demarcation is not intended to be inflexible or overly divisive, for, like the conditions of exile and diaspora themselves, there is a great deal of overlap involved. Some 'accented' films, *Yol* (Yilmaz Güney, 1982), for instance, envision the homeland itself (in this case Turkey) as a prison. Open-form chronotopic films commonly lend themselves to nostalgic, utopian and optimistic interpretations, while closed-form chronotopic films inevitably encourage dystopian and pessimistic readings.

'Accented' films which embody *both* open-form and closed-form chronotopes, argues Naficy, are evocative of Edward Soja's concept of 'thirdspace', which Naficy describes as a 'slipzone of simultaneity and intertextuality, [where] original cultures are no longer fixed.'[15] While the filmmakers in question can certainly be thought of as inhabiting a thirdspace of sorts, insofar as they belong wholly neither to the host country in which they reside, nor to the homeland which they have left, it is debatable to what extent their films inhabit this slipzone. Some of the films Naficy provides as examples of thirdspace chronotopicality, such as *Wavelength* (Michael Snow, 1967) and *The Great Sadness of Zohara* (Nina Menkes, 1983), seem to show a *transition* from closed-form to open-form chronotopicality, rather than a *synthesis* of the two forms to create a utopian 'thirdspace'; whereas other examples, such as *Calendar* (Atom Egoyan, 1993) and *A Tale of the Wind* (Joris Iven, 1988), seem to display a genuine oscillation between open-form and closed-form chronotopicality. By making thirdspace films, or acting 'thirdly or interstitially', as Naficy puts it, their makers 'resist both absolute essentialism and total integration to produce, instead, partiality and positionality', making the filmmakers and the films themselves 'moving targets, strategically adopting not only marginality and interstitiality but also at times *centrality*' (my emphasis).[16]

One of the foremost contributions Naficy has made to the study of émigré cinema has been to differentiate with great subtlety between the concepts of exile and diaspora themselves. For as obvious as such a distinction may appear, the terms are all too frequently conflated with each other. 'Exile', therefore, as Naficy explains, refers to 'individuals or groups who voluntarily or involuntarily have left their country of origin and who maintain an ambivalent relationship with their previous and current places and cultures.' Although it can be collective, exile is thus primarily a solitary or individual experience, in which the exile (or group of exiles) in question maintain a 'vertical and primary relationship' with their homeland, unlike people living in diaspora, whose consciousness is 'horizontal and multisited, involving not only the homeland but also compatriot communities elsewhere'. In other words, diaspora is collective by necessity. These important differences manifest themselves thematically and aesthetically, explains Naficy, in both exilic and diasporic films. The former are characterized by their 'narratives of retrospection, loss and absence', as well as by their emphasis on 'binarism and duality' and a 'cathected' relationship with the homeland. The latter are characterized by their emphasis on 'plurality, multiplicity and hybridity' and the 'performativity of identity'. This is not to suggest, however, that diasporic films do not also foster a vertical relationship to the homeland, while simultaneously encouraging a 'lateral relationship' to fellow diasporic communities, compatriot or otherwise.

Postcolonial ethnic and identity films by contrast are characterized by their overriding concern with 'the exigencies of life *here* and *now* in the country in which the filmmakers reside' (my emphasis). In their films, Naficy argues, there is no nostalgic longing for the homeland, but instead a focus on the process of assimilation or of 'becoming', of becoming, for instance, African-British or Chinese-American, what Naficy refers to as the 'politics of the hyphen'.[17]

Naficy posits a somewhat similar trichotomy in his writings on Iranian exilic television in Los Angeles. The first category or stage is *exilic* (programmes produced by exiles living in the host country as a response to and in parallel with their own transitional and provisional status), the second *transnational* (programmes imported from the homeland) and the third *ethnic* (programmes produced in the host country by long-established indigenous minorities). Iranian *exilic* television, therefore, by the nature of its very longevity, is in the process of becoming *ethnic*.[18]

In this respect Naficy's work represents something of a milestone in what has been a long academic debate regarding the nature of exile and diaspora. As indicated above, it is a debate distinguished by a tension between a decidedly essentialist and monolithic theorization of both terms and a more subtle, open-ended attempt at understanding how different exilic and diasporic subjects are affected by the experience of displacement in different ways.

Edward Said's celebrated essay *Reflections on Exile,* for instance, is one of the most important and influential pieces of writing on the subject of exile, in its attempt to articulate and give shape to what was a previously a very abstract concept, and in its theorization of exile as a mode of opposition to political, social and cultural orthodoxy. But it is perhaps guilty of perpetuating certain harmful stereotypes of exiles themselves in the number of sweeping generalizations it makes, most of them negative:

> Exile is a jealous state ... Exiles look at non-exiles with resentment ... No matter how well they may do, exiles are always eccentrics ... Wilfulness, exaggeration, overstatement: these are characteristic of being an exile ... Composure and serenity are the last things associated with the works of exiles ... Artists in exile are decidedly unpleasant.[19]

This is not to argue that Said's comments are necessarily untrue. On the contrary, they frequently are true. Nevertheless, they are true only at certain times, under certain circumstances and for certain groups or individuals. Despite its intentions, *Reflections on Exile* does as much to *define* as it does to *delineate*[20] the experience and the concept of exile, in a manner that is not always conducive to a deeper understanding of its manifold variations and complexities. As Zuzana M. Pick observes in her analysis of Chilean Cinema in exile from 1973 to 1986, not all exiles respond to their own displacement in a negative or defeatist manner. Indeed, many Chilean filmmakers, she argues, consciously emphasized in their works an exilic sensibility, both individual and collective, as a means of maintaining their political and social agency and countering their cultural disenfranchisement. Such a strategy, moreover, represents an inherent unwillingness to conform to the negative stereotypes associated with the condition of exile itself.

> If one looks at the 'catalogue' of films made by Chileans since 1973, the foregrounding of a consciousness of exile is paramount to the repositioning of works within a social

political and historical formation. This re-positioning implies a refusal to comply with the negative consequences of banishment. The disorienting alienation and marginality tend to prevent the exile from having an effect on a social and political context. By recognizing the privilege that the position of exile brings along, filmmakers have re-defined their practice as a means of cultural struggle. What I call the privilege of exile is the awareness of the possibility of this process. The capacity for operating dialectically within the heterogeneous allows the reaffirmation of political commitment and the re-contextualization as individual and collective identity.[21]

Some academics are, nonetheless, guilty of exaggerating what Pick calls the 'privilege of exile', the so-called liberating effect and the positive aspects of the cultural and aesthetic hybridity that the experience of displacement and marginalization entails. See, for example, Laura U. Marks' overly playful assertion that the 'minority artist *dances* along the border' (my emphasis), in her essay *A Deleuzian Politics of Hybrid Cinema*.[22] Indeed, academics such as Sophia A. McLennen have rightly criticized the overly theoretical and metaphorical reconceptualization of exile that has occurred over the past two decades or so. Removed from any sense of how exiles live their lives in the real world, McLennen questions the way in which the term 'exile' has gradually been divorced from its original connotations of 'anguish and loss':

> There are two flaws to this line of thinking. First, even if it were possible to experience a purely transnational existence, most of us recognize that globalization does not lead to a power-free, liberated, multicultural state of being. Second, the exile's material existence in a world requires that visas, passports and so on, in a world, that is, where the exile is forbidden to cross particular geographical boundaries, cannot be understood as existence free of the repressive nature of nationalism... in many scholarly works the term 'exile,' having lost its reference to a painful state of being, was empty of history and an association with material reality...[23]

McLennen's concerns are legitimate and well-founded. Contrary views of the experience of exile, however, are absolutely necessary in order to prevent an exclusively negative and monolithic understanding of the term or condition. In this vein, Winifred Woodhull, for example, has stressed the need to distinguish between, in her case, the various reasons for the relocation of many exiled 'intellectuals' to France in recent years:

> It is essential to draw distinctions within and between groups of émigré intellectuals who have come to France at different times and in various circumstances: those from other Western European countries, or from the U.S. and Canada, who have come mainly for reasons of intellectual and cultural affinity... and those for whom oppression in their native land is a central factor... those who have come from Eastern European countries as political and intellectual dissidents... and those who have come from Third World countries, particularly former colonies... to take up residence in France permanently or intermittently, for political, cultural, and intellectual reasons. Exile means something different in each case, and figures in the work of these individuals and groups in very different ways.[24]

One of the weaknesses underlying most academic literature on the subject of exile, as the writings of Said, Pick and Woodhull illustrate, is that it almost invariably concerns itself with the works of so-called intellectual émigrés. It is perhaps a truism to observe that the exiles whose experiences of displacement garner the most attention are those who possess the ability to articulate or express their opinions and feelings on the subject, via cinema, music, literature and other media. But it should be noted that the works of these 'intellectuals' do not necessarily speak for the many émigrés who suffer – or perhaps celebrate – their exilic existences in silence.

Therefore, although a degree of ambiguity often surrounds the concept of exile (is it external or internal, forced or voluntary?), *diaspora* by comparison may seem more straightforward and unproblematic a term to define. For Elazar Barkan and Marie-Denise Shelton, for instance, diaspora implies a certain degree of fixity, a sense of belonging and rootedness, that exile does not. Their differentiation between the concepts of exile and diaspora and the connotations that came to be associated with both terms following the creation of Israel in 1948 is especially useful in this respect:

> Exile connoted suffering, a negative term evoking displacement, refugee status and above all the myth of an eventual, and possibly soon, return. In contrast, diaspora came to mean a chosen geography and identity. Exile was largely revered for the cultural stamina of the exiled, their constant loyalty to the historical memory of the communal life, rejection of assimilation and struggle for authenticity and sacrifice.[25]

Nevertheless, developments in the study of diaspora have taken a somewhat similar route to those in the study of exile in recent years. In the first edition of the journal *Diaspora* in 1991, for example, William Safran sets out a rather restrictive set of criteria which an individual or group of people must fulfil in order to qualify as a diasporic community or member thereof.[26] Such prescriptive definitions, nevertheless, are hardly practical and fail to take into consideration the historical contingencies and particularities that are bound up with the establishment of any diasporic community. James Clifford's seminal essay *Diasporas*, therefore, represents an important step towards thinking constructively about not only how distinct diasporic communities come into being, but also how they continue to develop after their formation:

> What is the range of differences covered by the term [diaspora]? Where does it begin to lose definition?...we should be wary of constructing our working definition of a term like diaspora by recourse to an 'ideal type', with the consequence that groups become identified as more or less diasporic, having only two, or three, or four of the basic six features...Moreover at different times in their history, societies may wax and wane in their diasporism, depending on changing possibilities – obstacles, openings, antagonisms,

> and connections – in their host countries and transnationally...Whatever the working list of diasporic features, no society can be expected to qualify on all counts, throughout its history. And the discourse of diaspora will necessarily be modified as it is translated and adopted...Different diasporic maps of displacement and connection can be compared on the basis of family resemblance, of shared elements, no subset of which is defined as essential to the discourse. A polythetic field would seem most conducive to tracking (rather than policing) the contemporary range of diasporic forms.[27]

For Clifford, diaspora is a volatile condition, constantly shifting, yet at the same time traceable. As he asserts, if 'diaspora is to be something about which one could write a history...it must be something more than a name for a site of multiple displacements and reconstitutions of identity'.[28]

In a similar fashion, Avtar Brah has argued persuasively for the need to historicize the experience of displacement for each diasporic community. Furthermore, she points towards the need for a *pan-diasporic* sensibility to better comprehend the differences and similarities between distinct diasporic groups:

> The question is not simply about *who travels* but *when, how, and under what circumstances*? What socio-economic, political, and cultural conditions mark the trajectories of these journeys? What regimes of power inscribe the formation of a specific diaspora? In other words, it is necessary to analyse what makes one diasporic formation similar to or different from another: whether, for instance, the diaspora in question was constituted through conquest and colonisation as has been the case with several European diasporas. Or it might have resulted from the capture or removal of a group through slavery or systems of indentured labour...the *concept* of diaspora concerns the historically variable forms of *relationality* within and between diasporic formations. It is about relations of power that similarise and differentiate between and across changing diasporic formations. In other

words, the concept of diaspora centres on the *configurations of power which differentiate diasporas internally as well as situate them in relation to one another.*[29]

Such a commitment to relationality certainly seems to inform Naficy's methodological approach, as he utilizes his proposed chronotopic paradigm to highlight the differences as well as draw many enlightening parallels between a number of 'accented' filmmakers and their works. Moreover, as Naficy is careful to remind the reader, exile and diaspora are not mutually exclusive processes. They are instead 'fluid processes that under certain circumstances may transform into one another and beyond'.[30] Despite his welcome insistence on the need for locating different exilic and diasporic individuals or groups within their specific historical trajectories, it is precisely the wide-ranging scope of Naficy's book that, somewhat ironically, undermines some of the finer theoretical points of his work. For by attempting to incorporate all of the diverse forms of émigré filmmaking under the rubric of 'accented cinema', Naficy's work betrays an underlying aesthetic and theoretical determinism, indicated partly by his insistence on defining 'accented cinema' *in opposition to*, rather than *in relation to*, mainstream Hollywood cinema.

For Naficy, the relationship between 'accented cinema' and Hollywood cinema is one of mutuality and dependency, for although the process of making 'accented' films empowers their creators with a kind of self-determination, enabling them to 'move out of their disempowered "minority" status, conferred upon them by the majority', all that 'accented cinema' itself ultimately does is supply 'the sculpting lights that help define the major cinema's glowing visage'.[31] To what extent this argument is reconcilable with Naficy's earlier assertion that thirdspace 'accented' films and filmmakers are occasionally able to adopt positions of centrality is clearly open to question.

Indeed, as Alastair Phillips points out in his otherwise largely complimentary *Screen* review of Naficy's book, despite the impressive wealth of background and contextual information provided for most of the films considered, *An Accented Cinema*, by attempting to comprise and impose some form of unity upon such a wide variety of filmmaking styles, threatens to oversimplify the complex nature of the relationship between non-mainstream, 'minor' cinemas and Hollywood cinema:

> Although Naficy strives hard to clarify these specific histories, his work is also marked by the task of working towards a condensation or synthesis of the various tropes and principles operating in the largely minor cinemas he observes. And it is here that the broad dialectic between the marginal and the mainstream risks becoming too categorical...we also need to see Hollywood and other dominant film cultures in their temporally specific and perhaps surprisingly varied transnational contexts. In so doing, we may find more meaningful ways of illuminating their own distinctive practices of production and consumption that move beyond such received notions as 'the classic realist text'...[32]

The difficulty with Naficy's thesis, therefore, lies in the way it reduces émigré cinema's relationship with mainstream cinema to a simplistic Hollywood/anti-Hollywood binary opposition – first, because, as Phillips argues, it overgeneralizes and underestimates the complexity of mainstream Hollywood cinema on numerous levels; second, because it condemns many 'accented' films to their own secondariness. Although many of the films Naficy considers represent a clear challenge – aesthetic, economic and institutional in nature – to the ways in which Hollywood cinema entrenches itself both domestically and globally, surely any film which is made in or comes from a position of marginality, one that is worth its salt, so to speak, ultimately does more than offer itself up as some kind of alternative to mainstream Hollywood cinema. Furthermore, Naficy's argument risks overlooking the frequently antagonistic nature of the relationship between 'accented' cinema and the indigenous cinema of the particular host country from which it emanates. As is frequently the case, the indigenous cinema of the host country in question is engaged in its own battle with the cultural and economic dominance of Hollywood cinema.

There also remains the question of for whom precisely can this cinema be described as 'accented'. Naficy is most likely aware, as an Iranian-American émigré living and working in North America, that he is writing at a time of unparalleled economic and cultural imperialism on the part of the United States. Moreover, the term 'accented' certainly refers more to the unfamiliar narrative and aesthetic strategies that characterize so much émigré filmmaking than it does to the actual 'foreignness' of the various languages found within these films. Yet one of the problems with the paradigm of 'accented cinema' and the dialectic Naficy proposes between mainstream and 'minority' filmmaking is not so much that it presumes a complete familiarity with the codes and conventions of Hollywood filmmaking, or even that it over-exaggerates Hollywood's domination of domestic and international film markets. Rather, it is that it takes for granted the degree of acceptance of these codes and conventions on the part of 'Western' audiences on the one hand, and the monolithic nature of Hollywood's overwhelming presence in non-'Western', non-English speaking countries on the other, in a way that is being increasingly undermined in film studies overall. In a roundabout manner, the paradigm of 'accented cinema', somewhat perversely, merely serves to re-inscribe the global hegemony of Hollywood cinema at a conceptual level, as well as the division between East and West.

Although the undeniable value of Naficy's book lies in its commitment to raising awareness and improving the reader's knowledge and understanding of the international phenomenon that is the ever-increasing body of work made by displaced filmmakers from all over the world, as well as the modes of production, recurrent thematic concerns and stylistic features that connect them to varying degrees, I am hesitant to free the term 'accented cinema' from the boundaries of the inverted commas within which I have thus far chosen to circumscribe it throughout this chapter. Like its Third Cinema counterpart, which since its inception has been the subject of a constant theoretical re-evaluation, the term 'accented cinema' seems potentially far too broad a term to be of any practical use when considering the countless films that in a variety of ways fall under its rubric. The term 'accented cinema' refers potentially to films from anywhere in the world and covers a period of time ranging in Naficy's book from as early as 1949 (with Jonas Mekas's *Lost, Lost, Lost* not completed until 1976) and even earlier, right up until present-day 'accented cinema' and certainly beyond – an ambitious scope on enquiry, to say the least. As an idea or concept, 'accented cinema' is certainly useful, first, as a means of identifying the particular modes of production, common themes and aesthetic practices that undoubtedly distinguish many émigré films, and, second, because it proposes a new set of viewing skills (which include such diverse acts as reading, listening, translating and writing) that are necessary to more fully understand and appreciate the difficult and problematic nature of these films. The term also implies a more nuanced understanding of the concept of national cinema itself, by pointing to the existence of filmmakers and filmmaking collectives that operate at an almost subnational level, a point that is largely undermined by Naficy's insistence on positioning 'accented cinema' so strongly in opposition to Hollywood cinema. But to recognize the term 'accented cinema' as a distinct type of filmmaking unto itself – despite Naficy's warning against 'positing an all-encompassing grand Exile or great Diaspora' – runs the risk of transforming it into a totalizing category that paradoxically essentializes the very films it attempts to particularize.

As Naficy himself rightly observes, these 'accented' films are 'moving targets', they cannot be easily pinned down or comfortably categorized, for to do so would be contrary to and to deny them their itinerant nature. It is an unfortunate paradox that a work so strongly committed to tracing the shifting trajectories of émigré cinema should seek to *situate* this cinema so strongly in opposition to mainstream filmmaking. As Homi K. Bhabha might put it, émigré films and filmmakers remind us that the 'nation' is 'a liminal signifying space that is *internally* marked by the discourses of minorities, the heterogeneous histories of contending peoples, antagonistic authorities and tense locations of cultural difference'. They can be perceived as 'counter-narratives of the nation that continually evoke and erase its totalizing boundaries – both actual and conceptual – disturb those ideological manoeuvres through which "imagined communities" are given essentialist identities. For the political unity of the nation consists in a continual displacement of the anxiety of its irredeemably plural modern space.' Finally, émigré films provide a 'way of understanding how easily the boundary that secures the cohesive limits of the Western nation may imperceptibly turn into a contentious *internal* liminality providing a place from which to speak both of and as, the minority, the exilic, the marginal and the emergent'.[33]

The analysis of Iranian émigré filmmaking undertaken in this chapter, therefore, does not attempt to position this cinema in opposition to mainstream Hollywood or any other dominant mode of filmmaking, or to identify a range of defining aesthetic traits and thematic motifs that run throughout these films. Rather it attempts to explore and compare broadly the different ways in which Iranian émigré filmmakers have depicted the experience of displacement in their films and what these differences may suggest about the changing attitudes of the filmmakers themselves towards the condition of living in exile and diaspora. As noted above, this chapter aims to demonstrate how Iranian émigré filmmaking is characterized largely by a gradual, historical shift from a predominantly invariable and myopic outlook to a wider, pan-diasporic perspective. One of the potential problems with this argument, of course, is that it threatens merely to substitute one homogenizing paradigm for another, replacing 'accented cinema' with my own linear Grand Narrative. Without wishing to impose too strict a chronological trajectory upon these films, however, such a relatively open analytical schema will hopefully guard against any overgeneralizations and allow these films to *speak for themselves* as it were, in a manner that attempting to shoehorn them into the totalizing category of 'accented cinema' does not necessarily permit. Moreover, as noted in the introduction, the individual case studies of Naderi's New York films and Saless's German films, in chapters 3 and 4 respectively, are intended to provide a counterpoint to some of the methodological problems that inevitably underlie such a collective and comparative analysis.

This rest of this chapter in a sense attempts to outline the path that Iranian émigré cinema has forged for itself over the past twenty-five years, beginning with its immediate break with indigenous Iranian cinema, to one of its most recent and well-known incarnations, as Hollywood's vision of the Iranian experience of displacement, in the Oscar-nominated film *House of Sand and Fog* (Vadim Perlman, 2003). Nonetheless, it would be somewhat counterproductive to view these two locations (Iran and Hollywood) as strict nodal points, or to view the aforementioned overall shift in Iranian émigré filmmaking, from a strictly exilic to an openly pan-diasporic outlook, as in any way a straightforward or linear transition. For the path that Iranian émigré cinema has forged for itself during its relatively brief history is a circuitous and, despite the largely chronological emphasis of this chapter, a profoundly non-linear one. At certain points along this path, certain films have focused on the exigencies of life in exile and diaspora in a way that directly challenges a fixed or essentialized notion of identity, opening up traditional understandings of post-revolutionary Iranian cinema to even broader perspectives, as well as exposing some of the limitations of the concept of 'national cinema' itself as an organizational category. It is with these places in-between that the rest of this chapter principally concerns itself.

'A journey without end': *The Mission, Guests of the Hotel Astoria* and *Nightsongs*

We begin then with three films that are separated from each other by differences in location and subject matter and yet are linked, first, by the fact that they were all made within the decade immediately following the Iranian Revolution and, second, because they all reach remarkably similar conclusions regarding the effects of displacement upon their respective protagonists (particularly in relation to the symbolic closing shots of the first two films that are considered below). *The Mission* follows the efforts of Daoud Moslemi (Houshang Touzie) – an assassin who works for the mysterious 'Organization' – to kill an ex-SAVAK army colonel (Parviz Sayyad), now residing in New York City. *Guests of the Hotel Astoria* (Reza Allahmehzadeh, 1989) examines the various misfortunes of a group of Iranian exiles all interminably awaiting the arrival of their visas, their relatives and any news from home, in the Hotel Astoria in Istanbul, Turkey. *Nightsongs* focuses on the events in the lives of a Chinese-American family and their Chinese-Vietnamese cousin living in New York City's Chinatown. Even though *Nightsongs* does not take a specifically Iranian experience of displacement as its subject matter, the fact that it is directed by an Iranian émigré and shares an outlook similar to the other two films considered in this section distinguishes it as one of the foremost examples of an incipient Iranian émigré cinema.

The first of these films, *The Mission*, is strikingly reminiscent of the earlier thriller *The Day of the Jackal* (Fred Zinnemann, 1973) in terms of its subject matter, and the existential thriller *The Driver* (Walter Hill,

1978) in terms of its overall tone and the way in which it seemingly reduces its characters to the status of mere ciphers. In *The Mission*, it is noteworthy that even though we learn the assassin's real name, the film's end credits list Houshang Touzie's character merely as 'The Missioner'. Similarly, Parviz Sayyad's character is listed as 'The Colonel' and is never referred to by his actual name throughout the entire film. Neither do we learn the real name of 'His Eminence', Daoud's superior in New York City, whose orders Daoud has been instructed to obey unquestioningly by the 'Organization'. In *The Driver*, characters are likewise identified simply by their profession or by the function they perform (in the narrative and in society at large) rather than by their actual names (so that the film's two lead actors, Ryan O'Neal and Bruce Dern, are referred to only as 'The Driver' and 'The Detective' respectively).

The numerous exchanges throughout *The Mission*, between Daoud and the colonel's sister-in-law Maliheh (Mary Apick), in which they debate heatedly the pros and cons of the Iranian Revolution, demonstrate the extent to which the two characters represent opposing ends of the film's ideological spectrum. As Sheila Johnston observes in her *Monthly Film Bulletin* review of the film, it sets up an apparently explicit contrast between 'the strict principles of Islamic orthodoxy' (represented by Daoud and His Eminence) and 'Westernized liberalism' (represented by the characters of the colonel and Maliheh).[34] Reinforcing the idea that these characters are essentially types rather than fully rounded individuals, these exchanges between Daoud and Maliheh – in which Maliheh emerges as the most lucid and persuasive – though convincingly written and well acted, betray the film's tendency to didacticism.

Similar to *The Driver*, *The Mission* complicates the perception of its characters as nothing more than one-dimensional symbols of existential isolationism, primarily through the sympathetic performances of its three central protagonists. Johnston, for example, goes on to note how 'Sayyad's own engaging performance as the Colonel leaves little doubt as to where our sympathies are meant to lie'[35] in the film's overall ideological schema. Yet Touzie's performance as the assassin Daoud is if not more then at least equally affecting, conveying powerfully the ethical and spiritual crisis Daoud undergoes as he unintentionally befriends the colonel and his family, after rescuing the colonel one evening from some muggers in a subway station. A later scene, in which a brief smile flickers faintly, almost reluctantly across Daoud's face as the colonel laughs out loud upon realizing that the piece of paper stuck on the windscreen of his car is an advertising flyer rather than a parking ticket, reveals subtly Daoud's growing fondness for the colonel. As Daoud learns more about the colonel's background and character and, furthermore, that the colonel intends to publish a book revealing the names of corrupt clergy members in Iran, he begins to question the right of 'His Eminence' and the 'Organization' – whose authority he had previously accepted blindly – to command him to kill a man who in his own judgement appears to be innocent.

Indeed, the film takes great care to differentiate between the religious fundamentalism of the Iranian regime – the violent actions of which are never shown, but merely referred to through the dialogue between the characters – and the piety of Daoud himself. For instance, when Daoud arrives at his hideout – a cockroach-ridden apartment – at the beginning of the film, he is shown dutifully writing a letter to his mother and performing his prayers to Mecca with a gentleness and attention to detail that are more suggestive of peaceful devoutness than of fanaticism or extremism. The care and intricacy with which he performs his ablutions prior to praying is also mirrored by the way in which the camera understatedly, respectfully frames each stage of the ritual in a series of measured, static shots, as he washes his hands, forearms, feet and head.

Daoud's austere piety is also conveyed through his behaviour in general: his hesitancy to shake hands with Maliheh upon first meeting her; his refusal to drink alcohol or eat pork (in one scene removing the sausage from a hot dog roll, for fear it might be made of pork, despite the assurances of the street vendor from whom he purchases it that it is not!); and also the simplicity of the meals he prepares for himself (invariably fried eggs and bread). Moreover, Daoud is strongly differentiated from the morally corrupt and spiritually deficient members of the 'Organization', not only 'His Eminence', who, it is strongly suggested, orders the colonel to be murdered for personal motives rather than on orders from the 'Organization' itself (he fears the colonel might reveal him as an informer for the Shah's regime in Iran), but also his contact in New York City, Ghaffar (Kamran

Nozad). The small apartment in which Daoud lives and performs his prayers, for example, contrasts starkly with the opulent surroundings of the abode of 'His Eminence', while Daoud's humble piety finds its opposite, not in the figures of the colonel or Maliheh, but rather in Ghaffar himself, who guzzles greedily on bottles of beer as he implicitly threatens Daoud that he will be killed if he fails to execute the colonel by a certain deadline.

Daoud's moral and ideological distinction from his 'superiors' is further reinforced towards the end of the film, when he reveals that he was discharged from the army in Iran and tortured for refusing to open fire on a group of students holding a sit-in protest. Despite the film's obvious sensitivity to the predicament of the colonel and his family, its equally subtle portrayal of Daoud's dilemma reveals it as far from trying to align the viewer's complete sympathy with any one specific character or belief system. The film is far more interested in exploring shades of grey than it is in setting up a strict opposition between black and white, between 'right' and 'wrong'. Daoud himself remarks when he informs Ghaffar that he will not kill the colonel unless 'His Eminence' or the 'Organization' furnishes him with proof of the threat the colonel poses to the Iranian government: 'It's not clear who is the hunter and who is the prey'.

Furthermore, Daoud's disenchantment with the purpose and justness of his mission is not simply depicted as some kind of gradual conversion to liberal individualism or the 'American way of life'. Although Iran itself is quite clearly coded as a fanatical and violent country, the film does not portray the United States as somehow innately superior, or as a liberal utopia. The colonel refers to it as a 'jungle' in which everyone is either too scared or uncaring to help others, while Maliheh makes a similar observation upon thanking Daoud for rescuing her brother-in-law from the muggers in the subway station, remarking that seemingly he has not yet become 'Americanized'. Daoud's reluctance to carry out the assassination is paralleled by his increasing alienation from, yet growing fascination with, the society in which he finds himself. In a significant scene, Daoud, after performing his prayers for the first time in the film, experiences his first interaction with US culture: namely, watching on the television in his apartment the movie *Bus Stop* (Joshua Logan, 1956), starring Marilyn Monroe – perhaps *the* Hollywood symbol of

Americana, and all the connotations of sexuality, celebrity, glamour and tragedy that her star image encompasses.

Rather than serving to juxtapose crudely Daoud's asceticism and subdued religiosity with the crass consumerism and commercialism of Hollywood cinema, however, the scene marks the beginning of Daoud's ambiguous relationship to US culture itself. It is noteworthy, for instance, that Daoud watches *Bus Stop* on a small, dingy, black-and-white television screen. By distorting the original appearance of the film (originally shot in Cinemascope and Deluxe Colour) by drastically reducing the size of the image and draining it of all its vibrancy, the television puts a kind of distance between Daoud and the image, despite Daoud's attempts to literally *get closer to it* (he sits cross-legged on the floor like a child, his face right up close to the screen).

This ambiguous closeness to and yet distance from US culture and society is echoed in several other shots later in the film, particularly in the montage sequence which shows Daoud exploring New York City as he waits for proof from either 'His Eminence' or the 'Organization' of the colonel's guilt. Symbolically heavy-handed shots of Daoud leaning in anguish against a rail fence separating him from the city skyline in the distance, or wandering the streets of New York City aimlessly, the camera positioned at a low angle so as to emphasize the height of the buildings looming over him, are gradually replaced by less overwrought images of Daoud buying a giant pretzel from a fast-food stall and staring longingly at the woman who serves him in the store where he purchases some clothes, her long blonde hair flowing over her shoulders.

During these scenes the film reduces the United States to a series of iconic images or simulacra (Marilyn Monroe, giant pretzels and skyscrapers), though the overall effect serves more to illustrate Daoud's inability to see or reach beyond the surface of US society than to provide an authentic, accurate picture of this culture. Indeed, Daoud's capacity to experience the United States or New York City only *at a remove* as it were – significantly by the act of consuming (buying and eating food, shopping for clothes) – resembles the way in which the colonel and Maliheh are similarly reduced to 'experiencing' Iran by consuming images through viewing photographic slides of their homeland, which they are shown doing together towards the end of the film. Although one character's actions represent his attempt to understand and engage with a *foreign culture* and the actions of the others their attempt to remember and maintain a link with their *homeland*, the parallel is striking, nonetheless.

Ultimately Daoud's uncertainty and cultural dislocation lead to his downfall, as he decides not to proceed with the mission and return to Iran and is killed before his departure from Kennedy Airport, presumably by 'His Eminence' or the 'Organization' for his insubordination. The United States, therefore, offers no safe haven or refuge for either Daoud or the colonel, for either the assassin or the target. The colonel, finally realizing that Daoud was an assassin sent to kill him, tells Maliheh there is no safe place for him or his family to hide, as they drive home from the morgue after identifying Daoud's body in the film's penultimate scene. The film's closing images show a new, nameless assassin arriving at the address Daoud stayed at throughout the film, taking Daoud's place as it were, both physically and symbolically. Their similarity in appearance (their clothes, sunglasses, baggage), as well as the identical pattern of shots and camera angles used to portray their arrivals, reinforces the sense that the characters are trapped in a vicious cycle of violence.

Guests of the Hotel Astoria ends on a remarkably similar note, as its central female character Pari (Sohreh Aghdashloo) is also replaced, both physically and symbolically, by another nameless woman, who like Pari is mistakenly led to believe that giving birth to a child in the United States will establish legal residency for herself and her husband. The film ends with a close-up of the nameless woman's face as she smiles, presumably envisioning the happy future that awaits her and her family in the United States, just as *The Mission* concluded with a close-up of the face of the new assassin. Indeed in both films there appears to be no escape from the vicious circles of violence and disappointment set in motion by the characters' displacement. The closing shots of both films, the interchangeability of their respective characters and their various fates serve as powerful images of the depersonalizing and anonymizing effects of displacement, though in *Guests of the Hotel Astoria* this anonymity is partly due also to the episodic nature of its narrative and its large cast of characters.

The film nevertheless focuses primarily on the efforts of Pari and Karim (Mohsen Marzen), first of all to claim political asylum in

Holland and when that fails, to establish residency in the United States. Just as in *The Mission*, although Iran is never shown, it is once again coded as a brutal and violent country, through the dialogue spoken by the characters, as they relate their terrifying experiences of how they smuggled themselves into Turkey through treacherous mountain ranges; the letters which Mr Taghi and Mrs Mahin receive from their children, who are hospitalized and then imprisoned in Iran; the Persian language newspaper which Pari notices in the apartment of her friend upon her arrival in the United States, which tells of how five leftist collaborators against the Iranian regime – one of them her lover Mr Mohsehni (once again played by Houshang Touzie) – were executed in Iran; and especially the ominous performance of Marshall Manesh as Dr. Parto, the Persian language translator for the Turkish police and the character most clearly associated with the Iranian regime. An ex-SAVAK agent for the Shah, now working undercover for Khomeini's SAVAMA (he remarks, 'the two are the same'), Parto blackmails Pari into sleeping with the Turkish police when she and Karim are arrested, to save them both from imprisonment.

Turkey itself is portrayed in an equally unforgiving light. The touristic quality of the scenes that show Pari and Karim sightseeing in Istanbul as they go to apply for their visas (shots of them going on boat trips together and walking around Istanbul surrounded by pigeons) is quickly undermined by the corrupt characters they encounter, both inside and on those few occasions when they venture out of the hotel – from the Turkish police who perform midnight raids on the hotel, accepting bribes from the guests not to arrest them, to Turkish Ali, the counterfeiter who provides Pari and Karim with the papers and documents they need to leave the country, at extortionate rates. For the refugees seeking sanctuary in *Guests of the Hotel Astoria*, Turkey is a country inhabited by crooked policemen and opportunistic human traffickers.

Holland and the United States fail once again, however, to provide a safe haven for the protagonists, in the second instance exclusively for Pari, who is misinformed by one of the hotel's other residents that establishing residency in the United States is simply a matter of giving birth to a child there. After becoming pregnant as a result of her affair with Mohsehni (Karim believes the child to be his own) she successfully enters the United States using a fake passport, in the false hope that she and Karim will be granted full legal residency when she gives birth there. Indeed if *The Mission* concentrates primarily on the culture shock experienced as a result of displacement, then *Guests of the Hotel Astoria* focuses more on the bureaucratic problems facing immigrants when trying to claim political asylum or establish residency in another country; the film's approach though is at the expense of character development and without any particularly in-depth analysis of the actual legal difficulties involved. For instance, Pari and Karim are refused visas to enter Holland without any explanation. Similarly, when they fail to claim political asylum upon arriving in Amsterdam airport, the viewer is briefly shown their subsequent interrogations and strip searches, but never provided with any reason for their enforced return to Turkey. Although the lack of an official explanation in both instances serves to align the viewer's sympathy with Pari and Karim, who are equally clueless as to why they are refused entry, and may give an impression of the haphazardness and cruelty of the international immigration system, it is characteristic of how the film overall offers little insight into how such a system actually works.

The lawyer whom Pari and Tabatata'i (the brother of Mrs Zialli, with whom Pari initially stays upon her arrival in the United States) consult for advice on how Pari can establish legal residency seems likewise intended more to offer a blackly comedic critique of the uncaring nature of the US legal system, than to provide any insight into US immigration policy. His meaningless repetition of the phrase 'Y'know what I mean?' and the way he insensitively perceives Pari's death in childbirth as benefiting his efforts to help Karim obtain legal residency in the United States reinforce this view of his character.

The film also offers an interesting, implicit critique of the economic and social marginalization of other ethnic minorities in the United States, by portraying the affinity between Pari and Mrs Jones, the African-American woman whom Pari stays with after moving out of Tabatataii's home. Mrs Jones is clearly coded as working class, by the way she dresses and the way she speaks, and, with the exception of Tabatata'i and his wife, is the only character that expresses any kind of sympathy for Pari's dilemma. It is also perhaps significant to observe that the janitor who exits the elevator when Tabatata'i arrives at the hospital during Pari's childbirth is also African-American, unlike all of the hospital's administrative staff and doctors and other white-collar workers encountered in the film.

Although the spectre of 'Iran' and the threat of return loom large over all of the characters throughout the film, it is clear that the country itself, or rather the characters' memory of their homeland, acts as a source of comfort to them during their displacement. Within the hotel, the characters reminisce about Iran and 'experience' their homeland vicariously through television images and music. In this respect the film is none too subtle in its portrayal of the traumatic effects of displacement. In one scene, for instance, Mr Zialli (once again played by Kamran Nozad) collapses after drinking too much alcohol and threshes around on the floor of the hotel, bewailing his situation. Nonetheless, *Guests of the Hotel Astoria* effectively depicts the ennui of the émigré experience, as the characters wait in the hotel for days, weeks and months on end, for information about their own future and the fates of their families and friends. There is no strange fascination with the culture of the 'host' country, such as that displayed by Daoud in *The Mission*. Combining the tragic and uncertain fates of so many of the film's characters – Pari's death, Mohsehni's execution, Parvin's turn to prostitution (Parvin is the daughter of Mr and Mrs Zialli), Mr Taghi and Mrs Mahin's attempted return to Iran to be with their children – its depiction of the consequences of displacement is overwhelmingly negative in tone. Whereas *The Mission* manages successfully to interweave its heartfelt examination of the effects of cultural displacement with a compelling storyline, the dramatic impact of *Guests of the Hotel Astoria* is frequently (but not always) undercut by its one-dimensional characterization, its multiple narratives and the sheer number of scenarios it attempts to encompass. Somewhat fatal for the film and certainly the most unilluminating and distracting of these scenarios is the central – yet tawdry and irrelevant – romantic liaison between Pari and Mohsehni itself.

Because of its narrower focus on the experiences of just one particular family, *Nightsongs* by contrast constitutes an altogether more nuanced and emotionally involving study of the traumatic effects of cultural displacement. Because the group of immigrants in this instance are of Chinese origin rather than Iranian, the film, directed by Iranian émigré Marva Nabili, also significantly hints at the emergence of a pan-diasporic dimension to Iranian émigré cinema, although this dimension does not yet manifest itself as such within the diegetic world of the film. Unlike the residents of the Hotel Astoria, who are trapped both physically and symbolically in a state of temporariness and continual suspension, the characters in *Nightsongs* form a distinct diasporic community in the Chinatown of New York City, where they live and work. It is a community once again that is fractured heavily along generational lines; the film charts the growing conflict between the teenager Fung Tak Men (David Lee), who is ostracized and bullied at school because of his race and inability to speak good English, and his parents, Fung Leung (Victor Wong) and Fung Lai Ping (Ida F. O. Chung). Tak Men's growing isolation and estrangement from his family is portrayed in a similar fashion to Daoud's social alienation in *The Mission*, through numerous shots of Tak Men wandering the streets of New York City, itself a common trope for many émigré films. Where *Nightsongs* differs slightly, however, is in the absence of any of the colourful street life images that so strongly characterized Daoud's meanderings. There is no cultural allure or hidden delights on the lonely, bleak streets of *Nightsongs*' New York City, though the film does offer a similarly subtle critique of US consumerism, specifically when Tak Men examines the Japanese-themed display inside the window of what appears to be a Chinese department store, national culture being reduced to mere window dressing. There is, nonetheless, a gritty, desolate beauty to many of the shots of Tak Men walking around New York City, which is reminiscent of Chantal Akerman's *News from Home* (1977) and which when combined with the 'authentic', premodern, almost ethnographic quality of the traditional Chinese music playing on the soundtrack – which clashes noticeably with the film's contemporary urban setting – serves to enhance Tak Men's gradual withdrawal from the world around him.

The conflict between Tak Men and his parents, however, is not so much one of modernity versus tradition but rather centres around Tak Men's descent into the gang culture and warfare that pervade his neighbourhood. Once again this conflict results in death (Tak Men's father is gunned down by rival gang members in a failed attempt to kill Tak Men himself) and, in the figure of the film's central character, Tak Men's Chinese-Vietnamese cousin (Mabel Kwong), who comes to stay with the Fung family at the behest of her husband, an overwhelming sense of being dislocated not only culturally but also spiritually. Indeed, there is an ethereal quality to the character of Tak Men's cousin that is somewhat at odds with the film's realist setting but never threatens to undermine it. As she arrives at the airport at the beginning of the film, her husband's voiceover narration – in the form of a letter written to his relatives in New York City – informs the viewer that he has remained behind in a refugee camp in Malaysia to await news of the fate of their two sons, from whom they were separated during their flight from Vietnam. It provides hardly any information about his wife, not even her name, merely mentioning that she comes from an aristocratic background, a fact that is, nonetheless, important in subtly distinguishing her from the other members of the Fung family in general and the humble, crowded surroundings of their household.

Like the colonel in *The Mission*, Tak Men's cousin remains nameless throughout the entire film. Rather than threatening once again to reduce her character to the status of a mere cipher, however, her anonymity as well as her virtual silence through most of the film (she speaks on just a few occasions and even then only briefly) lend her an air of mystery and transcendence, as if she is somehow beyond words or language, and serve to intensify the film's portrayal of her private, spiritual unease. A strong sense of interiority and of her detachment from the physical world around her is also created by the frequent shots of her praying silently, presumably for the safety of her husband and children, and by the numerous internal monologues that punctuate the narrative, in the form of the poems that she writes in her journal.[36] In these poems she dreams of being reunited with her husband and envisions them both during happier times in their homeland. Indeed, one of the most striking features of these poems is the way in which they repeatedly draw an explicit parallel between the loss of her homeland and her separation from her husband, and her yearning to be reunited with them both. Such an analogy is significant as it highlights the strongly feminist perspective of the film, a perspective that was lacking, for instance, in *Guests of the Hotel Astoria* because of the scant psychological insight provided into that film's female characters, particularly Pari. The following extract from the journal of Tak Men's cousin, for instance, links the memory of her husband with the image of a river they used to walk alongside frequently, a vision that is returned to on numerous occasions during the film through her internal soliloquies:

> I have on my shoulders a touch of silence,
> And the gaze of your eyes.
> I stand a witness to your hell.
> You travel to another place,
> Your world becomes a stolen grave.
> But I have no fear for you.
> Many nights we walked along the riverbank,
> The sound of the water, a long, cooling song.
> Watching the faint shadows of the boats brush the river,
> At dawn when the fishermen pulled in with their catch.
> The air was salt-warm, the sea-wind heavy on our faces.
> My heart moves along that riverbank.
> I have not heard from you my husband.
> Let me hear your voice vibrate in the still of the night,
> Let us speak.
> I *am* lonely.
> I think of you and this river that binds us.
> I wish to feel it upon my body.
> Its rhythm is my source.

By interweaving the sensual imagery of her homeland closely with the memory of her husband, the homeland is envisioned as a thoroughly masculine construct, inverting the traditional male traveller–motherland dichotomy, problematizing what Janet Wolff has described as the notion that there is an *'intrinsic* relationship between masculinity and travel'.[37] Indeed, the way in which Tak Men's cousin is doubly displaced, out of place not only in the host society of the country in which she finds herself, but also within the family environment of the Fung household, recalls Clifford's statement that life for émigré women can be 'doubly painful – struggling with the material and spiritual insecurities of exile, with the demands of family and work and with the claims of old and new patriarchies'.[38] Despite the fact that such a statement – and by extension, the film itself – risks reinforcing the stereotype that women are somehow inherently more spiritual than men, and even though Tak Men's cousin is not subject to any new patriarchal claims within the Fung household itself, both she and Mrs Fung (along with many other women from immigrant and ethnic minority backgrounds) *are* subject to the manipulations of the seemingly kind but, in fact, exploitative manager of the sweatshop factory where they work, as well as to the inspections by the immigration authorities who randomly spot-check the factory and detain the female workers who lack the relevant identity papers. As Keya Ganguly has observed,

> immigrant women are *subject-ed* by the double articulation of discourses of cultural difference and patriarchy. This makes their attempts to negotiate their selfhood in daily life both more interesting and perhaps more exemplary of the contradictory conditions within which subaltern experience is represented and lived.[39]

Tak Men's cousin also appears in a sense to act as his guardian angel. She literally watches over him at times, albeit helplessly, as he becomes more deeply involved in his gang's criminal activities, while the fateful events leading up to the killing of Tak Men's father are witnessed largely through her eyes. The scene in which she saves Tak Men from the bullet that kills his father, moreover, demonstrates an almost preternatural prescience on her part, which is further emphasized by the way in which the viewer's perspective is restricted during this scene. The viewer never sees who shoots at Tak Men, while the sound of the gun firing is likewise concealed by the sound of the firecrackers exploding in the Chinese New Year celebrations Tak Men and his family are watching. All we see instead is a medium close-up of both Tak Men and his cousin, Tak Men occupying the foreground of the screen and his cousin – aptly enough – hovering just behind him over his shoulder, also watching the celebrations, until her eyes catch sight of something off-screen that clearly distresses her. She then dives on Tak Men and pushes him to the ground, saving his life, although the bullet hits his father as a result.

The almost wordless parting between Tak Men and his cousin at the bus station at the film's conclusion, as his cousin leaves not to be reunited with her own family, but instead to live with another surrogate family in San Francisco, further reinforces the impression that she is some kind of heavenly protector. After ascending the steps leading onto the bus, she turns to look down upon Tak Men affectionately one more time, her face framed by her flowing locks of black hair, before disappearing into the night.

If both *The Mission* and *Guests of the Hotel Astoria* tended to emphasize the ideological and legalistic aspects of displacement respectively, then *Nightsongs*, by way of its anonymous and otherworldly portrayal of Tak Men's cousin, highlights its spiritual ramifications. The fate of the characters – or, perhaps more appropriately, survivors – of all three films is nevertheless evocative of the closing lines of the final rumination of Tak Men's cousin, as she departs for San Francisco. Torn from their homeland, with no place of comfort or refuge, and plagued ceaselessly by violence, death and uncertainty, they are all seemingly bound on 'a journey without end'.

All three films considered in this section, therefore, share an overwhelmingly negative view of the experience of displacement. It would be wrong to suggest, however, that taken collectively they amount to an entirely homogeneous and undifferentiated view of life in exile. As the analyses above illustrate, *The Mission* and *Nightsongs* in particular depict the various effects of cultural dislocation with great insight and subtlety. Daoud's ambiguous relationship with US culture as well as the physical and spiritual isolation of Tak Men's cousin from the people and the world around her point towards some of the complexities and particularities of life in exile that challenge traditional monolithic understandings of the émigré experience. There is undoubtedly, however, an underlying determinism that serves to overwhelm the otherwise extremely nuanced portrayals of émigré life. Although *Nightsongs*, as noted above, in a sense represents the emergence of a pan-diasporic dimension in Iranian émigré filmmaking, none of the films considered above exhibit the kind of far-reaching diasporic sensibility that, as this chapter shall demonstrate, would come to characterize the works of other Iranian émigré filmmakers in the near future. Iranian filmmakers working in exile needed to first come to terms with their own hybrid sense of identity, before recognizing the parallels between their experiences of displacement, as well as their relationality to the experiences of other diasporic groups (as the film *America So Beautiful* testifies).

Being in the moment: *I Don't Hate Las Vegas Anymore* and *Walls of Sand*

> Diaspora does not refer us to those scattered tribes whose identity can only be secured in relation to some sacred homeland to which they must at all costs return... This is the old, the imperializing, the hegemonizing, form of 'ethnicity'... The diaspora experience as I intend it here is defined, not by essence or purity, but by the recognition of a necessary heterogeneity and diversity; by a conception of 'identity' which lives with and through, not despite, difference; by *hybridity*. Diaspora identities are those which are constantly producing and reproducing themselves anew, through transformation and difference.[40]
>
> (Stuart Hall)

Both *I Don't Hate Las Vegas Anymore* (Caveh Zahedi, 1994) and *Walls of Sand* (1994), directed by US filmmaker Erica Jordan, and co-produced, co-written and starring Iranian-American émigré Shirin Etessam, represent a significant development in Iranian émigré filmmaking. Both were made during the mid-90s, in spite of, or perhaps because of, the different backgrounds of the two filmmakers in question (Zahedi is a second-generation Iranian-American, while Etessam is an Iranian-born émigré working in the United States), both films signal a shift away from a focus or meditation solely on the harmful and traumatic effects of displacement, to an emphasis on the possibilities of positive change, and the need for self-adjustment and a cautious optimism about the future. Whereas *Guests of the Hotel Astoria* and *Nightsongs* both in their own particular way depict quite vividly the destructive effects of displacement upon family relations and the family unit, *I Don't Hate Las Vegas Anymore* and *Walls of Sand* by contrast, regardless of the different forms they employ – the former being ostensibly a documentary, the latter a more traditional dramatic narrative – emphasize the importance of the family as a source of personal strength, a site of reconciliation and hope, while also stressing the importance and complexity of individual identity.

I Don't Hate Las Vegas Anymore opens, as does Kiarostami's *Through the Olive Trees*, with the director directly addressing the audience, as Zahedi informs the viewer that the film they are about to watch has its origins in a screenplay he wrote two years ago during a family trip from Los Angeles to Las Vegas with his father, Ali, and his younger stepbrother, Amin. The screenplay itself was based on his own transcriptions of the dialogue he recorded during that journey, a journey he and his family made regularly ('every other weekend') when he was a child. Rather than an attempt to re-enact that script, however, explains Zahedi, the film is an unscripted though, as it shall emerge, not wholly unpremeditated record of yet another trip to Las Vegas he, his family and his film crew are undertaking (according to the film's opening intertitles, Zahedi's introductory monologue is recorded on the morning of Christmas Eve 1992, only a few hours before they are due to leave together). Zahedi describes the film and its improvisatory nature as primarily an 'experiment in faith', an attempt to prove the existence of God by leaving the film open to chance or divine providence, allowing events to unfold naturally and the film to take shape by itself as it were.

It is, moreover, he continues, a personal attempt to exorcize his own fears and frustrations about the lack of control over his life and confront his unwillingness to accept this lack of control. It gradually becomes clear that *I Don't Hate Las Vegas Anymore* also represents an attempt by Zahedi to reconcile the contradictory feelings of love and resentment he bears towards his own father. Indeed the long, loud, angry scream that Zahedi emits at the beginning of the film indicates to what a large extent the filmmaking process itself promises to be a form of emotional release for him. On two occasions during the lengthy car journey to Las Vegas, Zahedi speaks to the camera privately while his family members are absent, confessing to the viewer the shame he feels regarding his parents, particularly his father. On one level this shame clearly has its basis in his father's ethnicity (he mentions, for example, his father's 'funny accent') and on another, more universal level, in what Zahedi sees as his father's failings as a parent (later in the film he complains directly to his father about how he was never there for him when he was younger and how he never genuinely listens). Zahedi also acknowledges his self-resentment, his sense of shame at his own faults and the inherent paradox in wishing to show the viewer his father's cultural peculiarities as well as his shortcomings as a parent, while at the same time desiring to accept and come to terms with these peculiarities and shortcomings.

For all the openness and emotional honesty with which Zahedi speaks to the viewer, the film is equally at great pains to undermine the legitimacy of the images unfolding on screen and problematize the viewer's ability to readily accept the veracity of the events they are witnessing, a process that in no small way mirrors Zahedi's own problematic search for the 'truth', his own difficulty accepting and bonding with his father. The very first shot of the film is reflective of how it plays a variety of visual and aural tricks upon the viewer as a whole. Zahedi's apparently unrehearsed, confused, rambling delivery and twitchy body language – in addition to the way in which he converses offhandedly with his film crew behind the camera and is framed slightly off-centre, occupying the right-hand side of the screen as he speaks – lend the film an air of randomness, spontaneity and self-referential tone from the outset. The power and ferocity of the aforementioned scream that accompanies the film's opening credits – which fade in and out against a black background, disembodying the scream from Zahedi himself – is, however, strikingly incongruous with the seemingly timid, thin, neurotic figure of a man that eventually appears on screen.

The numerous ways in which the film violates the conventions of traditional documentary filmmaking – even though it is immediately clear that this is by no means a typical documentary – also aim to confound the viewer. While divulging the extremely personal information about himself, his family and his film crew, Zahedi admits he is a sex addict, his father a former 'womanizer' and his soundwoman Denise a recovering alcoholic with whom he once had a sexual relationship (in his subsequent film, *In the Bathtub of the World* (2001), Zahedi also openly admits to masturbating while fantasizing about one of the female students he teaches at film school).

Indeed the manner in which Zahedi tries to manipulate and implicate himself in proceedings is both morally suspect and far from objective, though it is certainly pertinent to one of his professed reasons for making the film in the first place, which is to test his own (un)willingness to surrender control over events. The most obvious example of Zahedi's unethical control freakery occurs during the very uncomfortable and prolonged sequence set in his hotel room on

Christmas Day after they have reached Las Vegas, in which he tries obstinately to persuade Ali and Amin to take ecstasy – which Zahedi describes to them as a 'love drug' – so they can all be more open and honest with each other. Through a deceptively subtle use of intertitles, the film works to cast doubt on the authenticity of the events that take place and the genuineness of all the participants involved. After failing to impose his own will upon both Ali and Amin, Zahedi takes the drug himself and asks his father and stepbrother to wait with him until it begins to work. They eventually depart, however, promising to return before the ecstasy takes effect, leaving Zahedi alone with his film crew. But when they return (later than promised, after Zahedi is already high), both Ali and Amin seem more than willing, even enthusiastic, to take part in Zahedi's shared drug experience. This is despite their initial reluctance to take ecstasy for fear of the effect it might have on Ali's weak heart – a stance which significantly Zahedi's film crew, notwithstanding their initial support for Zahedi, ultimately sympathize with. What follows, after another brief moment of hesitation over whether or not to take ecstasy (due to the fact that Ali has consumed some alcohol during his absence), is a seemingly drug-induced three-way conversation between Zahedi, Ali and to a decidedly lesser extent Amin. During this conversation Zahedi and his father speak quite candidly about their feelings towards one another, while Zahedi and his stepbrother also converse without the hostility that marked their previous exchanges in the film.

Almost immediately after this emotional climax or moment of catharsis, however, there follows a brief series of intercut monologues, apparently filmed the morning after the night of the shared drug experience, before the return journey to Los Angeles, in which Ali and Amin, as well as Zahedi's film crew, share privately with the viewer their thoughts about the film. During this montage sequence the assistant cameraman Steve confesses that he thinks neither Ali nor Amin actually consumed the ecstasy the previous night. His belief is ostensibly backed up, yet at the same time contradicted to an extent, by the intertitle which appears during the film's end credits sequence, informing the viewer that after they finished filming, Steve revealed to Zahedi that he found (only) one ecstasy tablet in the wastebasket of Ali and Amin's hotel room. The uncertainty that this intertitle and Steve's comments instil in the viewer's mind regarding the sincerity of Ali and/or Amin's behaviour prompts the viewer to consider whether or not they can trust this information (and if they cannot, why it is incorporated into the film at all). After all, Denise clearly states on camera earlier in the film that she saw Ali take his ecstasy tablet. So is Steve mistaken or lying, or was Denise herself complicit in Ali's (and/or Amin's) deception? Any opinion the viewer might reach will undoubtedly have a bearing upon their understanding of the scenes they witness earlier in the film. On the one hand it clearly threatens to undermine the integrity and intimacy of these earlier scenes, insofar as either Ali or Amin (and perhaps Denise, or maybe all three of them) misled Zahedi. On the other hand it may render these scenes all the more moving, in the sense that Ali and Amin both seemed genuinely to connect with Zahedi emotionally, regardless of the fact that neither of them, or only one of them, consumed the ecstasy.

The fact that we do not witness Zahedi taking an ecstasy tablet himself (perhaps the Zahedi family collectively deceive the film crew); Zahedi's earlier assertion to his crew that prior to filming they agreed the film should be half documentary and half re-enactment; the conflicting 'testimony' of Steve and Denise; the noticeably affected and artificial behaviour of Amin upon returning to the hotel room after Zahedi has (seemingly) taken the ecstasy, in direct contrast to the apparent naturalism of Ali's 'performance' earlier in the film; all these factors combine to make reaching any degree of certainty on the matter virtually impossible, just as Zahedi's own attempt to prove the existence of God is in itself an impossible undertaking.

Certain technical 'failures', such as the loss of sound and image, at vital points in the film, and the inclusion of these very failures into the finished product itself, also accumulate gradually to call into question the trustworthiness of the film and hence the filmmakers themselves. At one point, for example, during the initial stages of the shared(?) drug experience, another intertitle appears, informing the viewer that Steve accidentally loads 'the same already-exposed' roll of film into the camera. The resultant visual effect is an inverted image of Zahedi, at first apparently lying in bed speaking to the camera, superimposed over the image of him and his family seated on the sofa in his hotel room, obscuring our view of them as they talk to each other. The recurrence of this image at a later point in the film, *after* the shared drug experience, so that now it is the image of Zahedi seated on the sofa with his family that appears inverted on screen, superimposed over the image of Zahedi lying in bed addressing the camera directly, seemingly calls into question the overall chronology of the film itself, the very order in which the events themselves were recorded. Zahedi has spoken openly of the way in which he intentionally altered the appearance of the film to give an impression of disorder and incompleteness: 'Even filmically, I put in rollouts when they didn't really happen and I manipulated the images very drastically to give more failure than there was.'[41]

Somewhat ironically and perhaps intentionally, these technical 'failures' have the effect of heightening the emotional impact of certain scenes. One the most moving moments in the film, for example, occurs after both Ali and Amin have deserted Zahedi as he waits for the ecstasy to take effect. When it finally does, and it becomes clear that they have not yet returned, there follows a shot of Greg Watkins, the main cameraman, comforting Zahedi, who is visibly upset. The absence of any sound during this scene, or rather the conspicuous silence, puts the viewer at a distance from the brief moment of intimacy when Greg and Zahedi hug each other, lending the scene a sense of privacy, which stands out considerably in a film that has apparently been so emotionally candid and intrusive – albeit purposefully so – up until this point.

Through all of these manipulations and fabrications, therefore, the film somewhat paradoxically arrives at some kind of emotional truth, in a way that is strikingly recollective of Saless's description of cinema itself as a 'very beautiful lie'[42] and Kiarostami's suggestion that by analyzing different aspects of the lie,

> we can arrive at the truth. In cinema anything that can happen would be true. It doesn't have to correspond to reality, it doesn't have to 'really' be happening. In cinema, by fabricating lies we may never reach the fundamental truth, but we will always be on our way to it. We can never get close to the truth except through lying.[43]

Despite the apparent contradiction at the heart of such a statement, such a filmmaking 'ethic' indeed appears to have informed

Zahedi's own film and, moreover, provided Zahedi himself with a sense of inner peace by the film's conclusion. As Naficy observes regarding the film, the journey 'seems to have acted as an agent of family reconciliation and ethnic alignment for Zahedi.'[44] Standing before the camera once more, offering his final thoughts on how the past few days have changed him, Zahedi speaks touchingly of how he has finally learned to respect his father, mentioning one incident in particular when Ali gave Denise a bottle of wine as a gift, in spite of his knowledge of her drinking problem. His father's offering, explains Zahedi, was not an act of stupidity or insensitivity, but rather represented his father's acceptance of Denise, regardless of whatever faults she may have. Zahedi likewise seems more able by the film's end to accept himself, his father and the lack of control over his own life. As Zahedi remarks: 'I feel like I can be in the moment now. And I am.' His closing words are borne out in subsequent statements made in interviews after competing the film:

> I've only sort of caught up with myself in the last year [1994]. With *A Little Stiff* [Zahedi's first feature film, 1991] I was always frustrated that I should have been further along. I should have been more famous, more respected, more appreciated, richer. It always felt like it wasn't enough. Whereas now I feel like I'm right where I need to be and I feel very good where I am. I feel like I'm home.[45]

Zahedi, nonetheless, apparently cannot resist ending the film on a mischievously provocative note. As the film's final end credits roll, Zahedi's voice emerges on the soundtrack, attempting to articulate his thoughts on what he believes to be the 'true' meaning of the film. After a series of false starts and hesitations, he decides to begin again and the sound of a tape recorder cutting out is audible on the soundtrack. Zahedi's voice then emerges once more and offers a far more coherent explanation of the meaning of the film, in which he metaphorically equates his own father with 'God', a poetic explanation that is, nonetheless, undercut by Zahedi's final, irreverent exclamation of the word 'anyway'. The juxtaposition of these two versions of Zahedi's account of the film – the first seemingly improvised, the second prepared – serves as a microcosm of the entire film, reminding the viewer, in spite of the emotional 'high' the film concludes on, of the possible duplicity and ambiguity of the film and of the inherent dishonesty of the filmmaking process itself.

In spite of their similarly hopeful conclusions regarding the potential for change and acceptance, *Walls of Sand* differs from *I Don't Hate Las Vegas Anymore* insofar as it places a far greater emphasis on the specifically cultural aspects of its protagonists' disaffection and subsequent reconciliation with their family. The dilemmas that confront the Iranian-American Soroya (Etessam), in contrast to those faced by most of the protagonists of the films analyzed thus far, are not those of resistance or aversion to cultural assimilation, but rather of *overidentification* with US culture and the tension this creates between Soroya and her more traditional Iranian family.

Soroya's overidentification with US culture is represented both physically and symbolically by the way she dresses – at the funeral of her uncle, Soroya is clearly differentiated from other members of her family by the contemporary clothing she wears, which contrasts starkly with the more conventional attire worn by her cousin Mitra – and also by her relationship with an American man, Chad, which Soroya believes to be the main reason for her cousin's rejection of her. The film, however, begins where Soroya and Chad's relationship ends, their break-up leaving Soraya with no place to live and, lacking a green card, no means of seeking employment. Culturally disenfranchised by both her family and US society, Soroya resorts to sleeping in her car, lying about her race to prospective employers and attending self-help discussion groups in the seemingly vain hope of seeking some advice and guidance on her predicament.

At the same time, the film draws an explicit parallel between the cultural and economic isolation of Soroya and the alienation of its other central female character, Ellen (Jan Carty Marsh), who suffers from agoraphobia. Ellen hires Soroya as an au pair for her son Alex, not knowing that Soroya has been lured into applying for the position by Ellen's ex-husband, Tom, who is concerned about Alex's welfare. In return for a job in his company and a legal green card, Tom persuades Soroya to spy on Ellen and report back to him on any failings she may notice on Ellen's part with respect to Alex's upbringing.

Despite Soraya's initial concerns regarding the negative impact of Ellen's condition upon Alex (he is introverted and withdrawn and performs badly at school), her occupancy of Ellen's household actually has a kind of therapeutic and liberating effect upon Ellen herself. Although still confined largely to her bedroom and consumed with writing longing, unsent letters to her ex-husband, Ellen slowly begins to let her defences down and open up emotionally around Soraya. This psychological revival of sorts is conveyed visually by Ellen's increasingly relaxed and languorous body language, as well as the loose-fitting and more informal clothing she begins to wear about the house, in contrast to her previously inhibited behaviour and stern, school-mistress appearance. In one of the film's central scenes – central in terms of importance as well as its position in the overall narrative – the film emphasizes the connection between Soraya's presence and Ellen's growing openness, by intercutting between images of Ellen taking a bath and Soraya secretly reading one of her letters, a letter which itself speaks affectionately of the positive influence of Soraya's company. As Naficy observes, the sensuousness of the imagery, as well as the music and the voiceover that accompany it, spills over to infuse the relationship between Soraya and Ellen with heavily sexual overtones.

> The intercutting between the two women, one voicing what the other is reading, unites them, creating a charged homoerotic bond – although they are not in the same physical space. A lovely musical score that mixes Eastern and Western motifs symbolizes the coming together of the two women from different cultures. In the next scene, with knowing smiles, as though they have just shared a secret, they prepare a meal together for the first time and, like a couple, tend to various household chores and repairs. The lesbian eroticism is unmistakeable but subtle.[46]

The film utilizes this stylistic device on one more occasion later in the film for a similar purpose, when it intercuts between shots of Ellen burning some of the letters she wrote to Tom and Soraya leaping over several small bonfires she has built to mark the beginning of the Iranian New Year (Norouz). As the film cuts back and forth between both sets of flames, Ellen begins to relinquish her past, while Soraya learns to embrace her own. In this sense the blend of Eastern and Western music on the soundtrack also symbolizes Soraya's acceptance of her own hybrid identity as an Iranian-American. Indeed, Soraya's relationship with Ellen is mutually beneficial, significantly helping Soraya to open up and reconnect with Iranian culture. Soraya's behaviour in her regular discussion groups early on in the film, for instance, reveals the extent of her unwillingness or inability to acknowledge the 'root' causes of her own cultural, economic and social marginalization. She sneers and expresses indifference (sometimes comically, sometimes insensitively) as the various other members of the group speak (sometimes insufferably, sometimes poignantly) of their own emotional and psychological hang-ups, refusing to discuss her own problems. However, when Ellen shows Soraya some photos of her own brief trip to Iran from years ago, and when Alex asks Soraya to explain to him the intricacies of the ritual of Norouz, each opportunity acts as a kind of catalyst for Soraya to reflect upon her own past and her relationship with her family. A lengthy sequence towards the end of the film shows Soraya reconciling with her cousin Mitra and celebrating Norouz with her family and friends, leaving behind the ghost of her dead uncle that haunts and guides her throughout the film.

The following exchange between Soraya and Ellen during the dramatic climax of the film, in which Soraya helps Ellen to overcome her fears and step outside the house for the first time, to fool Tom into believing that Ellen does not, in fact, suffer from agoraphobia, furthermore underlines the crucial role that both women have played in each other's cultural and psychological reawakening:

> Soraya – Ellen, you can do this. You know, I was beginning to think that deep down we were a lot alike, but there's a big difference. I've been denying my past, where I come from and who I am and you can't let go of yours. Now if you and I are going to go through with this we have to be bigger people than we have been.
> Ellen – What if I panic?
> Soraya – Then just hold on a little bit tighter.

In the film's penultimate close-up shot of Ellen speaking to an anonymous off-screen confidant – presumably a psychiatrist, but almost as if she were directly addressing the viewer – we learn of the tentative progress she has made since overcoming her fears, as well as of Soraya's successful return to college. In a manner that is reminiscent of, yet decidedly more convincing and optimistic than both *Guests of the Hotel Astoria* and *Nightsongs*, *Walls of Sand* interweaves its tale of cultural, physical and psychological alienation with a strong feminist discourse. Considered in relation to *I Don't Hate Las Vegas Anymore*, both films clearly acknowledge the impossibility and undesirability of a utopian return to some original state of cultural stability or purity and point toward the need for a malleable, open-ended concept of individual identity that is, nonetheless, grounded in an awareness of one's own specific cultural background and family history.

Both of the films considered in this section, therefore, signal a clear shift away from the overwhelmingly negative portrayal of the effects of displacement found in earlier examples of Iranian émigré filmmaking such as *The Mission*, *Guests of the Hotel Astoria* and *Nightsongs*. At the same time, the newfound sense of optimism and freedom found in *I Don't Hate Las Vegas Anymore* and *Walls of Sand* is tempered by a knowledge of the pains of cultural assimilation and an acceptance of the innate hybridity of one's personal identity. The intensely personal and autobiographical nature of both films, however, does not easily allow for the incorporation or acknowledgement of other perspectives on the émigré experience. Which is not to suggest that either Jordan/Etessam and/or Zahedi are under any responsibility or obligation (moral or otherwise) to attempt to incorporate such alternative views into their films, or indeed that any of the films to be examined in the following sections of this chapter are any *less* personal than the films considered thus far. Rather it is to argue that *I Don't Hate Las Vegas Anymore* and *Walls of Sand* represent a decisive moment of transition in the historical development of Iranian émigré filmmaking, foreshadowing the emergence of a more far-reaching, though still underdeveloped, (pan-)diasporic sensibility. It is also to contend, as this chapter now goes on to illustrate, that the more recent examples of Iranian émigré filmmaking reveal a far greater awareness of how their own tales of dislocation fit into a wider global context of cultural displacement and diasporic formation.

The European connection: Reza Parsa and Susan Taslimi

If the analysis of the films in the two sections above bears more than a passing resemblance to Elisabeth Kubler-Ross's delineation of the five stages of mourning (Denial, Anger, Bargaining, Depression and Acceptance, though maybe not quite in that order), it is because the films themselves, without wishing to impose too strict or linear a trajectory upon them, clearly invite such a reading. In spite of the continued, equivocal emphasis on the vicissitudes of displacement in many of the films considered below, these works do not represent a return of the repressed, so much as they do a recognition that, to quote Stuart Hall, 'identity is always an open, complex, unfinished game – always under construction... It produces new subjects who bear the traces of the specific discourses which not only formed them but enable them to *produce themselves anew and differently*.'[47]

Both Reza Parsa and Susan Taslimi live and make films in Sweden. Parsa was born in Tehran and immigrated with his family to Sweden in 1980 at the age of twelve following the Revolution. He later studied directing at the National Film School of Denmark. Taslimi immigrated to Sweden in 1988, was born in the city of Rasht in northern Iran and is one of the country's most well-known actresses, noted for her portrayal of strong female characters, particularly in a number of films directed by Beyza'i, most famously as Na'i in *Bashu, the Little Stranger*. Along with other figures of the Iranian New Wave such as Sayyad, Naderi and Saless, Taslimi represents a powerful physical and symbolic link between the New Iranian Cinema and Iranian émigré cinema.

The connection between these two figures, other than the fact that they were both born in Iran and immigrated to Sweden, is the short film *Never* (1995), also known as *Border*. Directed by Parsa and made around the same time as *I Don't Hate Las Vegas Anymore* and *Walls of Sand* in the United States, *Never* stars Taslimi as Aisha, an illegal immigrant of Arab descent who takes a schoolteacher (Claes Ljungmark) and two of his pupils hostage and threatens to kill them unless the Swedish authorities grant her daughter Maryam (Nasim Kodadadi) asylum.

Throughout the film it is never revealed which country Aisha comes from. Taslimi speaks Arabic in the role, rather than Persian, which would have clearly identified Aisha as Iranian. This deliberate cultural non-specificity is characteristic of Parsa's subsequent films and illustrates the development of a pan-diasporic-cum-Middle Eastern sensibility in Iranian émigré filmmaking. His first feature-length film, *Before the Storm* (2000), tells the story of Ali (Per Graffman), a Muslim émigré living in Sweden, whose idyllic family life is disrupted when he is contacted by members of the terrorist organization he used to belong to in his unnamed country of origin. (Stephen Holden in his *New York Times* review of the film suggests that Ali hails from the Balkans.)[48]

Likewise, the suicide bomber (Cesar Saracho) who confronts the viewer in Parsa's more recent short film *Meeting Evil* (2002) never mentions the name of the country he lives in, the terrorist group to which he belongs, nor the name of the political party whose rally he is targeting. It is only apparent that the film is set in an Islamic country from the Arabic Saracho's character speaks at the film's beginning and from the brief glimpses of chador-clad women seen through the windows of the car as they pass by. With *Meeting Evil* at least, a direct response to the events of 9/11, this cultural anonymity was intended to give the film a universal dimension, which, according to Stephen Holden, in the case of *Before the Storm* makes the film seem 'grandiose and forced.'[49] What Holden's critique overlooks, however, is the degree to which Parsa refuses to pass any kind moral judgement on his protagonists. His films attempt to encompass the viewpoints of all his characters, showing the consequences of all their actions, whether they are innocent bystanders or terrorists, asking the viewer to make their own interpretations.

In *Never,* for instance, the potential sympathy for Aisha's plight is counterbalanced to a large degree by the opinions voiced, first, by the schoolteacher, who rightly insists that he and the schoolchildren have nothing to do with Aisha's predicament, and, second, by Eriksson (Sten Ljunggren), the main police officer on the scene, who angrily condemns Aisha for involving her own daughter in such a violent and dangerous situation. Indeed if the viewer has complete sympathy for any character in the film it is for Maryam herself, who falls devastatingly silent upon hearing her mother shoot herself behind the locked classroom door, thus committing suicide on realizing that the Swedish authorities will never accept her demands. Similarly, *Before the Storm*, by virtue of its greater length, represents a more wide-ranging and ambitious attempt by Parsa to display once again the even-handedness and impartiality he demonstrated in *Never*.

Somewhat similar to the plight of Daoud in *The Mission*, Ali is blackmailed into attempting to assassinate the Swedish politician Sanders (Claes Ljungmark once again), who is responsible for permitting the construction and shipment of two thousand military trucks to the regime in Ali's homeland. The courier for the terrorist organization (Nasrin Pakkho) that contacts Ali informs him that if does not undertake the assignment they will execute his former wife and son, whom Ali believed to be dead. The film nevertheless does not attempt to align the viewer's sympathy solely with Ali. The courier is accompanied throughout the film by her grandson Josef, who as she explains to Ali was blinded by a rocket from a military truck built in Sweden. When Ali decides to accept the assignment and infiltrates the hospital where Sanders is visiting his sick father, he discovers Sanders not to be a selfish, uncaring politician, but a son genuinely worried for his father's health. However, when Ali spares Sanders' life, in a subsequent sequence the viewer is shown Sanders (now wearing a neck brace after Ali's attempt to strangle him) signing the documents legalizing the shipment of the aforementioned trucks to Ali's homeland. The sequence continues to show quite graphically Ali's former wife and son being killed, not by the terrorists who held them hostage, but by missiles from the very trucks whose consignment they were seeking to halt. The incorporation of so many contrasting perspectives and scenarios into the film, far from legitimizing or condemning the actions of either Ali, the courier, the terrorists or Sanders, serves rather to present the viewer with a kaleidoscope of viewpoints and consequences, none of which can be totally accepted or dismissed with any degree of moral authority. This strategy is employed most audaciously in *Meeting Evil*.

The film itself is comprised almost entirely of what seems to be one single take of around ten minutes in length, in which the nameless suicide bomber directly addresses the camera in medium close-up from the back seat of his car, explaining why he is about to kill himself and a number of innocent civilians. The bomber does not directly address the viewer but is rather recording his own video message, initially to his wife, whom he then instructs to show the remainder of the tape to their daughter Nora some ten years later. The back of Nora's head is shown on those few occasions when the camera subtly, yet significantly, breaks away from the medium close-up of the bomber delivering his monologue to the camera, to what is essentially an over-the-shoulder shot from Nora's perspective as she watches her father on television. At these points, although Nora's face is not in view, the viewer is to an extent able to gauge her reaction to what her father is saying, by the way she holds her hand to head in a sign of distress, as she watches the posthumous video message left to her by her father.

On one other important occasion, however, the camera cuts away from the medium close-up of the bomber, not to an over-the-shoulder viewpoint from Nora's perspective, but rather to a close-up of the television screen, situating itself in an area that lies *in-between* Nora and her father. The cut is significant, because at this point in the film Nora's father utters the following words: 'They say I kill innocent people Nora, but there are no innocent people. There are only two options: with us or against us.' Aligned completely with neither Nora nor her father at this point, neither here nor there, the indeterminate and morally neutral position of the camera quite subtly undermines the deterministic and brutally reductive binary logic invoked by the bomber. Rather than inviting the viewers to make up their own mind at this point, or invoking a sense of moral ambiguity, the cut represents a very clear moral decision on the part of Parsa, as he distances the audience from the bomber at this vital moment.

The unsympathetic image of the bomber that emerges at this point is complicated, however, by the emotion he displays throughout the rest of the film, as he bids farewell to his daughter and remembers some of the acts of violence he has witnessed that drove him to become a terrorist in the first place. More importantly, the bomber's earlier remarks are offset by the final piece of advice he offers to his daughter: 'The worst thing you can do to your enemy is to think by yourself. Don't be stupid. People try to fool you. Always think by yourself. Don't be stupid. So, even what you've heard on this tape, you have to think for yourself.' Delivered once again in medium close-up, this supplication to open-mindedness and self-determination is a direct appeal not only to Nora, but also to the viewer. It is also reflective of the carefully balanced perspective that all of Parsa's films strive to present, which, when viewed in relation to the cultural anonymity of his central characters and the distinctly pan-diasporic sensibility of his films, represents a significant turning point in the evolution of Iranian émigré filmmaking.

Susan Taslimi's directorial debut by contrast is quite a different affair altogether. *All Hell Let Loose* (2002) deals quite specifically with an Iranian tale of displacement, examining the effect upon the lives of Serbandi (Hassan Brijany) and his family when his daughter Minoo (Melinda Kinnaman) returns home to Sweden from the United States, where unbeknownst to her family she worked as a stripper. It is also strongly implied via the flashbacks that punctuate the narrative that Minoo was involved in some form of prostitution or pornography. Upon Minoo's return the viewer also learns that Serbandi originally disowned her for getting pregnant by her ex-boyfriend Pontus (Ola Noreil). The film thus focuses mainly on the conflict between Serbandi and Minoo, and Serbandi's efforts to retain control over his entire family.

However, despite the film's renewed emphasis on the exigencies of displacement for a group of Iranian émigrés, it portrays the effects of cultural dislocation in a predominantly comical light. It thus provides an interesting counterpoint to the fatalistic outlook of the earlier Iranian émigré films considered above. *All Hell Let Loose* also examines, in much greater detail than any of the films analyzed so far, the generational conflicts brought about by the experience of displacement. Minoo, for example, lives not only with her parents, but also with her grandmother Farmour (Bibbi Azizi), Serbandi's mother. The film thus explores not only the tensions between father and daughter, between parents and their children, but also the fraught relationships between Farmour and the other members of Serbandi's household, his wife Nana (Caroline Rauf) in particular. In contrast to the films considered above, *All Hell Let Loose* apparently takes great glee in depicting the erosion of the traditional patriarchal structure of the Iranian family, as well as the weakening of traditional notions of Iranian masculinity, when they are transposed into a foreign context or culture. Serbandi, for instance, tries to pair Minoo off with his much older friend, the wheelchair-bound war veteran Karim (Kemal Görgö), who, despite losing both of his legs in the Iran-Iraq War, is considered by Serbandi to be a real 'man'. Serbandi's understanding of masculinity is based not so much upon a concept of physical wholeness or strength, but upon traditional Shi'i notions of male bravery and sacrifice (in other words, martyrdom).[50] His inability to comprehend the existence of other masculinities, let alone recognize their validity, is illustrated by the extreme distaste he exhibits upon first meeting Minoo's effeminate friend Bijan (Sunil Munshi), a hairdresser.

Serbandi's patriarchal authority is called into question, however, during an early scene in the film, when he is shown trying frantically to prepare a food delivery for the home-catering service he runs. As he rushes about the kitchen, his mother chastises him on more than one occasion for not being a real man, for doing 'women's work', hitting him as if he were a child. Indeed the insubordination, not only of Minoo, who eventually reconciles with Pontus, much to Serbandi's disapproval, but of all the female family members, illustrates both dramatically and comically Serbandi's gradual emasculation. Minoo's sister Gita (Meliz Karlge) meets with her fiancé (Dennis Önder) for sexual liasions behind Serbandi's back, while his wife, Nana, flirts constantly with Leif, the mechanic who comes round to fix her sewing machine regularly, at one point directly in front of Serbandi. Serbandi is furthermore contrasted physically with Leif. Short, overweight, with his swarthy complexion and balding head, Brijany stands in stark contrast with the tall, slim and Aryan-like Bjorn Söderback, the actor who portrays Leif.

Serbandi's failure to keep control over his family eventually erupts in violence, when he discovers that Minoo has reunited with Pontus. Restrained from attacking her only after Nana puts a pair of scissors to his throat, he locks Minoo in her room on the day of Gita's wedding, only for Minoo to escape and humiliate Serbandi by performing a striptease in front of the wedding guests on stage. This act of defiance and the show of sisterly allegiance performed by Gita, who runs up on stage and cloaks Minoo's partly naked body with her wedding dress, ring somewhat false, however, in light of the previous ease with which she and Nana submitted to Serbandi's decision to lock Minoo in her bedroom. It is in its depiction of the touching relationship between Minoo and Farmour, however, that *All Hell Let Loose* makes its most poignant statement regarding the potential for resistance to male tyranny through strong female bonds and the possibility of reconciliation between different generations.

Although Farmour speaks only Persian while Minoo speaks Swedish and English, the affection shown between the two and the joy Farmour expresses when Minoo arrives home – singing her to sleep and playing with her in bed – illustrates the potential for understanding between the two generations, despite their separation by language. Indeed from the very beginning of the film, Farmour is heavily associated with an 'authentic' sense of Iranian culture and heritage, an association that acts as a form of comfort to Minoo during her conflict with Serbandi. The opening shot of the film shows Farmour through an elaborately embroidered curtain anticipating her granddaughter's arrival and reminiscing of how she used to sing lullabies to her when she was a child. The languorous, mystical Eastern melody on the soundtrack, in conjunction with the slow billowing of cigarette smoke from her lips, as well as the languid camera movement, all serve to introduce Farmour as an apparently more spiritual and thoughtful person than the other members of her family, and as one who is more in touch with her Iranian heritage. It is significant that in the film's closing shot of the entire family – minus Serbandi – gathered around the wedding table after all the other guests have left, it is Farmour who beckons her son Serbandi to join them. From off-screen, Serbandi replies, 'I'm coming,' an indication perhaps that he will eventually come to accept his diminished authority as family patriarch and will attempt to etch out a new role for himself within the family unit. Farmour, therefore, at the film's conclusion, also acts as a potential bridge *between* generations, hinting at the possibility of a reconciliation between Serbandi and the rest of his family in due time.

The films of Parsa and Taslimi seem to be representative of a growing awareness on the part of Iranian émigré filmmakers of the inherent irreducibility of the Iranian émigré experience. Parsa's films, by way of the cultural anonymity of their protagonists, the deliberate non-particularity of their narratives and their considered moral objectivity, are informed by a manifestly pan-diasporic sensibility that emphasizes the similarities between experiences of displacement for all Middle Eastern émigrés, at the same time as it confounds monolithic understandings of these experiences. *All Hell Let Loose* by contrast explores the variability of factors, such as age and gender, which differentiate the experience of displacement *within* distinct diasporic formations.

As if to bear out this interpretation of the noticeable shift in Iranian émigré filmmaking, the two films considered in the following section – *Maryam* (Ramin Serry, 2000, USA) and *America So Beautiful* – reveal a further dimension to the evolution of Iranian émigré filmmaking, one that is heavily and explicitly informed by an intricate knowledge of the history, reception and formation of the Iranian diaspora in the United States.

Children of the revolution: *Maryam* and *America So Beautiful*

The emergence of both *Maryam* and *America So Beautiful* within such a short space of time of each other, in the years 2000 and 2001 respectively, is significant given their virtually identical subject matter. Although the events of the first film take place in New Jersey and those of the latter in Los Angeles, both are set during the outbreak of the Iranian Revolution, and both focus on the hostility and racism encountered by a group of Iranian-American émigrés as a result of the ensuing US hostage crisis. The extent to which both films parallel each other is borne out by a comparison of their remarkably similar opening credits, which both utilize a montage of documentary and news footage to chronicle the downfall of the Shah and Khomeini's subsequent return from exile. The opening credits of *Maryam* include images of US president Jimmy Carter toasting with the Shah in December 1977, during Carter's tour of the Middle East, a few weeks prior to the beginning of the protests that would eventually culminate in the Shah's flight into exile. The opening credits of *America So Beautiful* show Ayatollah Khomeini descending the steps of the Air France plane which brought him back to Iran after years in exile, on 31 January 1979.

Both sequences then take a slightly different route. *Maryam*'s goes on to show the kind of images that would come to be repeated endlessly on US television, of excited Iranian mobs crowding the streets of Tehran. In *Maryam*'s case, establishing this imagery in the viewer's mind early on in the film is crucial in laying the groundwork for the parallel the film eventually draws between the Iranian people's reaction to the Revolution and American public response to the subsequent hostage crisis. *America So Beautiful* employs actual footage of the American hostages being taken captive as Iranians overran the US Embassy in Tehran in November 1979, nearly one full year after Khomeini's return to Iran. Both sequences eventually conclude with a shot of Khomeini, though they are very different in terms of how they portray him. In *Maryam* the closing shot of Khomeini shows him reaching out affectionately to a young child, while in *America So Beautiful* the final image of Khomeini, gun in hand, his silhouette framed against a crowd of Iranians in the background, is far more mysterious and sinister in tone. These contrasting images of Khomeini, the former thoroughly paternalistic in nature and the latter militant, are reflective of the different visions of the man in both Iranian and US society.

Both films also use music to further contextualize their stories. *Maryam*'s opening credits for instance are accompanied – with an intentionally caustic irony no doubt – by The Cars 1979 song *Let the Good Times Roll* while *America So Beautiful* employs a wide-ranging disco soundtrack throughout. The latter film follows the exploits of Houshang (played by Iranian-American pop star Mansour), who works part-time in the grocery store owned by his uncle Hamid (Alan De Satti) and longs to get rich and live the American Dream. He steals money from his uncle to give to local disco owner Sahmi (Houshang Touzie), who promises to make Houshang a partner in his lucrative disco business. Sahmi, however, uses the money to fund covertly what appears to be a counter-revolutionary terrorist group inside Iran. By the film's conclusion, Sahmi is executed by members of the same group, apparently for keeping the money for himself and misleading them as to the size of the army he supposedly had at his disposal. Houshang's ambitions of improving his social and economic standing in US society are likewise destroyed.

In *America So Beautiful*, the attempt to contextualize its story of displacement and cultural alienation extends quite clearly to the film's visual style. As Johnny Ray Huston observes in his *San Francisco Bay Guardian* review of the film, its tale of family conflict, primarily between Houshang and his uncle Hamid, reveals a 'comic seriousness worthy of early Scorsese'.[51] The film's immaculate cinematography in particular only serves to bring to light more clearly the seedy and garish neon-lit streets of Los Angeles, in a manner reminiscent of Martin Scorsese's hellish vision of New York City in *Mean Streets* (1973) and *Taxi Driver* (1976), while the images of Houshang dressing in front of the mirror early on in the film, preparing to go out to Sahmi's disco, accompanied by Thelma Houston's *Don't Leave Me This Way* on the soundtrack, are deliberately evocative of John Travolta's character, Tony Manero, in *Saturday Night Fever* (John Badham, 1977).

Indeed the spectre of Tony Manero looms large over all the Iranian characters in the film, as they are advised on more than one occasion to conceal their ethnicity and pretend they are Italian-Americans, so as to avoid discrimination and to gain entry to the various discos scattered about Los Angeles. Such cultural mutability, however, does not provide the characters with a newfound sense of freedom or fluidity but only serves to increase their alienation from US society and from their own culture. In one scene, for instance, Houshang's friend Parviz (Fariborz David Diaan), the long-suffering taxi driver who puts up most of the money for Houshang's 'investment', berates a fellow Iranian in Hamid's store for changing his original name Dariush (the name of a famous ruler of the Persian Empire) to 'Disco Danny'. Unlike the film's other characters, Parviz dreams of returning to Iran to be with his family, predicting that the chaos following the Revolution will be over within 'one or two weeks'. The film, therefore, is careful to distinguish the differing responses to the Iranian Revolution by the Iranian-American community living in the United States at the time.

In *Maryam,* by contrast – despite the film's careful attention to period detail, such as the yellow ribbons the American families tie around the trees outside their houses in support of the US hostages – there is an unnervingly contemporary feel to the film's design and mise-en-scène, which lend the film a very topical edge. It was almost certainly this topical edge, in light of the events of 9/11 and the ensuing xenophobia experienced by Iranian and Arab-Americans living in the United States, which led Roger Ebert of the *Chicago Sun Times* to champion the film so strongly in 2002, although he had viewed the film two years earlier for the first time at the 2000 Hawaii Film Festival, and to remark that *Maryam* 'is more timely now than ever.'[52]

The film examines the impact upon the lives of an Iranian-American family, especially on the young teenage daughter, Maryam (Mariam Parris), when their devout Muslim relative Ali (David Eckert), Maryam's cousin, comes from Iran to live with them. Ali is staunchly in favour of the Revolution taking place in his homeland and, unlike Daoud in *The Mission*, is largely repelled by US society. The culture clash between Ali and his US relatives is initially played for comic effect (such as when Ali mocks Maryam for thinking that he does not know what a pizza is), as is Ali's aversion to US society (he begrudgingly accompanies Maryam to a roller disco, where he is offered drugs). This aversion is further exacerbated when the Shah travels to the United States for medical treatment. Outraged, Ali resolves to attempt to assassinate the Shah and is eventually forced to return to Iran after his fails to do so.

Perhaps the most striking aspect of *Maryam*, as noted above, is the way in which it draws an explicit comparison between the response of the Iranian people and that of the American people to the Revolution and the subsequent taking of US hostages. The footage of frenzied mobs of Iranians swarming the streets of Tehran which opens the film, representative as they are of the image of Iran that was circulated in the US media at the time, recalls Naficy's observations on the media's portrayal of Iran following the Revolution in the opening chapter of this book. These images are then paralleled later in the film by the even more violent and incendiary images of hysterical and angry Americans beating up peaceful Iranian-American protesters, burning the Iranian flag and chanting 'Bomb Iran!' Through the indirect juxtaposition of these images, *Maryam* highlights the similar types of patriotic fundamentalism and reactionary hatred taking hold in both countries. This comparison is supported by the racist abuse subsequently encountered by both Maryam and Ali at school. In one particularly uncomfortable scene, for example, Maryam's classmates imply she has facial hair, which they say 'must be a problem for you people.'

Both *America So Beautiful* and *Maryam*, therefore, strive to contextualize their narratives historically. The films also share an affinity with each other in their conclusions, insofar as their central protagonists begin to look beyond their own cultural displacement and recognize the validity of other cultural identities and émigré experiences. The final scene of *Maryam,* for instance, shows Maryam and Ali bidding farewell to each other at the airport, Ali having chosen to return to Iran after his failed attempt to assassinate the Shah (how his relatives manage to smuggle Ali out the United States with the police pursuing him is conveniently overlooked). The overly emotive score that accompanies this scene belies the understated and subtle exchange of glances between Maryam and Ali, as they seem to acknowledge their innate difference from each other, despite their shared Iranian heritage. There is an implied sense that Maryam's relationship with her cousin, fraught as it has been throughout the film, has enriched her understanding of her own identity and broadened her previously singular, culturally exclusive view of the world.

America So Beautiful concludes by demonstrating how Houshang's predicament resembles the fate of many other ethnic minorities in the United States, lending the film a multicultural and vividly pan-diasporic dimension, in a manner that is reminiscent of, yet different from, the pan–Middle Eastern sensibility of Reza Parsa's films. After his dealings with Sahmi fall through, Houshang, like Parviz, resorts to driving a taxi to support himself. The film's closing images, intercut with footage of Ronald Reagan's presidential inauguration and the safe return of the US hostages, show Houshang and a number of his fellow taxi drivers, of all different races, loitering about the same taxi rank. This montage sequence highlights the social and economic marginalization of all ethnic minorities in the United States in general. Although as director Babak Shokrian, the cast members and various reviews of the film have pointed out, the conclusion is also hopeful insofar as it represents Houshang's second chance of working slowly towards the American Dream, even if this dream is symbolized somewhat irreverently by the tacky figurine of the Statue of Liberty Houshang stands on the dashboard of his taxi. Indeed as Michelle Langford notes, the 'ragged Uncle Sam'[53] figure that pops up at various stages throughout the film serves to remind the audience (if not, alas, Houshang himself) of the superficiality of the American Dream he is chasing so desperately.

Although *America So Beautiful* and *Maryam* both locate their stories in the past, they are indicative of the way in which Iranian émigré filmmakers have acquired a sense of perspective and begun exploring the parallels between their own and other émigrés' experiences of displacement and cultural dislocation. Both Babak Shokrian and *Maryam*'s director, Ramin Serry, have spoken in detail of how their own experiences of living in the United States during the revolutionary period influenced their films. As Serry explains,

> The 'Maryam' character is largely based on me. Like her, I grew up in the U.S. without much connection to Iran. During the Iran-Iraq war, two of my male cousins fled Iran and came to live with my family. Mary's mixed feelings of curiosity and embarrassment regarding her cousin are based on my own experiences. I had a cousin named Ali who was very energized by the revolution. I used this for part of Ali's character. But Ali's feelings of frustration, resentment and struggle with his faith are actually based on me... I was born in the U.S. and, like Maryam, grew up thinking I was a typical American, until the hostages were taken and other kids started telling me that I was a foreigner. During that period, I was constantly called names and harassed. The hardest part about it was that some of the kids who harassed me were, otherwise, some of my closest friends. They weren't 'dumb' bullies. These kids were very intelligent and could be incredibly charming. This complicated the issue and, at the time, left me feeling very confused.[54]

Shokrian has made very similar remarks, echoing not only Serry but also Zahedi:

> The characters and customs within my own culture have always fascinated me. It made sense to make films about 'us'. I feel deeply compelled to embrace the generation before me, my own generation and the generation after me, to try and understand it, come to terms with it and to capture its essence. It is difficult to explain but it really comes out of love and the need to show this to ourselves and the rest of the world.[55]

A diasporic dimension that was absent from the earlier examples of Iranian émigré filmmaking considered in this chapter, therefore, manifests itself in *America So Beautiful* and *Maryam*. Although the latter film concludes by emphasizing the differences between cultures and the former film the similarities, both clearly embody a more open-ended and flexible understanding of ethnicity and of life as a first- and/or second-generation émigré, challenging established notions of the émigré experience as undifferentiated and monolithic.

However, the film with which we conclude this brief overview of Iranian émigré cinema, *House of Sand and Fog*, undoubtedly the most visible and well-known example of Iranian émigré filmmaking and yet in certain respects the most ambiguous, in many ways can be seen to signal a retreat from the diasporic sensibility displayed in the films considered above.

Recurring visions: *House of Sand and Fog*

Adapted from the American novel of the same name, directed by a Ukrainian-American émigré and starring a British actor in its leading male role, *House of Sand and Fog* does not overtly present itself as a prime example of Iranian émigré filmmaking. The film, however, does explore the tragic consequences of exile for an Iranian-American family living in Los Angeles, when its patriarch Massoud Amir Behrani (Ben Kingsley), a former colonel during the Shah's rule, purchases a house that is mistakenly repossessed from its former owner, an American woman named Kathy (Jennifer Connelly). The film also stars well-known Iranian émigré actress Sohreh Aghdashloo as Behrani's wife. Aghdashloo is a notable star of pre-revolutionary Iranian cinema, appearing in *Broken Hearts* (Ali Hatami, 1978), alongside Iran's most popular male movie star at the time, Behrouz Vossoughi, as well as in Kiarostami's *The Report*. Aghdashloo has also since gone on to star in a number of successful US television shows such as *24*.

Because of its subject matter the film naturally attracted a great deal of attention from Iranian-American media outlets in the United States. Many of these outlets praised Kingsley's amazingly quick mastery of the Persian language, even though he utters only a handful of words in Persian during the entire film. More commonly, however, discussions of the film focused on Aghdashloo's performance as Behrani's traumatized and reclusive wife, Nadi, a performance which earned Aghdashloo a nomination for Best Supporting Actress at the 2004 Academy Awards. In the same year, the prominent Iranian lawyer and human rights activist Shirin Ebadi was awarded the Nobel Peace Prize, in what many observers were quick to dub the 'year of Iranian women'.

The importance of *House of Sand and Fog* undoubtedly lies in the way it brought its version of the Iranian émigré experience to mainstream audiences, its story being one that is frequently overlooked and marginalized by the mass media. It is perhaps ironic, however, that this most visible and critically acclaimed manifestation of Iranian émigré filmmaking, viewed in light of the developments identified in the films above, is also arguably the bleakest and most deterministic. Asgdashloo's portrayal of Nadi and the overall outlook of the film itself are more reminiscent of her performance as Pari in *Guests of the Hotel Astoria* and that film's relentlessly negative view of life in exile, than it is of her performance as Maryam's mother in *Maryam* and that film's more balanced and nuanced examination of cultural difference (Aghdashloo also has a brief cameo in *America So Beautiful* as a famous exiled Iranian movie star). Indeed, the manner in which the death of Nadi recalls the death of Pari over a decade earlier could be seen to represent something of a step backwards in the evolution of Iranian émigré filmmaking, a return to the hopelessness and despair that characterized films such as *Guests of the Hotel Astoria*.

It would be wrong, however, to view *House of Sand and Fog* in this way simply because it does not fit neatly into the trajectory that this chapter has outlined thus far. On the contrary, despite the bleakness of its conclusion, in which Behrani kills himself and Nadi after the accidental shooting of their son Esmail (Jonathan Ahdout) by a police officer, *House of Sand and Fog* differs from many of the films analyzed above in a couple of important ways.

First, and perhaps most importantly, in contrast to films such as *Guests of the Hotel Astoria* and *Maryam*, *House of Sand and Fog* does not code Iran as a violent or evil country. Indeed, Behrani reminisces about his homeland with a great deal of nostalgia and longing. If we are to accept conventional understandings of the development of exilic and diasporic communities, and that nostalgia for one's homeland is something we might expect to wane over time and with each successive generation of émigrés, then *House of Sand of Fog* may appear somewhat backward-looking in this respect, coming as it does nearly twenty-five years after the Iranian Revolution. But the nostalgia that characterizes *House of Sand and Fog* is interesting and noteworthy in that it presents a different view of Iran from that found in other examples of Iranian émigré filmmaking. Behrani, for instance, speaks fondly of his homeland throughout the film and dreams, if not of returning one day, of recreating a simulacrum of his former home in the United States. His memories of Iran also serve as a form of comfort for him in his dying moments, when he suffocates himself, the flashbacks of his family playing joyfully on the beach by the Caspian Sea recalling the images that accompany the opening credits of the film. Iran, therefore, is a place to be longed for and hopefully returned to one day, not a place to be fled from and feared.

Second, *House of Sand and Fog* introduces the issue of class into its consideration of the Iranian émigré experience, in a much more overt way than the films analyzed above. One of the underlying causes of tension between Behrani and Kathy, besides their dispute over the ownership of the house, is their different class backgrounds, and thus the way in which Behrani resents his authority being challenged by a person he considers beneath him, let alone a woman. Behrani's family, it is revealed in the flashbacks at the beginning of the film, were clearly wealthy when they lived in Iran, owning a house that commanded an impressive view of the Caspian Sea. In the United States, by contrast, Behrani has to hold down two jobs in order to meet the expenses for his daughter's wedding as well as pay rent for the opulent flat that he and his family live in. It is the need to move into humbler surroundings that prompts his decision to purchase Kathy's house. It is probably obvious that many families who left Iran during the revolutionary period were those that could afford to leave; nevertheless, the fall in social standing of such families is an aspect of the Iranian émigré experience that has not often been depicted in film in the manner *House of Sand and Fog* does.

From the outset, *House of Sand and Fog* displays a pan-diasporic sensibility in its recognition of the way in which Behrani's downfall resembles the fate of other émigrés in the United States. An early sequence in the film, for example, shows Behrani shovelling asphalt as a roadside worker, just one of the several jobs he struggles to hold down. Behrani is shown quite clearly alongside workers from other ethnic minority groups, at one point ruefully watching a fellow co-worker of Asian descent eating a makeshift meal after they have finished their shift. The film's exploration, therefore, of certain previously overlooked aspects of the Iranian émigré experience, such as Behrani's fall in social status and his identification with other ethnic minorities, lends the film's portrayal of displacement more complexity and depth than its tragic conclusion might suggest.

The fact does remain, however, that the film lacks the strong feminist discourse that distinguishes other Iranian émigré films such as *Walls of Sand*; since Nadi is a very passive character, even though her passivity is clearly intentional. The film is a damning critique of patriarchy among other things. However, it is worth noting that, unlike her younger female counterparts such as Minoo in *All Hell Let Loose*, Nadi is a first-generation Iranian immigrant and as such arguably more vulnerable to traditional patriarchal structures. Yet *House of Sand and Fog* makes little attempt to explore the generational differences that may figure into the experience of displacement, sidelining Nadi and Behrani's daughter Soraya (Navi Rawat) after her marriage at the beginning of the film.

Although decidedly more polished than other examples of Iranian émigré filmmaking, *House of Sand and Fog* overall seems less sophisticated and nuanced in its portrayal of the tragic consequences of displacement. This is not to criticize the film as regressive in its outlook. It would be reductive to demand that it conform to the evolutionary trend identified in the films above. Its story, moreover, is one that undoubtedly does not receive enough attention in the media. But it does seem somewhat unfortunate, in light of the developments examined above, that the most visible and critically acclaimed tale of the Iranian émigré experience to date is also one of the bleakest and most deterministic.

Tracking post-revolutionary Iranian cinema

This chapter has attempted to outline the transformations in Iranian émigré filmmaking across Europe and North America over the past twenty-five years, in order to sketch a broader and more panoramic view of post-revolutionary Iranian cinema, which is typically understood as being synonymous with the New Iranian Cinema. Before attempting this it was necessary to outline criteria for the selection of films for the above analyses. This chapter has thus employed a broad definition of authorship in order to include films such as *Walls of Sand* and *House of Sand and Fog*, which although are not directed by Iranian émigrés can still certainly be regarded as formative examples of Iranian émigré filmmaking, by virtue of the presence of Iranian émigrés working at other levels in the filmmaking process. It was also necessary before attempting this overview to examine some of the main developments in the field of exile and diaspora studies in recent years, and to engage with some of the key theoretical arguments put forward in Naficy's influential contribution to the study of émigré filmmaking in general, *An Accented Cinema*.

After addressing these issues, this chapter then went on to demonstrate how Iranian émigré filmmaking is characterized largely by a gradual transition from an exclusively exilic to an inclusively diasporic and in some instances pan-diasporic perspective. It is this evolution, discernible in the works of Iranian émigré filmmakers working throughout Europe and North America over the past twenty-five years, that makes it possible to conceive of this contradictory group of films as a larger, collective body of work, aside from, though not entirely independent of, the fact that they are all made by Iranian émigrés, and regardless of the fact that they were all made outside of Iran.

During this evolution, Iranian émigré filmmakers have consistently addressed issues of cultural identity and national belonging, in ways that directly call into question traditional methods of organizing national cinemas along strict geographical boundaries. As observed above, the precise implications for the concept of national cinema will be discussed in greater detail in the conclusion to this book. What this chapter has striven to accomplish, however, is to present a wider view of post-revolutionary Iranian cinema, in just a handful of its various manifestations. This book also intends to highlight the limitations of viewing the New Iranian Cinema in isolation from all of the other different forms of Iranian filmmaking across the world, especially across Europe and North America. Put quite simply, the New Iranian Cinema is by no means representative of the entire spectrum of Iranian filmmaking taking place inside and outside of Iran. A more extensive view of the geographically dispersed nature of post-revolutionary Iranian filmmaking contributes to a wider understanding of indigenous Iranian cinema itself, and vice versa.

As noted in the introduction to this book, however, there are certain theoretical and practical problems with such a collective, comparative analysis as the one undertaken in this chapter, insofar as it risks glossing over some of the finer aspects of these filmmakers and their works. Chapters 3 and 4 of this book, therefore, examine in detail some of the émigré works of Naderi and Saless respectively, so as to provide a counterpoint to the methodological limitations of the approach adopted above, as well as to explore even further the links between the New Iranian Cinema and two of Iran's most influential and important filmmakers.

Postscript: back to Iran

Iran Is My Home (2003) is a seventy-minute video diary directed by Fariborz David Diaan. It relates Diaan's return to Iran, over twenty years after he moved to the United States for his education in 1976, and would no doubt make a fascinating comparison with Parviz Kimiavi's *Iran Is My Land* (1999), made upon Kimiavi's return to Iran after a near twenty-year absence, spent making mostly television documentaries in France.[56]

The image of Iran that emerges from Diaan's film is, to use a cliché, that of a country of contrasts. Pictures of perennial Hollywood movie star Tom Cruise are displayed in shop windows alongside pictures of Mohammed-Reza Shajarian, one of Iran's most famous classical Persian singers. Serene vistas of Iran's northern mountains clash with images of Tehran's bustling traffic and street life, and advertisements for Playstation on the sides of buses seem incongruous next to turbaned mullahs roaming the streets. Besides capturing the mythical, picturesque side of Iran, Diaan's diary seems as much intended to capture the everyday and commercialized side of the country, or at least the capital city of Tehran. The film is punctuated with shots of product logos, fast food restaurants and Western-imported movies, a side of Iran that runs contrary to stereotypes of the country and its people as somehow backward and/or hostile to foreign cultures, confounding the belief that a theocratic society such as that of Iran's is somehow incompatible with Western consumerism.

As well as being the well-known host of a television show aimed at Iranian expatriate groups in the United States, Diaan plays the character of Parviz in *America So Beautiful*. As Shokrian states in an interview, also available with the DVD of the film, 'I hope that the Iranians of America and the Iranians of Iran one day can share ideas and make films together, and that the Iranians from Iran can see these films.' Perhaps the most striking aspect of Diaan's film is the way in which he employs the medium of film to carry messages from Iran *back* to Iranian émigré communities in the United States. From the two young men he interviews in the Tehran bazaar who complain of the lack of jobs in the country, to the middle-aged man and woman who express their heartfelt good wishes to fellow Iranians in the United States, to the young woman who asks whether all the stereotypes she has of the United States are true, Diaan's diary allows the Iranians that he meets on his travels to communicate with Iranian émigrés in North America, if not exactly vice versa.

Iran Is My Home, therefore, represents a significant moment in the history of Iranian émigré filmmaking. Wholly collaborative efforts between indigenous Iranians and Iranian émigrés remain for the foreseeable future a political, practical and geographical impossibility. *Iran Is My Home,* nevertheless, symbolizes the first and perhaps only tentative step towards the conceptualization and the actual use of the medium of cinema as a means of forging links between the two groups, resulting in a film that reaches out to and addresses the concerns of Iranians living anywhere and everywhere in the world. With the screening of the film at the 2003 IFP/Los Angeles Film Festival, Iranian émigré filmmaking has finally begun to come full circle. With the following analyses of the émigré works of Naderi and Saless I hope to bring this book too, in a sense, full circle.

3

Close Up 1 – Amir Naderi

Having taken a step back so to speak in the preceding chapter, in order to better comprehend the diffuse and multifaceted nature of post-revolutionary Iranian cinema, this chapter, as well as the next, aims by contrast to zoom in and focus upon the works of two of this cinema's most important yet overlooked filmmakers in Naderi and Saless. The reasons for focusing specifically on the films of Naderi and Saless are twofold. First, despite the relative obscurity of their non-Iranian or émigré works, Naderi and Saless are arguably the two most prominent filmmakers to leave Iran during the revolutionary period (Saless in 1974, Naderi some 12 years later in 1986), after having played influential roles in the formation of what would come to be commonly referred to as the New Iranian Cinema. Second, their films do not comfortably fit into the evolutionary pattern outlined for Iranian émigré cinema in the previous chapter. Naderi and Saless's films represent divergences from this pattern, taking Iranian cinema even farther afield in new and interesting directions. Their films merit close individual analysis, not only because they provide a counterpoint to the methodological approach of filmmakers discussed in the previous chapter and highlight the limitations of an overly teleological understanding of the development of Iranian émigré filmmaking, but also because they promise to widen further our knowledge of the diversity of post-revolutionary Iranian cinema as a whole.

For instance, while the continuities between Saless's pre-exilic and post-exilic works are strongly apparent and will be explored in greater detail in the following chapter, Naderi's New York films represent a clear stylistic break with his Iranian works. Perhaps most strikingly, gone is the predominantly restrained and minimalist camerawork of films such as *The Runner* and *Water, Wind and Dust*, to be replaced by an extremely mobile camera, seemingly unfettered in its ability to travel everywhere and film everything. It is in trying to ascertain the extent to which this shift is indicative of, or these transformations attributable to, Naderi's own experience of 'displacement' that many of the tensions surrounding concepts of émigré filmmaking in general begin to emerge.

Naficy, for example, has argued convincingly that *Manhattan by Numbers* (1993), Naderi's second US-based film after the Iranian-US co-production *Made in Iran* in 1978, focusing as it does on the desperate attempts of its male protagonist, George Murphy, (John Wodja) to raise enough money to pay his rent and avoid eviction, can certainly be viewed as 'an allegory of the conditions of exile itself'.[1] Male protagonists are notable by their absence, however, in Naderi's subsequent films *A, B, C...Manhattan* (1997) and *Marathon* (2001). Although the central female characters of these films are all 'lost' in one way or another, be it physically, emotionally or psychologically, they do not deal with a culturally specific or even 'male' experience of displacement. Which is not to suggest that *A, B, C...Manhattan* and *Marathon* completely defy allegorical readings of Naderi's own particular experience of displacement simply because the central characters of both films are American and/or female. Rather it is to argue that viewing a film, especially one that is stylistically and thematically as complex as *A, B, C...Manhattan* or *Marathon*, primarily as an example of Iranian émigré filmmaking simply because it is directed by an Iranian émigré impoverishes the film to a considerable degree, closing it off to other possible readings. *Manhattan by Numbers* for instance, is as much about the hyperkinetic consumerism of US society as it is about the threat of homelessness. Admittedly, this may be a perspective that only an 'outsider' such as Naderi could offer. But *Manhattan by Numbers* ultimately resists any categorical understanding of its subject matter in relation to the background of its director, by the way in which George Murphy's search for his friend Tom Ryan becomes a journey of self-discovery, lending the film a transcendent, existential quality.

Likewise, any straightforward understanding of *A, B, C...Manhattan* or *Marathon* as being culturally transposed metaphors for Naderi's own experience of displacement is immediately complicated by the fact that both films' portrayals of displacement are explicitly *gendered*.

In these two films, rather than depicting his own experiences as an Iranian émigré living in New York vicariously through the plights of the films' central female characters, Naderi seems far more concerned with exploring a quite different subject altogether – namely, the place or role of women in the city.

Such an argument, however, does risk understating the extent to which Naderi's own experiences as an Iranian émigré inevitably determine the overall outlook of his films. After the following analysis of *A, B, C...Manhattan*, therefore, this chapter attempts a more balanced reading of Naderi's subsequent film *Marathon*, the central character of which is once again female (although in this instance she is a decidedly *lone* female protagonist, in contrast to the three female protagonists of Naderi's earlier film). *Marathon* is once again set in New York City, though on this occasion the film's focus extends beyond the confines of the borough of Manhattan. The film's portrayal of urban dislocation, however, is less contingent upon an understanding of the film's protagonist as a woman, than is the case in *A, B, C...Manhattan*. As a result, perhaps due to its altogether narrow focus on a day in the life of one central female character, it is possible after watching *Marathon* to draw specific conclusions regarding Naderi's own personal attitude towards the city in which he now lives and works.

This chapter attempts an analysis of two of Naderi's more recent New York films, an analysis that is ever mindful of, yet not overly reliant on, an understanding of these films as the work of an Iranian émigré filmmaker. Such an analysis will serve not only to help us think outside of the potentially restrictive paradigm of 'accented cinema' but also to extend even further our knowledge of the scope and variety of post-revolutionary Iranian filmmaking.

Sidewalks of despair: *A, B, C...Manhattan*

Born in the southern Iranian port city of Abadan, Naderi is a wholly self-trained and self-educated filmmaker. In interviews he has spoken of how he learnt about filmmaking as he grew up, by watching Hollywood movies starring the likes of Fred Astaire and Charlie Chaplin, before eventually embarking upon his own filmmaking career.[2] His film *The Runner* was the first post-revolutionary Iranian film to garner serious international attention when it was discovered at Venice and later won the top prize at the 1985 Nantes Three Continents Festival. Perhaps more than Kiarostami's *Where Is the Friend's House?*, *The Runner* can be credited with kick-starting interest throughout Europe and North America in what would come to be known as the New Iranian Cinema. Naderi's subsequent film *Water, Wind and Dust* was banned by the Iranian government during the mid-80s and was not released until after Naderi had already moved to the United States. Some ten years after his departure, Naderi made *A, B, C...Manhattan*, a film distinguished as much by its depiction of women as by its portrayal of the famous New York City borough. Indeed the two are intimately connected with each other, the film examining and contrasting the different ways in which its three central female characters experience the urban maze of Manhattan's Lower East Side.

Recent studies of representations of the city in cinema, influenced heavily as they are by the writings of Henri Lefebvre and more recently Soja, are characterized by their distinct emphasis on what has been described as the supposed 'spatial turn' within film studies itself.[3] Such studies have provided many insightful and thought-provoking analyses of how the city – in this case New York City in particular – has been represented in film. Soja, for example, insists on the need to rethink conventional, *historical* conceptions of the city or the 'urban experience' in 'spatial' terms, as heterogeneous, fragmentary and multi-sited rather than homogeneous, continuous and monolithic. Similarly, many studies focus on how certain cinematic representations of the city and its traditionally marginalized inhabitants (be they non-white, gay, female, etc.) explore the racial, sexual and gender differences and inequalities which challenge archetypal visions of the city as a site of 'white', 'male' and/or 'heterosexual' power or dominance. Elisabeth Mahoney's illuminating essay on *Just Another Girl on the I. R. T.* (Leslie Harris, 1992)[4] is a good example of this kind of analysis. Indeed by means of a brief comparison between her examination of the film's opening credits and the opening images of *A, B, C...Manhattan*, it is possible to illustrate how some of the stylistic and visual techniques employed in the latter film serve to undermine the female protagonists' sense of autonomy and self-control.

In her essay, Mahoney acknowledges the influential work of feminist philosophers, urban theorists and geographers such as Gillian

Rose, Elizabeth Grosz and Doreen Massey, and their contributions to a better understanding of how women live in urban environments. Massey, Mahoney explains, is especially critical of postmodern theorists such as Soja and David Harvey, whose work, she argues – despite their definition of the 'postmodern condition' as a site of eclecticism and conflict – merely continues to peripheralize and objectify the marginalized subjects who already suffer from a severe 'critical 'ghettoization''.[5] Mahoney adopts a similar line of argument in her analysis of three films: the aforementioned Leslie Harris film, as well as *Falling Down* (Joel Schumacher, 1993) and *Night on Earth* (Jim Jarmusch, 1991). Whereas the two latter films, argues Mahoney, reinforce traditional male/female gender divisions, portraying their female characters as either domesticated or exoticized 'others', Harris's film by contrast imbues its female protagonist with a strong sense of individuality and self-determination, and most importantly, a 'sense of rootedness in the city' (the film is set in Brooklyn).[6] Indeed, Mahoney identifies a number of aesthetic features at the very beginning of the film that provide its protagonist Chantal (Ariyan A. Johnson) with a strong feeling of individuality and autonomy within *and* over her surroundings.

> The long sequence with the opening credits shows Chantal travelling across town and partly because she narrates to the camera and partly because of the movement and music of the scene, there is a sense of ownership, articulation and visibility which is extremely rare in representations of women in urban space... Chantal's relationship with the urban space of the 'projects' throughout the film enables her to work through larger questions of power and territory in both public and private space. Most importantly, the space which she occupies in the city and in the text is not a marginal or silent space; she is not the 'other' against whom the urban spectator defines 'himself', but rather, through her act of self-representation in the city, Chantal offers up a direct challenge to the traditional cultural positioning of women as other, as metaphor, as spatial ground, in masculine experience and appropriation of public space.[7]

Just Another Girl on the I. R. T., therefore, imbues its central character with a discernible sense of independence and expressiveness through its use of direct address, music and camera movement. By contrast, the opening images of *A, B, C...Manhattan* – a series of black-and-white still photographs, which introduce the film's three female protagonists, and which become a recurring motif throughout the film – suggest a strong feeling of stasis and entrapment. The voiceovers that accompany these still images, each spoken by the photographed character herself, inform the viewer of each character's name and age and provide important information about their hopes and desires. Colleen (Lucy Knight), for instance, states that she wants to be a photographer, which gives her a kind of 'authorial' presence as she speaks over the film's opening images. Indeed, some of the photos are visible on the wall of Colleen's apartment in the film's opening sequence, although it is actually Kate's point of view with which the viewer is first aligned when the narrative begins. She also states that she wants to smoke and drink less, and be a good mother to her daughter, Stella. The wishes of Kacey (Erin Norris) are somewhat less profound, explaining that she wants 'to quit getting screwed over all the time' and to 'sleep for 10 hours straight'. Kate (Sara Paul) by contrast says that all she wants to do is simply 'make music', a statement that is reinforced by the ensuing shot of her walking along a street with a guitar strapped to her back.

The tone of each voiceover also gives the viewer an initial impression of each character's personality. Colleen's voice sounds markedly more weary and jaded than Kacey's livelier, more energetic tones, while Kate's voice is extremely subdued and quiet, giving a distinct impression of introversion and shyness, as she curtly utters her name and age and ponders for a moment before deciding what it is exactly that she wants to do with her life. The composition of each photo is also suggestive, as the opening close-up shots of Colleen's face show her looking off-screen to her left, as if she is continually distracted by something, unable to concentrate on what is in front of her. The following shots of Kacey emphasize the clothes she is wearing: sunglasses, a large black cap and a short silver jacket with a chain hanging from it and studs around the collar, as well as a spiky dog collar – a veritable picture of the rebellious teenage punk rocker. The close-up shots of Kate's face, however, seem to show her glancing sideways at the camera momentarily, as if she is hiding from it, an image which seems to fit perfectly with the reserved and evasive tone of her voice. Her face is also partially concealed by her long, black, wavy hair and what appears to be a patterned wall cutting down the left-hand side of the frame.

Moreover, no sense of 'space' emerges from any of the images. Indeed, were it not for the film's title, it would not be possible to construe where the film is set from these opening images. Whereas the female protagonist of Harris's film exudes a strong sense of freedom, confidence and authority, Naderi's female protagonists are characterized initially by their immobility and uncertainty.

Set over the course of one day, the film relates the harrowing events in the lives of Colleen, Kacey and Sara, all of whose lives appear to be centred around men or, as in Colleen's case, the absence of a male figure. It is their respective struggles to take control of their own lives which links them all and forms the overarching theme of the film (although the only time in the entire film in which all three characters meet each other and are on screen at the same time is in the opening scene, when Kate visits Colleen and Kacey's apartment to enquire about renting a room there, reflecting the often disconnected and fleeting nature of city life). Kate, for instance, yearns to get out of her incestuous and destructive relationship with her brother Stevie (Nikolai Voloshuk), while Kacey searches desperately (and ultimately unsuccessfully) for her elusive ex-boyfriend Johnny O, who has apparently stolen her dog TJ in a fit of rage upon discovering that Kacey left him for another woman named Tricia (Carla Bedrostan). Colleen, however, sits in her local bar, run by sympathetic bartender Janet (Rebecca Nelson), brooding all day over her decision to give up her daughter to a new family. Although her exact reasons for doing so are never fully revealed, it appears to be her inability to cope with raising a child by herself and the absence of a traditional family unit that compel Colleen to give up her daughter. As she remarks during one of her many internal monologues,

> It's hard to raise a little person in the city. Everything's so dirty, everyone's so cold. Except at Mona's. It's a bar. But it's the closest thing to a family that Stella or I have. That's pretty screwed up, isn't it? I guess it is. I know it is. Maybe

that's why I'm doing what I'm doing. Today is the day Stella's gonna go to a new family...

Whereas the viewer is quite clearly invited to sympathize with the plights of Colleen, Kacey and Kate, all of the film's male characters are portrayed in a rather unsympathetic light. From the anonymous man carrying a bike who barges past Kate as she climbs the stairs to Colleen and Kacey's apartment at the very beginning of the film; to Charles (John Connolly), who is attracted to Colleen but too shy to reveal his feelings; to the hypermasculine, sexually predatory and infantile loafer Milo (Jon Abrahams); to the barfly Louis (Arnie Charnik), who brags endlessly about his previous sexual conquests and cruelly belittles Janet; the men who populate Naderi's film are characterized by their insecurities, their insensitivity, their misogyny and, as in Stevie's case, their neuroses. Charles, for instance, seems to be the perfect match for Colleen. Indeed he appears to be the only 'decent' man in the entire film, playing with her daughter Stella as if he were her father. But he lacks the courage to tell Colleen how he feels. His endearing shyness, indicated at one point in the small gesture he makes (and captured only fleetingly by the camera) when he removes his hat and brushes his hair to one side with his hand when Colleen first passes him by in Mona's, contrasts starkly with the exhibitionism and misogynistic bravado of Milo, who hits on Colleen from the moment he enters Mona's, much to the annoyance of Charles. Milo even relates and literally enacts the imaginary story of how he seduces a 'beautiful woman' (Colleen) and humiliates her 'asshole' boyfriend (Charles) in a bar, which concludes with him 'nailing' the woman 'in the toilet'.

It is in its depiction of the possessive, abusive relationship between Stevie and Kate, however, that the film makes its most powerful comment about the need of its female protagonists to free themselves from their dependency upon the men in their lives (with the exception of Colleen, who nevertheless haunts Mona's with Charles, Milo and Louis throughout the film). Relatively early in the film, via a voiceover which accompanies another series of black-and-white still photographs of Kate and Stevie lying in bed together in their apartment (which could not possibly have been taken by Colleen this time), the viewer is informed by Kate that she wants to end her relationship with

Stevie. When she and her brother moved to New York, she explains, 'things started to change', they did not have to 'pretend' anymore. Even though exactly *how* things changed and *what* they were pretending to be remains undisclosed, Kate's desire to break up with Stevie is explicitly linked with their move to the city, thus seeming to suggest that the city itself offers a newfound sense of freedom for Kate, though the exact nature of its role is revealed to be more ambiguous as the film progresses. Indeed the city seems to threaten, at the same time as it promises to facilitate, her search for independence

The city is portrayed symbolically as a potential prison, for instance, during the final climactic encounter between Kate and Stevie towards the end of the film, atop the roof of the building where Kate records music with her band. The scene is filmed entirely in one virtuoso, uninterrupted ten-minute take that follows the characters all over the building as they argue with each other. The unsteady and almost perpetual movement of the camera reflects not only the general sense of confusion and disorientation experienced by both characters, but also the particular sense of entrapment experienced by Kate as a result of her brother's possessiveness. At one point in the scene, for example, as Kate informs Stevie that she intends to move out of the apartment they currently share, a distraught Stevie comes up behind Kate, who stands in the foreground of the shot, and wraps his arms around her, embracing her. As he does so, the camera begins to circle around both of them, so the viewer can see Stevie kissing the back of Kate's neck through her hair, which he also caresses with his hands. As the camera moves further round, Kate gradually disappears entirely, as the back of Stevie's black overcoat fills up most of the screen, engulfing her completely. As the camera comes full circle around to its previous position, Kate begins to tell Stevie that she has already decided to move out, and that she will try continuing to cover her end of the rent until Stevie can find a new place to live by himself. As she speaks, Stevie reaches his left arm across her chest, almost across her throat, as if he were going to strangle her, while his other hand creeps slowly up onto her right shoulder, as he holds on to her more tightly. The movement of the camera mirrors the way in which Stevie's arms enfold Kate, adding to the sense of her restriction and captivity. All the while Stevie's actions are juxtaposed against the backdrop of the decidedly bleak and snow-covered Manhattan rooftops, explicitly drawing a parallel between his refusal to relinquish Kate and the way in which the city itself looms over both of them, threatening to overwhelm them. Despite all of the 'change' the move to New York instigates in Kate's life, therefore, throughout the film the city is typically portrayed as a site of confusion and dislocation for all of the female protagonists, and in this scene, via an analogy to her suffocating relationship with Stevie, as a potential prison for Kate.

This sense of imprisonment is captured early on in the film, during the scene set in Kate and Stevie's apartment, and once again is intimately linked with the style of camera movement Naderi employs. As the camera tracks back from Kate in a straight line as she gets out of bed – after pushing Stevie off her – and walks into the bathroom, the linear and restricted movement of the camera emphasizes the narrowness and cramped nature of the apartment, the claustrophobic nature of the scene reflecting Kate's own sense of entrapment. This is also implied by the intrusive behaviour of the camera, and how it mirrors the way in which Stevie constantly invades Kate's space. For instance, the camera follows Kate into the toilet as she sits down to urinate, whereupon Stevie's forearm enters the left-hand side of the frame, right hand outstretched, as he orders Kate to hand over the toothbrush she is holding in her mouth. Kate turns the handle towards him, only to grip onto the toothbrush briefly with her teeth before Stevie yanks it free.

Throughout the remainder of the scene, Stevie's behaviour demonstrates further how he infringes on Kate's space, ordering her to move over as she sits in the bathtub so he can climb in with her, constantly leaning in towards her, forcing her finally to physically push him away. As he steps out of the bathtub, he grabs her legs and holds her underwater for a few moments, as if to restate his control over her. The way the camera lingers over the image of Kate lying underwater, forearms raised beside her head and turned upwards, evokes very strongly John Everett Millais's famous painting of Ophelia drowning, and consequently William Shakespeare's play *Hamlet*, which itself contains heavily incestuous overtones. The overall effect of the scene is to show the overbearing and fraught nature of Kate and Stevie's relationship, and how Stevie encroaches, at times quite violently, on Kate's sense of space and independence, an encroachment that is displayed not only by Stevie's domineering and abusive behaviour, but also by the invasive movement of the camera itself.

The apparent insensitivity and unrelenting gaze of the camera is illustrated later in the film, during the scene in which Colleen finally gives up her daughter Stella. At first the camera seems to maintain a respectful distance from the exchange between Colleen and Stella's 'new' family, filming the handover – which takes place on the sidewalk outside Mona's – from within the bar itself, through the window, so the viewer cannot actually hear anything that is said between the two parties. The distance of the camera from the events unfolding on screen, although underplaying the emotional impact of the scene, rather than alienating the viewer from Colleen's plight, paradoxically renders the scene all the more poignant, precisely because of the way in which the camera maintains its distance and respects Colleen's privacy.

However, when Colleen re-enters the bar, the camera follows her (once again) into the toilet, as she leans her head against the wall, her back to the camera. The camera then comes right up beside her, as if trying to get a look at her face, at which point Colleen turns away, almost as if in response to the intrusive presence of the camera itself, and leans against the other wall across from her, before looking at her reflection in the mirror hanging over the sink. The prying movement of the camera at this point in the scene is very much at odds with the previous compassion it had seemingly displayed towards Colleen's distress.

Kacey, by contrast, initially displays a degree of familiarity with her surroundings that Kate and Colleen do not. For instance, she visits her fellow squatter friends in the neighbourhood and chats with them at several points. However, as she gradually fails to track down her dog, her ex-boyfriend Johnny O and her estranged lover Tricia, the frequent tracking shots of Kacey wandering the streets of her neighbourhood, endlessly putting up posters for her missing pet, show her increasing alienation from her surroundings. Indeed, rather than successfully inscribing Kacey into the space she occupies or the landscape she moves through, Naderi's use of prolonged, extremely mobile tracking shots show Kacey moving in conflicting directions and looking confusedly around her, reflecting her growing bewilderment as she wanders the streets randomly, constantly searching but never actually getting anywhere, much like George in *Manhattan by Numbers*. When Kacey finally does track down Tricia, she attempts to seek comfort in her arms, only to be turned away. At precisely the moment when a long take would perhaps have been best suited to capturing fully Kacey's happiness on finding Tricia, a series of disruptive jump-cuts – beginning when Kacey embraces Tricia, only to have her affections spurned – serves not only to break up the continuous 'flow' of the camera movement (quite literally), but also to reflect the disconnected and unreciprocated nature of Kacey's feelings towards Tricia.

Although the camera tracks very closely the movements of the film's three central female characters, the overall effect is not so much to imbue these characters with a sense of autonomy or centredness, but, on the contrary, to infuse them with a sense of vulnerability and disorientation. Indeed, rather than moving 'with' Colleen, Kacey and Kate, the camera appears to function independently of them, exercising its control over them and imposing its watchful eye on them when it pleases, in an insidious rather than voyeuristic manner. That the constant sense of motion evoked by the film's camera movement seems to be reflective of the protagonists' inability to cope with the hectic pace of city life, and to take control of their own lives, is made explicit at one point when Kacey says to Tricia, 'I just need everything to stop so I can catch up!' In this sense, the series of black-and-white still photographs that punctuate the narrative at various points throughout the film take on an added importance. It is only during these temporary pauses in the narrative, these brief moments of stasis (which are also accompanied significantly by the protagonists' internal monologues), that Colleen, Kacey and Kate are truly able to express themselves coherently and speak their minds. During these vignettes, in contrast to majority of the film, the viewer is permitted access to the most intimate thoughts and desires of these characters.

Given that Colleen, Kacey and Kate are able to express themselves only when their images are 'frozen' on screen, the film would seem to reinforce traditional stereotypes of women in cinema as passive objects. The conclusion of the film, however, is particularly striking, in the way in which Colleen and Kate apparently begin to exercise their control over the camera, by literally stopping it in its tracks with a single direct glance. For instance, as the editing intercuts between the three characters during the film's closing moments, after they have all seemingly reached a turning point in their lives (Kate has left Stevie, Colleen has given up her daughter, and Kacey has finally abandoned her search for her dog), Colleen turns her head and looks over her shoulder directly into the camera, bringing it to a sudden halt. The effect is jarring, particularly given the obtrusive presence that the camera has exercised thus far in the film. Likewise, as the camera once again encircles Kate as she stands on a street corner looking aimlessly around her after her altercation with Stevie, her eyes bring the camera to a standstill directly in front of her as she stares straight into it.

Although it is certainly suggestive that Colleen and Kate should possess the ability to 'confront' or 'stop' the camera so to speak by the end of the film, to what extent all three characters have been empowered by the events that have occurred remains ambiguous. Emanuel Levy, for instance, in his *Variety* review of the film, has argued that it 'seldom persuades that its director really understands his female characters' complex psyches and souls'.[8] Such an argument, however, fails to take into account the care and attention with which the film delineates the plights of Colleen, Kacey and Kate, as well as the predominantly sympathetic and non-judgemental attitude Naderi displays towards his characters, despite the aggressive nature of the camerawork noted above. However, despite the emotional upheavals they all experience by the end of the film and the cathartic nature of the conclusion itself, the overall impression of their lives remains one of confusion and aimlessness. The picture of Manhattan that emerges from the film is not simply, in general terms, one of loneliness and disaffection, but one of especial hostility to the hopes and dreams of its female inhabitants.

Filling in the blanks: *Marathon*

In *A, B, C... Manhattan*, Kacey's lost dog TJ functions as a metaphor for something else that is missing in her life (whatever that other 'something else' may be). Likewise, the obsession of *Marathon*'s protagonist, Gretchen (once again played by Sara Paul), with beating her own personal record of completing seventy-seven crossword puzzles in one day is symbolic of her need to impose some kind of order or control over her life and the hectic city in which she lives (which, once again, is New York City). As Dave Kehr notes in his *New York Times* review of the film, 'By performing this strange, private ritual…in the most public and chaotic of places [mostly the New York City subway system], Gretchen seems to be waging her own private war against the meaningless din of urban existence. As absurd as her gesture may be, it is one way of imposing order on arbitrariness.'[9]

Indeed, *Marathon* is as much an anatomy of New York City as it is a character study. As the film begins, the editing intercuts between images of Gretchen doing her crossword puzzles on a subway train, and shots of a map of New York City on the wall of the train beside her, which is itself broken up by the camera into parts according to its five constitutive boroughs: Queens, the Bronx, Brooklyn, Manhattan and Staten Island. The concept of New York City itself being a 'puzzle' of sorts, a labyrinth that Gretchen needs to navigate, is developed further by the subway station signs which the viewer frequently catches sight of as the train doors open and close. Signs such as '41st Street' and '196th Street' correspond to the numbered clues Gretchen reads in her crossword puzzles, while the frequent shots of the interweaving railway lines form a visual link with the interconnected blocks of empty, white boxes Gretchen fills in. This parallel is made explicit towards the end of the film, when the screeching sound of the subway trains accompanies a series of shots of the numerous crossword puzzles Gretchen has stuck all over the walls of her apartment (see figure 5).

As for Gretchen herself, the viewer never learns of the reasons behind her compulsion to perform this 'marathon'. It is revealed, however, via a series of voiceovers spoken by her mother, in the form of telephone messages left on Gretchen's answering machine, that Gretchen's ritual it is an annual tradition she inherited from her mother (whose own personal record, the viewer is informed, is eighty-six puzzles). These messages occasionally accompany images of Gretchen either walking through the subway or along the street, and it is through these messages that Gretchen's mother offers her daughter advice (not to drink too much coffee, the several different ways of spelling the word 'omelette'). The mother's clear concern for her daughter's well-being also hints at some previous trauma in

Figure 5 *Marathon*

Gretchen's life, her mother at one point going so far as to say, 'I know you need all that noise to concentrate, but it's just not safe for you anymore.' What exactly happened in the past, however, remains undisclosed. That Gretchen has essentially followed in her mother's footsteps perhaps suggests a family rivalry, a desire to outdo her mother. Indeed the way Gretchen's mother constantly calls up her daughter to enquire how the marathon is proceeding implies a desire on her part to relive the experience vicariously through her daughter. But even this relationship is left unexplored. Gretchen and her mother never actually speak to each other at any point in the film.

Gretchen's apartment also contains no clues as to her personality, her background or her occupation, covered as the walls are almost completely by hundreds of crossword puzzles, although it is revealed – as the camera passes over some notes from previous years strewn about the apartment – that Gretchen has been undertaking this 'marathon' on a yearly basis since 1992. Gretchen's reasons for doing the marathon, therefore, are not as important as the actual marathon itself and the effect it has upon her.

In this sense, the use of sound itself plays an integral role throughout the film. Initially, Gretchen relies on the discordant noise of the subway trains to help focus her attention on the task confronting her, their repetitive rumbling noise providing a kind of mental vacuum for her in which she can concentrate her thoughts. As the film progresses, however, it becomes clear that the constant noise bombarding Gretchen's senses begins to overwhelm her and hinder her in her efforts to complete her 'marathon'. Thus the use of sound begins to reflect Gretchen's growing confusion and isolation from the people and the environment around her, a separation that is also communicated visually by the numerous shots of Gretchen with her fingers in her ears, or standing *in-between* the sliding doors which connect the train carriages in the subway, her eyes closed, physically shutting herself off from the cacophony of noise around her. At one point, the babble of voices in one of the subway stations Gretchen passes through dies down, to be subsumed entirely by the low buzzing noise of her handheld fan, which she holds close to her face. As soon as she turns the fan off, however, the voices immediately come surging back to the surface of the soundtrack once again. The extremely subjective use of the sound at these points is vital to establishing a link between Gretchen and the viewer, particularly in a film that contains so little dialogue. As the viewer shares these introspective moments of silence with Gretchen, they gain access, however briefly, to her subjective point of view and are allowed to experience the incessant (dis)harmony of noise as she experiences it.

Gretchen's increasing (and somewhat extreme) alienation from the people and the city around her is also manifested in her inability to concentrate when she hears human voices distinctly over the tumult of noise surrounding her. For instance, in one scene she rides through the city atop a tourist bus, the sound of the traffic emanating from below providing a suitable background noise for her to focus her thoughts. However, she has to leave the bus when the tourist guide begins to speak through a microphone to the other passengers. Similarly, when she arrives home from her journey, she tries to recreate the noise of the subway trains in her apartment by playing taped sounds that she presumably recorded herself. However, when she hears a distinct voice in the background making an announcement over a tannoy loudspeaker, she rushes quickly over to her stereo to fast-forward the tape.

Gretchen's mounting frustration with her inability to focus, as she falls further and further behind schedule, eventually reaches breaking point, as she turns on all the taps in her kitchen and bathroom, and all of her electrical appliances, such as her washing machine, microwave, radio, alarm clock and stereo, to create as much noise as possible before storming out of her apartment. Her outburst acts as a kind of release, however, for when she returns she decides to make one final attempt to break her record before time runs out. Significantly, she does so unaccompanied by the simulated noise of traffic or subway trains, or even the steady ticking noise of the pendulum clock, which she slams down comically upon finding it a distraction.

Unlike *A, B, C...Manhattan*, *Marathon* does not conclude on a seemingly equivocal or downbeat note. Gretchen clearly overcomes her dependency on noise to complete her marathon – or figuratively speaking, her addiction to the chaos of city life and her struggle to impose order upon it. The closing images of Gretchen leaning out of her apartment window, looking at snow falling on a calm and still New York City, having broken her own record by half a puzzle, give a sense of resolution to *Marathon*'s narrative that its predecessor *A, B, C...Manhattan* significantly lacked.

Whereas the conclusion of *A, B, C...Manhattan* left its female protagonists in a state of spatial and psychological limbo, there is a strong sense by the end of *Marathon* that Gretchen has effectively exorcized her demons, that she has decided to accept rather than resist the complexity of city life and is at peace with herself. Moreover, as the camera moves further and further away from Gretchen, leaving her behind, physically detaching itself from her perspective as it were, to focus on the film's closing image of a picturesque and serene, snow-caked New York City skyline, it becomes possible to discern Naderi's personal vision of his adopted hometown.

The way in which the camera takes the viewer away from Gretchen's perspective to provide an 'impossible' bird's-eye view of New York City encourages the viewer to understand these closing images as a personal tribute of sorts on Naderi's part to the place in which he now lives and works. Naderi, therefore, may very well continue to look at US society through the eyes of an outsider, as the largely disaffected and restless nature of his characters would strongly suggest. But the ruthless and grime-stained dissection of underclass city life that so strongly characterized *A, B, C...Manhattan* has in *Marathon* come to be replaced by a vision of New York City which, although just as rigorously schematic in its outlook as its predecessor's, on this occasion is infused with a hopeless romanticism as well.

Iranian cinema in focus

> Amir Naderi was a very good photographer. I edited the film *Harmonica* for him. He really likes me...But, well, Amir Naderi should know that he is not John Ford, even though all his life he has tried to be John Ford. He should know that he cannot ride on the crest of the wave of the American cinema. The American cinema is monopolized by a group of wealthy businessmen. Today's American cinema is not even the classic cinema of the U.S. It has declined and swallows a person such as Amir Naderi.[10]
>
> (Sohrab Shahid Saless)

One question that Saless's observation prompts is whether Naderi even wants to ride on the crest of the wave of US cinema or whether he even regards himself as a disciple of Ford, or as a Ford imitator. Indeed, far from contributing to or redefining Ford's epic vision of the Western landscape and 'the Frontier' via the medium of US cinema, as the above analysis of *A, B, C...Manhattan* and *Marathon* demonstrates, the films Naderi has directed since leaving Iran (all low-budget and decidedly small-scale in nature) seem more concerned with exploring this cinema's relationship with that most *urban* of US cities – New York City. In this sense, Naderi's US films have much more in common with the gritty, hand-held, on-the-street style of many New York 'indie' films, perhaps most notably films such as *Rhythm Thief* (Matthew Harrison, 1994). One of the effects of much 'independent' New York cinema, of course, has been to debunk archetypal, romanticized representations of New York City in mainstream Hollywood cinema, both classical and contemporary. As Leonard Quart has noted,

> There are films like the frothy, forgettable *You've Got Mail* (Nora Ephron, 1998), which recently turned New York's Upper West Side into an urban paradise just as Woody Allen did in a more difficult decade for the Upper East Side's streets in *Manhattan* (1978). What one remembers after

watching this film are the affluent, smart-looking people sitting in cafes; the montage of distinctive, beautiful small stores opening on a sunlit morning; and side streets filled with handsome brownstones and blossoming trees. There are no homeless people camped on the sidewalks, just a glistening, pedestrian-filled, brightly coloured urban neighbourhood that anybody in the audience who likes cities would want to live in...A film like *You've Got Mail* goes back to Hollywood's version of New York as a dream city, evoked in musicals like *On the Town* (Stanley Donen and Gene Kelly, 1949) and *The Band Wagon* (Vincente Minnelli)...constructing New York as a dream city is less an act of will or a selective vision in the late 1990s than when Woody Allen was creating it in the dark days of the late 1970s. There are enough radiant surfaces and genuine urban beauty to focus on in New York – so the dream city does not have to seem utterly fabulistic.[11]

Naderi, by contrast, despite the immaculate cinematography of some of his films, like most of his New York 'indie' predecessors and contemporaries, paints an alternative picture of New York City, one that is largely devoid of its familiar landmarks and picturesque vistas. Indeed, the image of New York City that emerges from Naderi's US films is an altogether less glossy, dirtier and seedier vision of the city than that which is so often seen in mainstream Hollywood cinema. As Andrew Sarris observes in his review of *Manhattan by Numbers*, 'I am indebted to Mr. Naderi for plunging into the gritty experience of Manhattan without an airbrush on his lens. Of course, he couldn't afford one, but he has made a virtue of necessity all the same.'[12]

Naderi's films, therefore, begin to raise some of the problems that confront us when considering those works made by Iranian émigrés that do not necessarily fit neatly into the evolutionary path outlined for Iranian émigré filmmaking in the preceding chapter. On the one hand, the unmistakeable differences between Naderi's Iranian and US films would suggest a clean break with his filmmaking past upon moving to the United States and, therefore, perhaps the emergence of an exilic outlook or an outsider's perspective in his émigré works. On the other hand, to understand Naderi's films purely in terms of his own experience of displacement is to prejudge these works and close them off to other readings. As the above analyses are intended to illustrate, although slight glimpses of Naderi's personal vision of New York City can be detected at certain points in *Marathon* and even *A, B, C...Manhattan*, both films address and explore many other themes and issues that are by no means wholly contingent upon an appreciation of their director as an Iranian émigré filmmaker.

Paradoxically, therefore, Naderi's émigré works expand our knowledge of Iranian émigré filmmaking, and the various forms of post-revolutionary Iranian cinema in general, while they resist assimilation into such potentially restrictive categories. Considered in close detail, they reveal not only the inability of traditional notions of 'national cinemas' to account for émigré filmmakers such as Naderi, but also the contradictory nature of post-revolutionary Iranian cinema as a whole.

Where does this leave a filmmaker such as Naderi? Are his works simply neither here nor there, or are they capable of occupying more than one position, of belonging to more than one cinema at the same time? As noted above, although Naderi may not be part of the John Ford School of filmmakers to which Saless presumes Naderi wishes to belong, his films clearly fit into a more recent history of New York independent cinema, most closely associated with the work of John Cassavetes and contemporary 'indie' filmmakers such as Jim Jarmusch. It is Naderi's affinity with this particular aspect of US cinema (which is just as amorphous and contradictory in its conceptual make-up as Iranian cinema) that most clearly identifies him as an American filmmaker, and as one of Iran's most important directors. This book now goes on to pose these questions in relation to the works of a far more prolific Iranian émigré filmmaker, this time working in Europe. For through his German works, Saless symbolizes, perhaps more strongly than any other filmmaker considered thus far, the fundamental yet frequently incongruous nature of the links between the New Iranian Cinema and its émigré counterpart.

4

Close Up 2 – Sohrab Shahid Saless

> Look at the case of [Sohrab Shahid] Saless. He left Iran during the shah's time. He lived in Germany twenty-five years and made fourteen films there. But when he died, all the German publications called him an Iranian filmmaker... Then, when I spoke to Simon Field three years ago about showing a retrospective of his films at the Rotterdam Film Festival, he said, 'But he's not Iranian – he made most of his films in Germany.' So he can't be appreciated as part of any national cinema. What does that say about 'us'?[1]
>
> (Mehrnaz Saeed-Vafa)

Saeed-Vafa's comments encapsulate some of the main problems that confront us when considering the films of Saless, and for that matter, any émigré filmmaker (and by 'us' I mean myself and the readers of this book, though Saeed-Vafa's 'us' could refer to any number of film festival organizers, cinema audiences, film critics, and academics alike living and working in Europe and North America). Her statement exposes the limitations not only in trying to understand the works of émigré filmmakers such as Saless solely in terms of their directors' national origins, but also in the practice of viewing national cinemas themselves as being organized purely along geographical boundaries. Saless and his films certainly seem to have been the victims of such longstanding tendencies.

Saless left Iran when the Shah's regime stopped production of his third feature film (*Quarantine*), just as Iranian cinema was beginning to receive international attention, and arrived in Germany at a time when the New German Cinema was hitting its full stride in the mid-70s. Separated from the Iranian New Wave (a movement he helped to initiate before its 'interruption' by the Revolution) and overlooked in academic circles as an important part of the New German Cinema – a fact that is as much due to the unavailability of his films, as well as their problematic and uncompromising nature, as it is to his nationality – Saless has fallen through the cracks of film history, suspended in a kind of extraterritorial limbo.

Because of his liminal status as an émigré filmmaker, as well as the relentlessly dark, pessimistic and claustrophobic tone of his films, the image of Saless as the exiled Iranian filmmaker par excellence has been established and solidified posthumously in a remarkably short space of time following his death in Chicago in June 1998. For example, in the program for the 2003 Third Diaspora Film Festival in Toronto – which was known in its first two years specifically as the Iranian Diaspora Film Festival – there was a brief section devoted entirely to Saless, entitled 'The Legend'. The festival also had a tradition of concluding each year with a rare screening of one of Saless's films. Additionally, in an earlier essay on his films, Saeed-Vafa calls Saless 'the greatest Iranian director working in exile',[2] while Naficy maintains that his 'critically dystopic films, his successful but marginalized career as a filmmaker in Germany, and his reasons for finally leaving his adopted homeland for yet another exile all point to a deep undercurrent of exilism in his life and oeuvre'.[3]

Saless is also credited – along with other New Wave filmmakers such as Kimia'i, Mehrjui, Kiarostami, Naderi, Kimiavi and Beyza'i – with pioneering the use of a number of stylistic and narrative techniques in Iranian cinema. Briefly, these include the use of long takes and long shots; the use of non-professional actors; and a non-dramatic, minimalist, observational style of storytelling – elements that have since become the hallmarks of almost every other internationally acclaimed Iranian director and that, therefore, characterize the New Iranian Cinema as a whole. Given his influential role in the history of Iranian cinema, and the extent to which his German works undoubtedly lend themselves to exilic readings, Saless's body of work would appear to be the ideal case study with which to demonstrate the existence of an Iranian émigré cinema. That is not quite the approach, however, that I wish to adopt in this chapter. For as the previous chapter on Naderi's New York films illustrates, there are definite problems in repeatedly imposing an exclusively exilic reading upon the works of émigré filmmakers, let alone a filmmaker such as Saless, whose overall *oeuvre* manifests such clear aesthetic and thematic continuities. Not least among these problems is that it risks reducing Saless's films to merely one level of meaning – namely, of being reflective (subconsciously or otherwise) of the state or condition of living in exile. It also risks overlooking the similarities between Saless's pre-exile and post-exile films (though Saeed-Vafa's well-judged essay certainly cannot be accused of this).

Moreover, such readings tend to undervalue the versatility Saless displayed after arriving and subsequently embarking upon his filmmaking career in Germany – a fact that should hardly be surprising, considering Saless originally studied cinema and filmmaking in Paris and Vienna before making his first short documentary films in Iran, although he would later dismiss such studies as 'stupid'.[4] Compared to other Iranian filmmakers working outside Iran, only Allahyari in Austria has been as prolific in terms of feature film production. That the consistency of vision of a filmmaker such as Saless should be neglected in favour of foregrounding the exilic aspects of his cinema thus seems particularly selective, especially when other émigré filmmakers – such as Max Ophüls, to provide a deliberately incongruous example – seem to resist wholly exilic readings or interpretations of their works, precisely because they appear to display such striking versatility and continuity throughout their careers (in Ophüls case, numerous films in four different countries, in four different languages). Of course, there are many differences between the kinds of films Ophüls directed and those Saless made, as well as between the specific circumstances of their respective exiles (a European in America and a Middle Easterner in Europe), but this is not my point. My point quite simply is that Saless's films are far too rich and complex to be viewed exclusively as exilic works, merely because they are directed by an Iranian émigré.

On the one hand, there is undoubtedly a very strong autobiographical streak running throughout all of Saless's films, none more so than *Roses for Africa* (1991), in which the film's male protagonist, Paul (Silvan-Pierre Leirich), who longs to leave Germany and join his brother in Africa, is by Saless's own admission the director's alter ego. As Saless stated in an interview conducted by Naficy in 1997, just a year prior to his death, 'Paul's attitude and behaviour is exactly like mine. Whatever he does, I do. I wanted to see myself on screen as I am.'[5]

Considering Paul's alcoholism and self-destructive behaviour, this is disarming honesty on the part of Saless, revealing the director's own sense of despair and isolation in German society. On the other hand, Saless's German films do not depict a particularly *Iranian* experience of displacement. Although nearly all of his films touch on the theme of displacement in one way or another, it is mainly on a broadly physical (*Roses for Africa*), psychological (*Diary of a Lover*, 1977), generational (*A Time of Maturity*, 1976; *The Willow Tree*, 1983) or racial (*Hans – A Boy in Germany*, 1985) level, rather than on a specifically cultural one. The exceptions to this rule would be *Far From Home* (1975) and *Addressee Unknown* (1983). However, both of these films take not Iranian but *Turkish* experiences of displacement as their subject matter.

If the question of national cinema can no longer be reduced to an issue of mere geography, then it equally cannot be reduced to an issue of authorship. Claiming that *A Time of Maturity*, for instance, is an example of an Iranian émigré cinema, collective of otherwise, simply by virtue of the fact that it is directed by an Iranian émigré shows scant regard for the narrative strategies and thematic content of the films themselves. In this case it also seems somewhat ethically dubious, given that the filmmaker in question has explicitly stated, 'I do not belong to the Iranian diaspora cinema.'[6] To read a 'classical' Hollywood film such as *Letter from an Unknown Woman* (1948) as an exilic work, simply because it is directed by a German émigré in Max Ophüls, would likewise be problematic.

Saless's films are also not viewed in relation to the national cinema of the host country in which he lived and worked after leaving Iran; in this case (West) German cinema of the 70s, 80s and early 90s, or to give it its popular appellation, the New German Cinema. Naficy stresses the need to avoid examining the films of exiled directors such as Saless as completely separate from the national cinema of their host countries, because the two, he rightly points out, influence each other. But the thematic parallels that Naficy lists between the films of the New German Cinema and their exilic counterparts – such as 'a preoccupation with homeland...a utopian yearning for faraway utopian places...a homesick nostalgia for the past...a schizoid perception of the present, loss of identity and belonging, and a desire for social others and foreigner'[7] – serve to generalize rather than clarify the complex nature of the numerous parallels that can be drawn between Saless's films and those of his New German contemporaries. Even Saeed-Vafa's description of Saless as a 'major filmmaker' of the New German Cinema, in her short documentary film on Saless, seems somewhat unsubstantiated, with little explanation as to how and why Saless is important to the New German Cinema movement itself. Indeed, Saless is continually omitted from any histories or studies of the New German Cinema. As Naficy observes, 'Eurocentric scholars in Europe and North America have paid little attention to him, treating him as more of a guest than a contender.'[8]

Despite these problems, it is not my intention to counter an exilic reading of Saless's films by arguing for their inclusion into the canon of films that make up the New German Cinema, or to somehow demonstrate the 'Germanness' of Saless's émigré films. Neither is it my intention to underplay the benefits of regarding Saless's German films as valuable examples of émigré filmmaking. Rather the aim of this chapter, much like that of the preceding one, is not only to provide a contrast to, as well as highlight the limitations of, the collective analysis of Iranian émigré filmmaking conducted in chapter 2, by way of a more focused individual analysis of Saless's *oeuvre*, but also to open up Saless's films to alternative readings, something that seems essential if they are to acquire any relevance outside of the limited frame of reference in which they have so far been discussed. For what struck me upon my own first viewing of many of Saless's films, conditioned as this viewing experience was by much of the literature referenced above which I had read prior to viewing them, was not their exilic overtones, but rather their portrayal of (what at this point I refer to only vaguely as) the 'everyday'. Indeed I would go so far as to argue that it is this thematic and stylistic trait, rather than a relentlessly morbid obsession with depicting the traumatic effects of life in exile, that can be seen as constituting the defining characteristic of Saless's *oeuvre*. The obvious criticism of such an argument is that it merely substitutes one restrictive paradigm for another. On the contrary, it is my hope that a consideration of Saless's portrayal of the 'everyday' will make clear some of the tensions and inadequacies that arise when viewing his films solely as examples of an Iranian émigré cinema.

This chapter then concludes with an examination of the similarities, as well as the differences, between the films of Saless and Kiarostami. The parallels between their respective styles and *oeuvres* – the former being arguably Iran's most influential pre-revolutionary filmmaker, and the latter Iran's foremost post-revolutionary filmmaker – constitute one of the most significant and compelling links between the New Iranian Cinema and Iranian cinema in exile and diaspora and will hopefully serve to bring this overview of post-revolutionary Iranian filmmaking to a fitting conclusion.

Saless and the 'everyday'

The concept of the everyday itself, or what exactly can be considered to constitute the 'everyday', has traditionally been notoriously difficult to define. After all, what may be a daily occurrence or practice for a filmmaker working in early 70s Iran may differ greatly from the everyday routine of a filmmaker working in West Germany at the same time. Ivone Margulies, in her study of the 'hyperrealist everyday' in the films of Chantal Akerman, has shown how cinematic representations of the everyday throughout the twentieth century have been closely linked to the ever-evolving debates concerning concepts of cinematic realism.[9] *How* to represent the everyday has thus been a constant problem for filmmakers from different countries and eras alike, one that is not without its political and ethical implications. As Rey Chow states in her essay on the uses of the everyday in *The Road Home* (Zhang Yimou, 2000) and *In The Mood for Love* (Wong Kar Wai, 2000), the 'everyday' is a precariously vague and abstract concept that is extremely vulnerable to ideological abuse.

> The everyday is an open, empty category, one that allows critics to fill it with critical agendas as they please. This is why both its defenders and its detractors can use it to stake their political claims, either as the bedrock of reality, the ground zero of cultural representation, or as a misleading set of appearances concealing ideological exploitation, a collective false consciousness.

'For these reasons,' continues Chow, 'it is perhaps less interesting simply to unravel the argumentative pros and cons around the everyday as such than to consider specific uses of the everyday in representational practices...'[10] In Saless's case, his representation of the everyday can be understood as forming a critique of the societies in which he lived and worked – of the Shah's grand modernization plans for Iran and its infrastructure, which left so many 'ordinary' Iranians behind in its wake, and of German society's intolerance and latent racism – a critique sustained throughout his entire career. It can also be understood as offering an alternative to more traditional or dominant forms of filmmaking, such as not only Hollywood cinema but also other forms of filmmaking popular within Iran and Germany. As Saless himself wrote, the types of films that dominated Iranian cinema screens during the 60s when he was a teenager were characterized by their escapist and melodramatic tendencies:

> Aside from such new works [such as *Downtown* by Farokh Ghaffari], the market was predominated by run-of-the-mill Iranian and Indian films: singing, dancing, weeping and all that jazz. I always looked for real life in them but I could see little. Or in Chekov's words 'they did not mirror the realities of life as they were.' This made me think of going to film school when I was only sixteen.[11]

In contrast to popular films of the period in both Iran and Germany, Saless's films are characterized by their emotional reticence and undramatic tone. There are certainly no musical numbers – and hardly any weeping – in any of Saless's films. Indeed he has expressed his aversion to the excessive use of music in cinema in general, and the way music is typically used to manipulate the viewer's emotions, describing it as 'cheating'. 'For me,' Saless states, demonstrating his preference for ambient noises, 'the sound of the wind, thunder, or drops of water serve as music.'[12] This observation is certainly borne out by Saless's films, most of which contain little non-diegetic music or none whatsoever.

In a similar manner, Saless wrote a short but scathing essay criticizing what he perceived to be the increasing Americanization of the West German film industry, as well as the penchant for classic literary adaptations so prevalent among New German Cinema directors – or as Saless puts it, the laziness in rescuing 'dead geniuses from the grave', so as to increase their chances of receiving funding for their projects. In typically contrary fashion, Saless's own literary adaptations (with the exception of *The Willow Tree*, an adaptation of a short story by Anton Chekov) are of works by more recent and obscure German writers. *Roses for Africa,* for instance, is an adaptation of the novel of the same name by the modern German novelist Ludwig Fels. The wartime novel *The Blue Hour* (1977), by the German-Jewish writer Hans Frick – a novelist who seems to have been largely overlooked by German literary scholars, in the same way that Saless has been overlooked by German film scholars – was the inspiration for *Hans – A Boy in Germany*. Overall, Saless's essay reveals a clear anger and disenchantment reminiscent of his frustration with the film industry in Iran.

> The reality of life today in the Federal Republic of Germany is increasingly not to be found in our films. The excuse offered is that this won't make any money. It has no economic potential. Culture is culture and business is business! Didn't you know that?... All those young people running around without a job and turning to drugs and alcohol. All those separated women living alone with their children. Children who instead of a father often get to know five uncles, one after the other. Aren't those worthy topics? In a democratic system like that of the Federal Republic one would think that criticism should be allowed. That one might be able to tell somber stories based on the facts. The public is always willing to listen. It's interested in learning something about the society in which it lives.[13]

The image of Saless that emerges most strongly from the quotes above, therefore, is that of a socially conscious director, frustrated by the difficulties in making films that explore the everyday problems of the marginalized and forgotten people in society at large. It is this frustration, more than a recalcitrant self-pity or bitterness at his own exile, which seems to have motivated Saless, influenced his directorial style, and informed the melancholy, inherently undramatic and subdued nature of many of his films.

My understanding of Saless's representation of the everyday is most heavily indebted to Andrew Klevan's theorization of the everyday in narrative film as a process of undramatic disclosure. Basing his argument upon the claim that most narrative films are 'in an overtly dramatic, melodramatic or comic idiom...tapping the visually expressive potentialities of the art and satisfying the needs of the audience', Klevan examines how some films 'organize their narratives around a range of life experiences unavailable to the melodramatic mode as it has developed in world cinema' – namely, 'life experiences based around the routine or repetitive, the apparently banal or mundane, and the uneventful'.[14] Among the four films that Klevan analyses in depth – *Diary of a Country Priest* (Robert Bresson, 1950), *Loves of a Blonde* (Milos Forman, 1965), *Late Spring* (Yasujiro Ozu, 1949) and *A Tale of Springtime* (Eric Rohmer, 1990) – he identifies a variety of stylistic and performative narrational techniques, ranging from subtle camera movement, positioning and framing, to body language and the repetition of simple yet significant gestures performed by the actors on screen, such as the way they bow their head or a particular way of sitting. These techniques, asserts Klevan, reveal a preference for more restrained and understated modes of narration, which stand in contrast to more traditionally expressive and dramatic forms of storytelling in cinema. Such different modes of narration, explains Klevan, referring specifically to a scene from *Loves of a Blonde*, require the viewers to reposition themselves in relation to the film's more indirect means of revealing information: 'Viewers need to redirect their interest, therefore, from the possible suspense provided by plot questions, and instead reorientate themselves to the scene's alternative form of organisation. They should become attuned to its pattern of prevarications.'[15]

Klevan, therefore, does not pretend to offer a definitive concept of the 'everyday' as much as he aims to illustrate how complex emotional states and seemingly commonplace and repetitive daily events and actions can be portrayed in film in an essentially undramatic yet meaningful manner. Indeed, the word 'disclosure' itself implies a more discreet method of narration, one that is more concerned with gradually *divulging information* and encouraging attentiveness to small details than it is with *telling a story* as such by means of significant plot revelations and clear-cut character motivation. Naderi, for instance, has described some of his own Iranian films, which share many similarities with those of Saless, as examples of 'anti-plot' or 'anti-story' filmmaking.[16] However, as Klevan explains, a lack of narrative drive and psychological transparency does not necessarily equate to an indifference to, or disavowal of, plot and character development altogether:

> The presence of clear continuity ... prevents us from bracketing them as non-narrative films, or from categorizing them as not interested in narrating any story at all ... The respecting of spatial and temporal continuity, but not causal or teleological integration, encourages one to conclude that nothing is happening, or that matters are not developing apace. This, however, is to overlook the 'more complete visual field', which is an integral part of film's narration, to miss the broader sense in which films are narrated and to need more urgently than ever to be oriented to the 'oblique strands of narrational strategy.'[17]

These 'oblique strands of narrational strategy' are better appreciated, continues Klevan, by closer attention to a film's 'narrative patterning' – the way in which banal, everyday events and acts are shown repeatedly, with 'slight, but crucial, variations'.[18] For example, there are two scenes in Saless's first feature-length film, *A Simple Event* (1973), involving the film's central character, a young boy (played by Mohammed Zamani), which I find particularly moving. In the first scene, the boy arrives home and, after closing the door behind him, looks down at an empty mattress lying on the floor, where his recently deceased mother used to sleep. In a later scene, also set in his home, he eats a makeshift dinner of bread and a soft drink. I find these scenes moving, however, only in the context of several other scenes already witnessed earlier in the film, which show the boy arriving home – either from school or from helping his father in his illegal fishing activities – and tending to his sick mother, or eating a hot meal prepared for him by his mother as he sits perched on the window ledge, in contrast to the aforementioned scene where he eats by himself, standing up rather than sitting down. The images of the boy eating alone thus reveal his sense of loss and solitude, while an everyday object such as a mattress is imbued with meaning, acting as a reminder of the mother's absent presence. Indeed, Saeed-Vafa notes how the repetition of the simple act of eating reflects the boy's changing emotional state throughout the film.

A similar strategy is employed in *Still Life* (1974) and *A Time of Maturity*.[19] On the first two occasions when the railway worker (Z. Bonyadi) and his wife (H. Safarian) are shown sharing a meal together in *Still Life* – in the second instance with their son also – their reticence and unhurried manner of eating suggests a familiarity with and ease in each other's company. On the third occasion, however, the act of eating reveals the insolence and disrespectful nature of the young railway worker who is sent to replace the husband when he is forcibly retired. As the young man greedily wolfs down the food prepared for him, the wife looks on silently, a look of what appears to be quiet but palpable disdain on her face. Likewise, in *A Time of Maturity*, the recurring scenes of Michael (Mike Henning) eating alone – the first time at breakfast, as he tiptoes quietly about his mother's apartment so as not to wake her up as she sleeps; the second time at dinner, as he sits by himself while his mother (Eva Manhardt) puts on her make-up before going out to work as a prostitute; and the next two occasions at supper, as he eats alone while his mother is out working – gradually reveal his growing isolation.

Repetition is a narrative device found in all of Saless's films, in Paul's incessant drinking in *Roses for Africa*, in Herbert's increasingly enervating trips to the supermarket in *Order* (1980), in the anti-Semitic notes Hans receives and in Michael's painting of his flat in *Diary of a Lover* (the same Michael who appears in *A Time of Maturity*, now an adult, *Diary of a Lover* being a kind of follow-up to the earlier film).[20] As Saeed-Vafa remarks, repetition in Saless's films 'goes beyond serving the idea of the passage of time and routine or even a philosophical statement about life. It also provides a reference for us to measure and notice the shifts in the characters' emotions and their inner trauma.'[21]

The notion of the repetition of everyday routines – and the variations within those routines – providing a reference for the viewer to notice otherwise hidden or imperceptible changes in the characters' emotions is displayed most powerfully in *A Time of Maturity*, in the mother's daily removal of her make-up when she arrives home from work every night. This routine is depicted on three separate occasions throughout the film, each time with barely noticeable but significant differences, with 'slight, but crucial variations'. Indeed the layout of images from these three sequences below is intended to show how the repetition of certain actions by the characters, and of certain shots and camera angles across these three sequences, enables the viewer to recognize them as following largely the same order overall – albeit in more abbreviated or extended forms, as the same but different. The sequences also reveal Saless's reliance on the viewer's ability to notice the variations between the three sequences, at certain points inviting the viewer – once again, as the layout of images hopefully demonstrates – to fill in the blanks, so to speak.

The viewer, therefore, is introduced to this routine in the opening scene of the film, which is around ten minutes in length. The opening long shot shows a darkened room, with some light shining in through a window in the centre of the screen (figure 6.1). There is no movement for over two minutes as the opening credits roll, the only audible noise being a clock ticking away in the background. Eventually the silhouette of a young boy is visible moving past the window (figure 6.2), and a light flicks on off-screen, shedding some light on the room and revealing a bed and some crumpled sheets in the corner. A cut shows the boy getting himself a drink of water from the tap in the kitchen, before returning to the preceding long shot of the room (as seen in figure 6.1). The boy reenters the screen to go back to bed, pausing midway and returning to the kitchen to turn off the light before doing so. There is another lengthy pause of around forty seconds or so, before there is the sound of a lock being turned. A cut to the front door shows the mother entering the apartment (figure 6.3) – the light from the landing outside allows the viewer a brief glimpse of her figure and her clothes, and it is heavily implied that she is a sex worker by her manner of dress and the time at which she arrives home – and then returns to the long shot of the darkened room. Entering screen right, her outline moves faintly across the room and past the window, where she turns on a light above her make-up table (figure 6.4), revealing a drab and sparsely decorated apartment. Sitting down in front of a mirror, the camera looking over her shoulder so we can see her reflection in the mirror (figure 6.5), she proceeds quite laboriously to remove her necklace, her blouse, her shoes, her earrings, her jewellery and – in a close-up of her reflection (figure 6.7) – her lipstick and her fake eyelashes, wiping her face clean before getting up and going into the kitchen. This process, intercut with a few shots of her son lying in bed (figure 6.6), takes around three and half minutes to complete. The unchanging and impassive expression on her face as well as the habitual nature of her movements indicate the extent to which this daily ritual is a matter of routine for her. In the kitchen, her dual status as loving mother and sex object is touchingly combined as she, in her underwear, makes a sandwich for her son's school lunch the next day (figure 6.8), which she leaves for him on a table with some change from her purse (figure 6.9). She then smokes a cigarette in bed before finally going to sleep (figure 6.10).

Some forty minutes later into the film, the viewer is again shown this routine, but on this occasion with some notable ellipses. The sequence begins once more with the same static long shot of the darkened room (figure 7.1). This time, however, there follows only one relatively brief shot of Michael lying in bed asleep (figure 7.2), before there is a cut to his mother entering the apartment through the front door, wearing an outfit similar to the one she wore earlier (figure 7.3). When she crosses the room and switches on the light above her make-up table (figure 7.4), the camera initially maintains a distance as she begins to remove her make-up, before cutting to the over-the-shoulder shot of her reflection in the mirror (figure 7.5). She removes her make-up in exactly the same manner and in much the same order as before, this time keeping her blouse on, however. As expected, there is a cut to her son lying in bed (figure 7.6). Instead of returning to her reflection in the mirror, however, she is shown making another sandwich in the kitchen (figure 7.7). A lengthy close-up of the sandwich lying on the table replaces the earlier shot of the mother moving about the apartment, taking some money out of her purse, and laying it on the table beside the sandwich. On this occasion, her hand simply enters the close-up shot to throw some money on the table (figure 7.8), and the sequence ends, as before, with a shot of her smoking a cigarette in bed (figure 7.9). In comparison with the opening sequence, this sequence lasts only roughly three and a half minutes. However, as suggested above, the repetition of certain actions by the mother (opening the front door, switching on the light, removing her make-up, making the

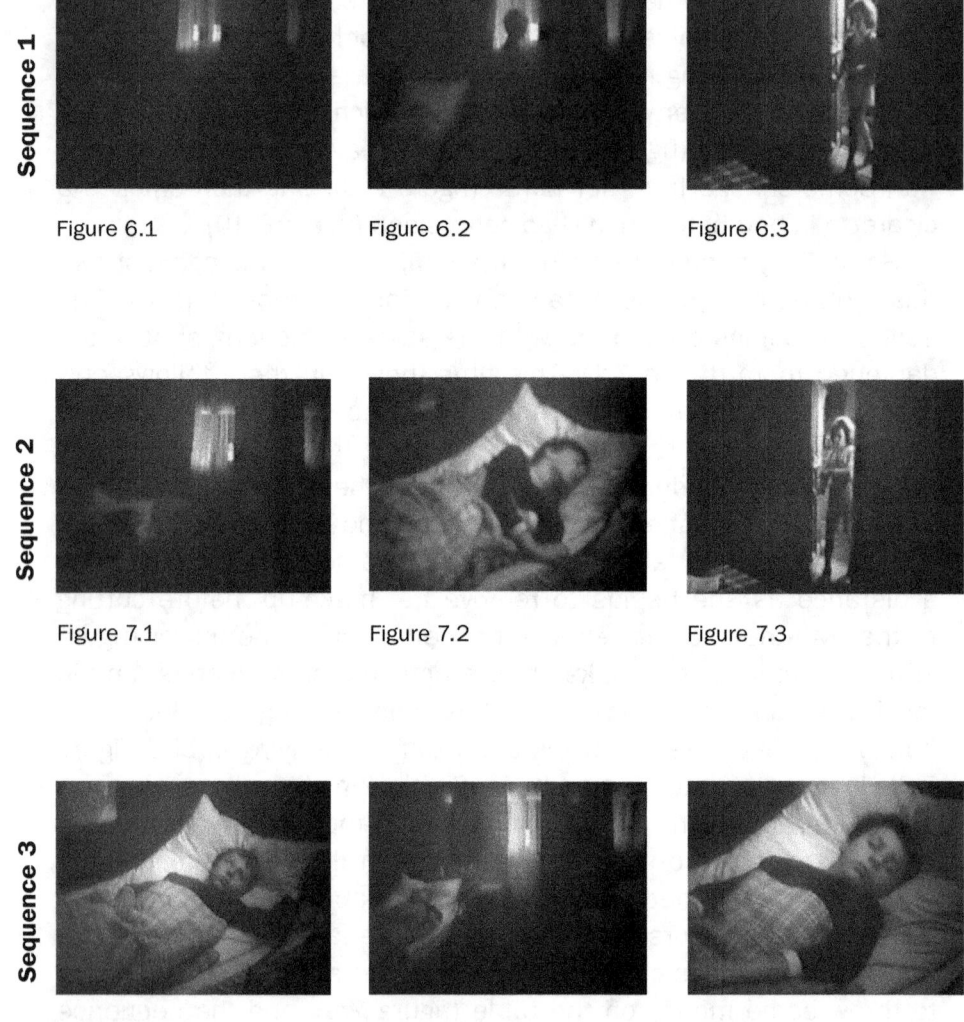

Figure 6.1 Figure 6.2 Figure 6.3

Figure 7.1 Figure 7.2 Figure 7.3

Figure 8.1 Figure 8.2 Figure 8.3

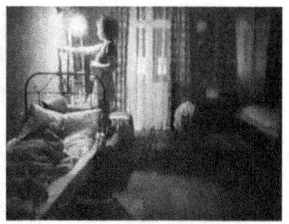

Figure 6.4

Figure 6.5

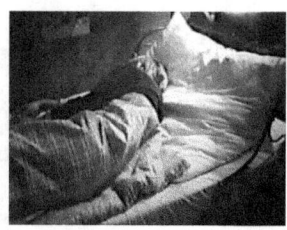

Figure 6.6

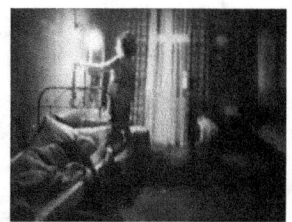

Figure 7.4

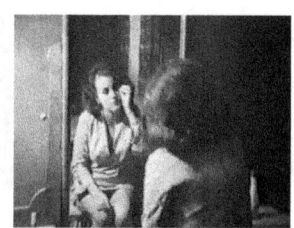

Figure 7.5

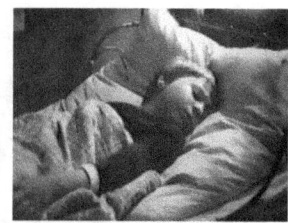

Figure 7.6

Figure 8.4

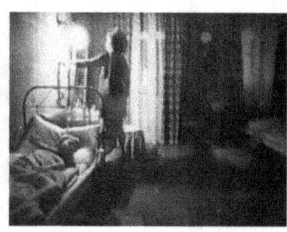

Figure 8.5

Figure 8.6

Sequence 1

Figure 6.7   Figure 6.8   Figure 6.9

Sequence 2

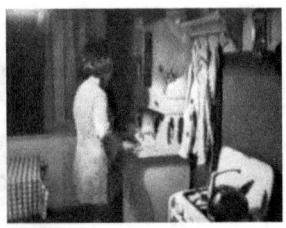 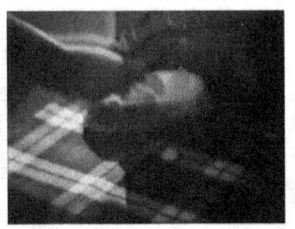 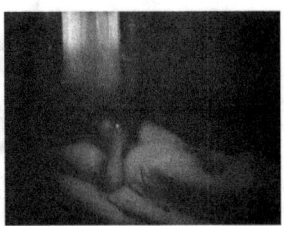

Figure 7.7   Figure 7.8   Figure 7.9

Sequence 3

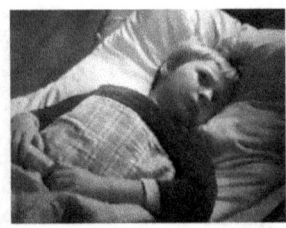  

Figure 8.7   Figure 8.8   Figure 8.9

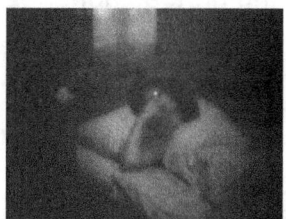

Figures 6.1–8.11 *A Time of Maturity*

Figure 6.10

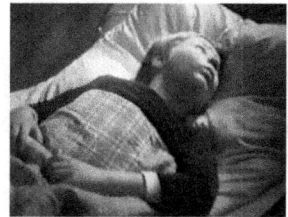 

Figure 8.10   Figure 8.11

sandwich, laying the money from her purse on the table, and smoking her cigarette) and of certain shots and camera angles (figures 6.1 and 7.1, 6.3 and 7.3, 6.4 and 7.4, 6.5 and 7.5, 6.6 and 7.6, 6.9 and 7.8, and finally 6.10 and 7.9) allows the viewer not only to recognize the second sequence as recollective of the first, as adhering broadly to the pattern established in the opening scene, but also to discern the slight ellipses that occur.

The viewer may regard the repetition of these events as self-indulgent or pointless, and the time devoted to them as disproportionate to the amount of narrative information or character development they relate. But the repetition of these events and the ellipses that curtail their duration call upon the viewer to remember in their entirety the events that they witnessed in the first sequence, engraining within the viewer at an (un)conscious level, it would seem, the mother's routine and the series of actions and images that comprise it, setting up a number of expectations for what will ensue in the third sequence.

On the third occasion that this routine is shown, a noticeable change in the mother's behaviour reveals her pain and distress, while a similar deviation from the established pattern of shots and camera angles used to depict this routine serves to undercut the potentially dramatic effects of such a shift. As Ivone Margulies might put it, Saless – like Chantal Akerman in *Jeanne Dielman, 23 Quai du Commerce, 1080 Bruxelles* (1975), a film which *A Time of Maturity* resembles remarkably (like *Jeanne Dielman* from the child's point of view, minus the murder scene) – establishes 'a formal and a behavioural paradigm only the better to expose its underside'.[22] The sequence begins slightly differently this time, opening with a shot of Michael lying in bed awake (figure 8.1), seemingly waiting for his mother to arrive home. There is a cut to the familiar long shot of the darkened room (figure 8.2), before returning to the previous shot of Michael, who closes his eyes and pretends to be asleep (figure 8.3) when he hears the key turning in the lock on the front door. His mother then enters the apartment (figure 8.4), crosses the room and switches on the light as before (figure 8.5). On this occasion, however, she pauses briefly to inspect her face in the mirror before sitting down (figure 8.6). A shot of Michael opening his eyes and surreptitiously listening to his mother (figure 8.7) precedes the familiar over-the-shoulder shot of his mother's reflection in the mirror. This time, however, she does not begin to remove her clothes or her make-up but instead leans into the mirror slightly, examining her face and gently touching what appears to be a bruise near her mouth, though it is barely perceptible to the viewer (figure 8.8). Visibly upset, she then hangs her head and begins to cry (figure 8.9). Her grief is all the more unexpected and striking given her previous lack of emotion, and the scene would not be as effective had the time not already been taken to establish her usual impassivity as commonplace and invariable. It is also significant that, in contrast to the previous sequences in the film, the viewer's point of view on this occasion is subtly yet clearly aligned with that of Michael's, from the opening shot (figure 8.1) onwards. As the sequence begins the viewer waits with him for his mother to arrive home, is privy to his pretence to be asleep, and shares his concern when he hears his mother crying. As soon as this disturbance occurs, the scene suddenly concludes. There follows one more shot of Michael in bed, a look of concern on his face (figure 8.10), before the camera reverts to the previous long shot of the room (figure 8.11) and, instead of lingering on the scene, gradually fades out to black.

Given the extent to which *A Time of Maturity* depends upon repetition, and the way in which it emphasizes temporality – that is, the sheer length of time it takes for events to unfold on screen, as well as the differences in duration it accords to these (repeated) events – there are clear comparisons to be made here between Saless's films and the structural/materialist practices of European and North American avant-garde filmmaking (the parallel with Chantal Akerman, for instance, has already been noted). Like a great deal of so-called structural/materialist filmmaking, Saless's films encourage an active spectator, inviting the viewer to recognize and contemplate the repetition of certain scenes, events, objects and shots, and to notice the slight deviations (or 'prevarications' perhaps) from these established patterns. There are tensions, however, between the kind of viewing experience Saless's films offer and what Stephen Heath identifies, first, as the effect of repetition in structural/materialist film, which is to break or problematize straightforward viewer identification (although Heath acknowledges that *all* films solicit primary identification with the image even if they lack the potential for secondary identification provided by particular characters within the world of the film); and, second, the intention of structural/materialist filmmaking overall, which is to produce a sense of disunity in the viewer, often by self-reflexive means (and thereby disrupting the potential for complete, unchecked ego-investment offered by unmediated primary identification with the image). As Stephen Heath argues, in contrast to traditional narrative cinema, which typically offers the viewer a more or less fixed, stable position of subjectivity, the practices of structural/materialist filmmaking address

> not a spectator as a unified subject, timed by narrative action, making the relations the film makes to be made, coming in the pleasure of the mastery of those relations, of the positioned view they offer, but a spectator, a spectating activity, at the limit of any fixed subjectivity, materially inconstant, dispersed in process, beyond the accommodation of reality and pleasure principles. 'Boredom' is a word which is sometimes assumed by the film-makers with regard to their films, the boredom which is the loss of the imaginary unity of the subject-ego and the very grain of drive against that coherent fiction.[23]

Despite their often painstakingly slow and methodical pace, Saless's fiction films have clearly discernible and easily understandable narratives. Moreover, unlike many structural/materialist films, Saless's films always feature at least one central character (sometimes several, as in *Utopia* [1983]) with whom the viewer can identify, even if this identification is strategically problematized, as much by those characters' passivity and lack of narrative agency as by the seemingly redundant repetition of narrative information, as will become evident in the following analysis of *Hans – A Boy in Germany*.

Furthermore – besides the repetition of certain authorial signatures, such as the use of long takes and long shots, which may serve to remind the informed viewer that they are watching a Saless film – Saless never seeks to break down the unity or reveal the constructedness of the diegetic world he portrays on screen. As Olaf Möller observes, Saless would more than likely have regarded such self-reflexive devices as 'a con game, diversion, or excuse', a distraction from the social 'realism' his films strive for. Indeed, it is this filmmaking ethic that perhaps most clearly distinguishes Saless from the self-reflexive practices of contemporary Iranian filmmakers such as Kiarostami, Panahi and the Makhmalbafs.

Ultimately Saless's films exist somewhere in-between the practices of experimental structural/materialist filmmaking and those of traditional narrative cinema. Saless's films, continues Möller, set out to 'confront the viewer with a hard, precisely aimed slap'.[24] By 'slap' Möller means the way in which Saless carefully structures his portrayals of the everyday so as to shock viewers, rather than alienate them, when an especially traumatic or significant event disrupts his characters' daily lives.

The closing moments *A Time of Maturity* are once again a good illustration of this 'shock affect' strategy. The scene in question shows Michael arriving home early from school one day to see, in a reflection in the mirror, his mother performing fellatio on one of her clients. It begins with a long shot of Michael entering the apartment through the front door, the camera positioned at the opposite end of the room so that the mother's bed is hidden from view. Just as Michael has finished closing the door and hanging his key up on the wall, there is a sudden cut (almost a jump-cut) to a medium close-up of the mirror with the reflection of his mother giving oral sex to one of her clients. The cut appears sudden because up until this point in the film, the viewer has been accustomed to watching the characters perform nearly all of their daily tasks in their entirety, usually in protracted, uninterrupted long takes. The cut away from Michael, therefore, slight as it may seem, appears abrupt because it occurs unexpectedly in mid-action and is violent in the manner it momentarily tears the viewer's point of view away from that of Michael's. Because the viewer sees Michael's mother giving oral sex before Michael himself actually sees it, the shot is thus made more shocking than it might otherwise have seemed, had it been revealed, for instance, by a slight camera movement, or motivated causally by a shot of Michael gazing off-screen at something, as the next shot shows him doing transfixed to the spot upon seeing the reflection in the mirror and seemingly hidden from his mother's view by the kitchen door. This shot in itself is somewhat disconcerting, because for the first time in the film there appears to be a minor yet noticeable breakdown in spatial continuity. First, Michael does not occupy the position that he did prior to the shot of his mother's reflection in the mirror, for he has clearly moved from the background into the middle ground of the shot. Furthermore, a cut back to the reflection in the mirror and a slight zoom in seem to confirm it as a point-of-view shot from Michael's perspective, which seems impossible given the order of shots so far. Or does Michael himself assume this perspective after the viewer/camera has already done so? However the viewer may choose to interpret it, it seems clear that the shock of Michael's discovery is complemented and intensified by a similar disorientation in the spatial organization of the scene itself.

Michael's muted reaction to the sight of his mother performing oral sex also seems incongruous with the presumably traumatic consequences of his discovery. He does not express anger, grief or sorrow. Instead, removing his schoolbag slowly from over his shoulder and laying it quietly on the floor next to the table, keeping his eyes fixed firmly on the reflection in the mirror, he merely turns around, silently exits the apartment – looking back once before leaving – and goes down the flights of stairs to the lobby on the ground floor. As he sits and waits for the client to leave, the film ends. Although the scene provides a climax of sorts to the narrative, the conclusion of the film itself is very subdued and open-ended. There is no emotional confrontation between Michael and his mother, and Michael's feelings at his discovery remain undivulged, the blank expression on his face rendering them incomprehensible. Indeed, Saless does not go on to explore the traumatic effects of the event upon Michael until his subsequent film *Diary of a Lover*, which contains an equally shocking conclusion: in the film's penultimate scene, the dead body of Michael's lover Monika is discovered under his bed by police officers searching his apartment, a discovery that Saless portrays once again with self-restraint and nonchalance typical of his style. (The closing image of the film is of Michael wearing a straitjacket, imprisoned in an asylum.)

Saless's thoroughly unemotional and undramatic manner of depicting these shocking events is often unnerving, because stylistically it accords the events themselves an equivalence with the other mundane and unexceptional incidents which comprise the characters' everyday routines, an equivalence that is at odds with their unexpectedness and their frequently traumatic effects. In this respect Saless's strategy once again seems to bear a striking similarity to the strategy Margulies identifies at work in Akerman's *Jeanne Dielman*, where a process of 'diegetic indifferentiation' between the scenes of housework and the scenes of prostitution neutralizes the importance – in the 'hierarchy of spectacle' – of the 'fictive obscenity' of the latter scenes, 'revealing a complicity between narrative procedures and narrated acts and gestures'.[25]

Such a strategy can also be seen at work in *The Willow Tree*, the film that perhaps most expertly demonstrates Saless's meticulous attention to the construction of the 'everyday', and his method of shocking the viewer by dramatically undercutting those events that disrupt the daily order of things. Indeed the opening twenty minutes of the film appear in many respects to be a microcosm of every film Saless ever made, the culmination of his filmmaking style, displaying all the hallmarks of his directorial technique. In *The Willow Tree*, not one take seems overlong or drawn out, not one shot misplaced. The shocking event – in this instance, a murder – is all the more startling for this precision when it occurs.

The film begins with the miller Arkhip (Josef Stehlik), sitting on the small jetty that juts out into the lake next to his mill, fishing with a makeshift rod made from a stick and a piece of line, in a quite idyllic pastoral setting. The opening shot – a slight zoom in on Arkhip's inverted reflection, undulating on the surface of the lake – is the first of a number of images hinting at the old man's transience. A close-up of Arkhip's bearded, aged face shows him reaching out to grab hold of the line. Then a brief shot of a small fish being pulled out of the water is followed by a long shot of Arkhip unhooking the fish, putting it in a bucket behind him, and throwing the line back into the water. There follows an extreme long shot of Arkhip's mill, a large willow tree standing beside it. A horse-drawn coach appears on the horizon behind the mill, its arrival also announced by the chiming of bells attached to the horses' collars.

A long shot of Arkhip perched on the edge of the jetty shows him looking off-screen to his right over his shoulder at the coach descending the path next to the mill. Another extreme long shot of the mill, repositioned slightly so as to include Arkhip sitting on the jetty, then shows the coach moving rapidly past the mill, eventually disappearing off the right-hand side of the screen. A cut to a panning shot of the carriage – a closer long shot which shows two men aboard – follows the coach as it moves quickly along the path running alongside the edge of the lake and into the distance. A considerably slower panning shot then shows Arkhip getting to his feet, picking up his bucket and hobbling slowly towards his mill as the opening titles of the film roll.

The first interior shot of the film shows Arkhip entering the mill, putting his bucket on the floor and moving over to the stove, before fading to black. The fade to black – less immediate than a cut – suggests the slow passage of time and adds to the sense of Arkhip's life unfolding at a leisurely, unhurried pace, a mood that has already been generated by the use of long takes and the body language of Arkhip himself. The two subsequent shots that follow are long shots in terms of both distance *and* duration – one shows Arkhip preparing food on the stove and the other has him sitting on his bed, eating the food he has just prepared. These shots conclude with fade-outs as well. The colour scheme of the mill itself is one of resounding greyness, matching the shade of Arkhip's faded and ragged clothes. His slow, considered movements; the drabness and lifelessness of his clothing and the interior of his house; and the shots of him fishing, preparing his meal and eating alone; all point toward the repetitive, rhythmical and solitary nature of his existence.

It is unclear whether the first shot of the ensuing sequence – a long shot of Arkhip once again fishing on the jetty – occurs on the same day, the following day, or at a later point in time. The chiming of bells that emerges on the soundtrack anticipates the impending reappearance of the coach and acts as a segue into the panning shot of the coach that follows, in which the carriage once again follows the path that runs past the mill and alongside the lake. It is virtually identical to the panning shot from the first sequence, the only difference being that on this occasion the shot concludes with a fade-out, rather than another cut to Arkhip on the jetty.

An extreme long shot of Arkhip's mill follows the fade-out from the panning shot, the smoke emerging from the chimney suggesting that perhaps Arkhip is once again preparing a meal. Another long shot of Arkhip sitting on his bed and eating his food follows, the sound of a fly buzzing around him as he eats confirming his utter loneliness and isolation. A close-up of Arkhip's wizened face as he eats precedes a fade out to black. The sequence concludes with another combination of a long shot and a close-up, this time of Arkhip asleep in bed. It is now nighttime, and the sound of crickets chirping is clearly audible in the background. Similar to the second time the viewer witnesses the mother removing her make-up in *A Time of Maturity*, this second sequence in *The Willow Tree* effectively condenses the events of the opening sequence into the space of three minutes and a mere seven shots.

Four shots precede the appearance of the coach in the third sequence; an establishing shot of Arkhip's mill, similar to the previous shots of the mill in the first two sequences; a medium close-up of Arkhip sitting on the jetty, the sunlight reflected off the surface of the lake shimmering over his immobile face; a shot of the float on his fishing line bobbing on the surface of the water; and a long shot of Arkhip perched on the edge of the jetty, the sound of bells chiming in the distance once more anticipating a cut to an extreme long shot of the coach emerging over the horizon next to Arkhip's mill. The coach is moving noticeably slower this time, the horses trotting rather than galloping as they were before, the bells also chiming less rapidly as a result. These slight changes – in the movement of the coach and the chiming of the bells – alert the viewer to the differences between the arrival of the coach on this occasion and its two previous appearances in the film thus far. Moreover, only one man is driving the coach this time as it moves from the background into the middle ground of the shot and comes to a stop in front of Arkhip's mill. A shot of Arkhip looking back over his shoulder at the cart precedes the very first close-up of the driver (Peter Stanik) as he looks about him suspiciously, as if to make sure no one is around. He eventually steps down from his seat and moves round to the rear of the cart – failing to notice Arkhip, who, seated on the jetty, is looking on silently – and climbs on board, revealing the other coachman to be asleep in the back of the cart, as the driver looms over him, the camera positioned so that we are looking down over the driver's shoulder at the sleeping coachman. Then the murder occurs.

A frontal medium shot of the driver shows him looking down at the other coachman off-screen, followed by a close-up of the latter as he sleeps unsuspectingly, before returning to the previous over-the-shoulder perspective. The driver looks around one more time as he reaches down off-screen to his right to pick up a mace, which he then bashes over the sleeping coachman's head four times. The first blow is represented in a medium shot of the driver as he swings the mace and brings it crashing down on the sleeping coachman's head off-screen, followed by another close-up of the latter's face, a trail of blood now visible on his forehead. A rear medium long shot of the driver and the coach shows the second blow, the head of the mace clearly connecting with the coachman's skull with a sickening, dull thudding noise. The final two blows are shown from a distance, in a side-on extreme long shot of the coach.

Like Michael's reaction to his discovery of his mother and her client in *A Time of Maturity*, Arkhip's reaction to the murder in *The Willow Tree* is quiet and understated. He merely waits for the driver to leave, before taking the bagful of money the driver hides in the trunk of the willow tree next to his mill to the local authorities (only to have the local authorities gradually pilfer all the money for themselves). Rather than merely serving to render the murder all the more shocking by underplaying its dramatic impact, the stark and emotionally detached portrayal of the murder in *The Willow Tree* also mirrors the disturbing brutality and coldness of its execution. Saless's use of sound is especially important in this respect and illustrates his preference for natural sounds rather than music in his films. The dull thud of the mace connecting with the coachman's skull, for instance, is particularly jolting on a soundtrack which up until the murder scene has been almost entirely composed of sounds of nature, such as birds singing, crickets chirping, and flies buzzing. The *unnatural* clubbing noise of the mace and even the slight clinking of its chain as the driver handles it, insignificant as they may seem, are, therefore, integral to the scene's disconcerting and visceral quality. Moreover, in such an apparently prelapsarian setting as the woodland surrounding Arkhip's mill, the murder seems to take on an almost mythical, primeval resonance. The only other scene in Saless's *oeuvre* with which the murder scene in *The Willow Tree* seems comparable is the prostitutes' collective killing of their pimp at the conclusion of *Utopia*, a murder that is perhaps equally shocking in its casual violence and restrained portrayal.

It is significant, however, that one of the most violent moments of Chekov's short story is completely elided from Saless's film adaptation. When the coachman returns to the scene of his crime to retrieve his bag of money, only to discover it is gone, he attacks Arkhip:

> The driver sprang to his feet, gave a roar, and threw himself on Arkhip. He beat him and beat him. He beat his old face unmercifully, then threw him down on the ground and stamped on him. When he had finished beating the old man, he did not go away but stayed on at the mill and lived there with Arkhip.[26]

The driver does certainly stay on and live with Arkhip at the end of Saless's film, but the savage beating is omitted, perhaps because, somewhat ironically, Saless found it far too dramatic an event to portray. The driver instead turns up one day out of nowhere like a ghost, seemingly haunted by the crime he has committed, disappearing into the lake at the end of the film.

For all of Saless's subtlety, however, there is arguably an occasional heavy-handedness to his directorial style, a stubbornness in his refusal to allow the viewer to identify or empathize straightforwardly with his characters, by means of none-too-subtle distancing strategies which seem incompatible with Klevan's notion of the everyday in narrative film as a process that avoids assertion or overemphasis. The mother's death scene in *A Simple Event* is a prime example of this heavy-handedness and illustrates Saless's relentlessly understated way of portraying sometimes the most harrowing of events (as does the title of the film itself). The scene is comprised almost entirely of one long, uninterrupted take – a long shot of the one room that forms the house that the boy and his mother and father live in. The boy has been sent by his father to fetch a doctor to examine his sick mother. The boy and the doctor enter the room through the door on the left-hand side of the screen, the camera panning slightly to follow the doctor as he moves past the mother – who lays motionless on a mattress on the floor in the background – and rests his medical bag on a table on the other side of the room. Taking a stethoscope out of his bag, he then goes over to the mother, moving into the background of the shot himself to examine her. During the examination he does not utter a word and keeps his back to the camera, obscuring the camera's view of the mother also. The shot is composed so that the doctor and the mother occupy mainly the centre of the screen, though they are slightly off centre to the left-hand side. The boy and the father stand to the left and the right of them respectively, looking on, and stay completely still and silent during the examination. Indeed what is perhaps most noticeable during the scene, besides the sheer length and stillness of the take, is the obtrusive noise of a dog barking continually in the background, in the absence of music or any other noise whatsoever on the soundtrack.

The two medium close-ups of the boy that briefly break up the take do nothing to heighten the emotional tone of the scene. The first close-up shows the boy leaning forward and peering curiously off-screen to his right. There follows no point-of-view shot, however, even though the boy's off-screen gaze could easily motivate one. The second close-up occurs when the doctor stands up and coolly pronounces the mother dead before packing his medical bag and leaving the house. The boy shows no visible signs of emotion but instead merely bows his head, as if he were accepting his mother's death as a simple fact of life. When the doctor leaves, the boy and his father remain still and do not speak to each other. The father appears to begin to weep as he raises his hand to his face and leans against the wall of the house. But his physical distance from the camera obscures and minimizes the emotional impact of the gesture. Indeed, the stillness and silence of the actors on screen, the minimalist soundtrack, and the camera framing and positioning, all work together – as suggested, perhaps somewhat forcefully – to frustrate the viewer's possible emotional involvement in the scene. At two and a half minutes in length, the take is absolutely unrelenting in its fixity and its detachment from the plight of the characters on screen.

By contrast, a similar technique is used to considerable emotive effect in *A Time of Maturity*, when Michael's mother breaks down in tears in front of the mirror. As mentioned previously, as soon as the mother begins to cry, there is a cut to the familiar long shot of the room (figure 8.11). In one sense the cut clearly distances the viewer from the mother as she cries, undercutting the emotional impact of the scene as opposed to heightening it, as a well-timed close-up of the mother's face as she weeps might have done. Nevertheless, the cut to a long shot and the subsequent fade to black paradoxically render the scene all the more moving, as it indicates a sensitivity towards the mother's distress, a reluctance to exploit or dwell voyeuristically upon her moment of anguish. Or, to put it another way, the camera and hence the viewer seem to show a deference to her suffering by physically extricating themselves from the scene. The same argument could indeed also be applied to the mother's death scene in *A Simple Event*, which also fades to black relatively quickly after the doctor pronounces the mother dead.

The ambiguities surrounding Saless's portrayal of everyday manifest themselves most powerfully in *Hans – A Boy in Germany*, particularly around the portrayal of the film's main character, played by Martin Pasko. The film, which as noted above is an adaptation of Hans Frick's novel *The Blue Hour* and largely autobiographical in content, tells the tale of a half-Jewish boy living in Nazi Germany with his mother and grandmother. His father, a Hungarian Jew, fled Germany before the outbreak of war. In his portrayal of the everyday racism rife in German society during the Nazi era, Saless creates a darkly cynical critique of how that racism carries over into post-war German society.

Hans: a film from Germany?

That the title of *Hans – A Boy in Germany* is evocative of Hans Jürgen Syberberg's epic *Hitler – A Film from Germany* (1978) seems particularly apt, Saless's film providing a characteristically less grandiose, though in some respects equally ambitious, counterpoint of sorts to Syberberg's sweeping account of the Second World War and the Holocaust as the omega point of German (and by extension, European) civilization. In *Stranded Objects*, an insightful examination of mourning in post-war West German cinema, Eric L. Santner argues that Syberberg's vision of history as a 'single apocalyptic *grand récit*'[27] implies less a concern with initiating a 'labour of mourning than a reinscription of grandiose refusals to mourn: quests for a regressive return to origins, and ultimately for oblivion', a strategy 'more akin to an exorcism than to the labour of mourning'.[28] (This is despite Syberberg's impressive examination of 'the gears of the most powerful politico-cinematic machinery ever known'.)[29] Saless's portrayal of the 'everyday' also clearly differs from Edgar Reitz's understanding of the concept of 'everyday history', or *alltagsgeschichte*, a term originally coined by German historian Martin Broszat, and envisioned in Reitz's monumental film *Heimat - a German Chronicle* (1984, over fifteen hours in length). As Santner notes, Reitz's portrayal of daily life in the idyllic village of Schabbach – which is irrevocably altered by the encroaching forces of modernity, fascism, and ultimately, Americanization – essentializes a way of life that probably never existed in the first place, betraying a melancholic regret for the destruction of an allegedly 'authentic' German way of life, rather than marking the beginning of a long overdue process of mourning or *trauerarbeit*. As the German historian Omer Bartov has remarked, '*Heimat* is a film not about memory but about amnesia, that is, about the absence of memory and all that can be remembered and must nevertheless be erased.'[30]

If Syberberg and Reitz, whose films Santner describes as 'the two most ambitious attempts by recent German artists to create works of national elegiac art', are both responsible for an abstraction and romanticization of German history, Saless by contrast exposes the underside of German society during the Nazi era, focusing on the sinisterly casual, everyday racism endemic to Germany during that time, and how that racism lingers on in German society after the end of the war. Indeed, if *Heimat* and *Hitler - A Film from Germany* are both in their own ways films about amnesia, about the need to rewrite history, then *Hans - A Boy in Germany* is a film about the inability to forget or change the past, and the way in which the past returns to haunt the lives of Hans and his family, particularly his mother Eva (Imke Barnstedt). As Eva remarks, when her son returns home following the end of the war – after fleeing one day upon discovering men dressed like Gestapo agents knocking on the front door – to discover his grandmother Oma (Yane Bittlova) has died during his absence: 'Perhaps today we will forget.'

However, troubled by nightmares and growing ever more paranoid, Eva is unable to forget the cruelty of her neighbours, who continue to slip anti-Semitic notes under her front door calling her a Jewish whore, even as Hans attempts to hide the notes from her. Just like her mother Oma, who wishes to die and is confined to her bed for most of the film, Eva's inability to overcome the past transforms into a desire for oblivion. The final image of Eva, bed-ridden and catatonic, illustrates vividly that she is slowly suffering the same fate as her mother. Moreover, Eva and Oma's desire for oblivion is matched by their racist neighbours' desire for another kind of oblivion – namely, to banish the last trace, the last rem(a)inder of Jewish existence from their midst. It is indeed telling that Hans finds the single-word imperative 'Verschwinde!' or 'Disappear!' scribbled on one of the notes he discovers slipped under the front door one day (it is the anti-Semitic notes which form *the* recurring motif throughout the film).

As Ritchie Robertson has argued, a disturbing development in post-war German literature has been the tendency to depict Jewish characters as anonymous and – metaphorically speaking – *invisible* figures, via a process of de-individualization.[31] Such a process furthermore reflects a disturbing shift in post-war German society overall, not from a denial of complicity and responsibility to an acceptance of the past and the beginning of a belated process of empathy with Jews as victims of the Holocaust, but from the perception of German-as-perpetrators to Germans-as-resistors,[32] and finally to Germans-(themselves)-as-victims. In her provocative essay on the representation of Jews in the films of Rainer Werner Fassbinder – a director who certainly did not shy away from portraying Jewish characters in his films – Gertrud Koch claims, for instance, that Jews serve as nothing more than a mere foil for the sufferings of Fassbinder's non-Jewish protagonists. Taking such films as *In a Year with Thirteen Moons* (1978), *The Marriage of Maria Braun* (1979), *Berlin Alexanderplatz* (1980), *Lili Marleen* (1981) and *Veronika Voss* (1982) as illustrations of her argument, Koch contends that although Jews are not portrayed as mere helpless victims, in Fassbinder's *oeuvre* they are nevertheless presented as abstract, almost metaphysical beings. 'Untouchable, cold, aloof, unattainable, unapproachable' and 'arrogant', they are far removed from and seemingly immune to the earthly torments of the flesh endured by Fassbinder's other, non-Jewish characters:

> In Fassbinder's work Jews are not wanton, rich, seductive, power-hungry or amoral. But neither are they included among the tormented victims, oppressed minorities, and suffering creatures like many of Fassbinder's characters. They could be called anti-figures, almost abstract ... Although Fassbinder

never makes use of malicious anti-Semitic clichés in his films, there lies at the root of his creation an anti-Semitic motif, which often manifests itself in the form of a philo-Semitic stereotype: the picture of the Jew as the strict patriarch and man of intellect, law-abiding and austere... At the same time, they function as a screen for the projection of a narcissistic yearning for love as in *In a Year With Thirteen Moons*. The displacement and repression of suffering and sacrifice is absorbed into a cosmos of physical self-mutilation, in which the Jews are allotted the ambivalent role of judges over life and death.[33]

Providing several revealing analyses of Jewish characters from Fassbinder's works – perhaps most compellingly, the figure of Nachum from *Berlin Alexanderplatz* – Koch argues that amidst these dispassionate and highly generalized representations of 'Jewishness', there is little, if any, room left for empathy with Jews as victims, at least of physical suffering, unaffected as they seem to be by the worries and pain of the corporal world.[34] Moreover, as Bartov has observed, the most troubling aspect of this desire to render Jewishness as ever more abstract and inscrutable, as a means of suppressing the painful memories of the past and prioritizing self-empathy, is that on a psychological level it seems worryingly similar to the attempt made by the Nazis fifty years earlier, to physically exterminate Jewish 'difference' from German society:

> One is hard put to think of any German film or work of fiction devoted to the Jewish experience of genocide... While not absent, the victims remain anonymous and faceless; the evil, whatever the causes attributed to it, is in the deed (and its effects on the perpetrators), not in the application to individual human beings. This is a type of representation not unrelated to the Nazis' own perception and representation of the victims as constituting targets for their actions totally lacking individual identity.[35]

As Bartov argues, 'empathy begins with the self and is therefore deeply rooted in a narcissistic view of the world'. The gradual effacement or displacement of the victims of the Holocaust (not only Jews, of course) is hence 'a crucial precondition for the representation of German victimhood'.[36] Their presence is a 'fundamental obstruction to self-empathy'.[37] It is films such as *Heimat* and *Hitler – A Film from Germany,* therefore, which have prompted scholars such as Santner to observe that 'Jews are being displaced by the event of their own destruction...[they are] no longer available as the signifier of ruptures and disturbances one would like to banish from the inside (of the self, the family, the city, the *Reich*)...the Holocaust now figures as the placeholder for the decenteredness and instability experienced as so painfully chronic in contemporary German society.'[38]

The Holocaust and any images of Jewish victimization associated with it are also conspicuous by their absence in Saless's film. As Hans struggles to survive in his racist neighbourhood, all the major events of the Jewish genocide significantly occur off-screen. Reasons for this could, of course, include simple budgetary constraints, or strict adherence to the film's source material, rather than a desire to completely efface any images of Jewish persecution from the film altogether. Saless, however, in keeping with his previous films, once again problematizes straightforward identification with his protagonist, not through the use of long shots and long takes, but paradoxically by means of a basic technique traditionally used in cinema to provoke empathy in the viewer: the close-up. Indeed, the film is full of prolonged close-ups of Hans's blank, expressionless face, in which he displays no intelligible emotion or reaction whatsoever to the events occurring around him.

The scene in which Hans goes to the munitions factory where his mother works, to discover the foreman attempting to rape his mother (in a scene reminiscent of the closing moments of *A Time of Maturity*), is perhaps the most striking example of this distanciation technique. A long shot of Hans initially shows him entering and crossing the yard of the factory, drawn to the voice of his mother shouting at the foreman to stop. A close-up of Hans's face then shows him gazing off-screen to his left, whereupon there is a cut to a point-of-view shot of the foreman forcing himself upon Eva. In the next shot – a medium close-up of Hans – he merely continues to stare vacantly (into the camera) at the scene unfolding before him. The use of a frontal close-up here is particularly striking, emphasizing as it does the utter emptiness and stillness of Hans's expression as he moves slowly forward, gradually filling up more of the frame. Eventually the foreman notices Hans's presence, desists and leaves, while Hans helps his mother to her feet. But Hans's apparent lack of emotion and his unresponsiveness to the scene leaves the viewer with the uneasy question of just how much longer he would have continued to watch impassively before he was noticed. Other prolonged close-ups of Hans's face, such as those that show Hans lying in bed between his mother and grandmother, during which he learns important details about his mother and father's past, are also characterized by their emotional emptiness and only serve to render his true feelings even more unreadable. Even Martin Pasko's stilted performance and his mannered, dispassionate delivery of his lines appear intended to alienate the viewer. At certain points in the narrative it even seems misleading to describe Hans as a 'protagonist' at all. For as Klevan explains, 'Protagonists in most narrative films tend to disturb order or act to resolve disruption: this is what lends films their drive, as the protagonist either disrupts or searches for solutions to situations'.[39]

Hans by contrast, rather than being the force that drives the narrative forward (although he certainly becomes more forceful and defiant towards the end of the film), wanders aimlessly around the streets of his neighbourhood and glides through the first half of the film seemingly unfazed by the racist taunts of his neighbours and the destruction caused by the frequent air-raid bombings. On the one hand, Saless and Pasko's unemotional depiction of Hans may seem to be merely yet another addition to a long line of insensitive, morally suspect portrayals of Jewish characters in German cinema, wholly inappropriate given the delicate and provocative nature of the film's subject matter. On the other hand, Saless's minimalist style once again works strategically to prevent the film from lapsing into an overwrought, emotionally manipulative tale of one boy's struggle to survive in Nazi Germany. As Annette Insdorf has noted, for example, many Holocaust films have, somewhat crudely, '[yoked] childhood and Judaism together to express weakness and victimization'.[40] Rather than facilitating a transferral of victimhood from Jews to Germans (or vice versa), Saless's non-representation of the Holocaust and of all the iconography associated with it – combined with his unemotional depiction of Hans – works to avoid fetishizing or dwelling voyeuristically on those bankrupt images of Jewish suffering which have become virtually synonymous with the Holocaust through their circulation and repetition in films and television programs. Michael E. Geisler has noted the trend in post-war German cinema and television, especially in those films and programs which do not even attempt to portray the Holocaust diegetically, towards recycling familiar images of Jewish suffering, particularly 'archival materials, photographs, and flashbacks', to lend themselves an aura of legitimacy and false pathos.

> Being relegated to the position of referent and instrumentalized in the interest of narratives whose main concerns lay elsewhere, these sequences and photographs of mass murders and gas chambers, of torture and dehumanization became part of what Anton Kaes has called the 'iconography of the Nazi era': a set of disposable, interchangeable, dehistoricized images that can be inserted into any historical narrative, no matter how trivial, to give it a simulated authenticity and a sense of tragic depth.[41]

In *Hans – A Boy in Germany*, small acts of humanity and inhumanity stand in for or replace those images of oppression and genocide, or of mercy and survival, which would typically be expected from a film taking the experiences of a Jew in Nazi Germany as its subject matter, especially in a post-*Holocaust* (Marvin J. Chomsky, 1978) context.[42] In one scene, for example, the sadistic Nazi officer Martin White (Hans Sander) marches a group of prisoners (whether they are Jews or POWs is unclear) through the streets outside Hans's home. As Hans watches the prisoners, he notices Peter Schwab (Ulrich von Bock), the kindly shopkeeper whom Hans refers to as 'Uncle Peter', handing out slices of bread surreptitiously to the men as they march by. Saless's method of revealing Peter's kindness towards the men is particularly effective in its understatedness and restraint. A medium close-up of Peter – a point-of-view shot from Hans's perspective – shows him watching the men as they pass him by in the foreground of the shot, intermittently blocking Hans's view of Peter as they do so. When the last Nazi officer has finally passed Peter by, the camera pans down slightly, seemingly arbitrarily, to catch sight of Peter hurriedly reaching into his pocket and handing slices of bread to the prisoners. The sight of the men's bodies moving past the front of the camera and obscuring Hans's view of Peter's actions adds to the feeling of randomness surrounding the shot, giving the impression that Hans and the viewer are catching a brief glimpse of humanity amidst the scenes of persecution.

In another scene, during his flight from home, Hans tries to give some water to a carriage full of prisoners who are being transported by train, only to be stopped by a Nazi soldier, who kicks over the bucket of water he is carrying. Saless on this occasion employs a long shot – which shows the soldier glaring down at Hans as he casually tips the bucket of water with his foot – to emphasize the deliberate, detached nature of his cruelty. In both of the above scenes, minor, understated acts of compassion and brutality – the passing out of bread, the denial of water – take the place of those familiar and emotionally provocative images of Jewish victimization recycled endlessly by so many films and television programs before them.

It is significant, therefore, that only after the end of the war does the mise-en-scène of Saless's film begin to resemble that of a Holocaust film, the grim young offenders' institute in which Hans is interned – for impersonating an American soldier over the telephone – resembling very strongly a concentration camp of sorts. In one scene, set in the refectory where Hans eats with his fellow inmates, the camera pans slowly across the hall to focus on a guard reading a newspaper ironically entitled *Die Neue Zeitung* (or *The New Times*). But, as Hans discovers, there is nothing 'new' about post-war Germany at all. Although the extremely clumsy characterization of many of the American soldiers in the film undermines to an extent the parallel the film makes between wartime and post-war German society and the continuing intolerance Hans encounters, Saless's subtle repetition of certain motifs – or certain patterns of behaviour on the part of specific characters – established earlier in the film makes clear that the Allied victory brings no liberation of any kind for Hans and his family from the racist abuse they received before the end of the war, or any change in the mindset of the German people and their attitude towards Jews.

Hans's girlfriend Nora (Eva Vejmalkova), for instance, who is quite clearly differentiated from Hans by her blond hair and her visibly 'Aryan' appearance, and who throughout the film grows noticeably uneasier in Hans's presence and scorns his suggestions that Germany will eventually lose the war, grows ever more distant from him towards the end of the film, refusing to even look at him or speak to him during their last 'conversation', treating him as if he were indeed 'invisible'. Likewise, Hans's racist neighbour, Mrs Marbach, remains steadfast in her prejudice towards Hans and his family. In one striking scene, Hans boldly performs the 'Sieg Heil' salute in front of her as she is hanging her washing out to dry, mocking the racist insults she directed at him earlier in the film. The fact that Mrs Marbach is shown performing such a mundane and everyday task as hanging her clothes on a washing line is important, as it indicates where the unsettling power of Saless's portrayal of the 'everyday' in *Hans – A Boy in Germany* truly lies: namely, in its depiction of 'ordinary' Germans, not as unwitting agents of or reluctant participants in the racist policies of the Nazis, but predominantly as willing and complicit supporters of the violence and hatred perpetrated by their leaders. Hans also continues to receive the anti-Semitic notes which are slipped under his front door. Significantly, Hans never discovers those responsible for the notes. Their origin remains unknown, their racist content reflective of the collective mindset of post-war Germany as a whole, rather than attributed to one particular individual.

In stark contrast to all of his other films, however, Saless chooses to conclude *Hans – A Boy in Germany* on a cautious note of optimism, a note that nonetheless does not appear forced or contrived but seems quite appropriate and suitably ambiguous in its tentativeness and uncertainty. The final image of Hans sawing through the metal bars that cover the window in his kitchen, in defiance of his neighbours, is a quietly understated picture of his will and determination to survive.

Saless and Kiarostami: the Iranian connection

Having considered Saless's émigré works to some degree in relation to other films of the New German Cinema, it is worth examining briefly his ties with the New Iranian Cinema, most notably this cinema's most well-known and acclaimed filmmaker, Kiarostami. As stated at the beginning of this chapter, the purpose of this comparison is not only to underline the importance of Saless's works and the link they represent between the New Iranian Cinema and Iranian émigré filmmaking, but also to bring this analysis of post-revolutionary Iranian filmmaking, in its various guises, in a sense back to where we started, with indigenous Iranian cinema. This circular movement is, however, not intended to insulate or close off Iranian cinema to further discussion, for indeed this book has only scratched the surface of the complex relationships and various connections between the New Iranian Cinema and its émigré counterpart. It is rather meant to reinforce the argument that a better understanding of both the New Iranian Cinema and Iranian émigré filmmaking can be attained if they are viewed in relation to one another, rather than as two completely distinct entities.

The parallels between the works of Kiarostami and Saless will be clear to anyone who as ever seen any of their films. Indeed, it is a comparison that is made with a relatively fair degree of frequency in much of the literature on the New Iranian Cinema. It is a comparison that nonetheless never really extends beyond the superficial. Elena, for instance, on several occasions in his book on Kiarostami, notes the director's apparent indebtedness to Saless's seminal film *A Simple Event* (and by extension the indebtedness of fellow Kiarostami disciples such as Panahi and Ghobadi). Elena, however, never really goes into any great detail about the exact nature of the affinities between the works of these two directors. On the one hand, this is largely due to Kiarostami's own coyness and notoriously deliberate reluctance to reveal or acknowledge his own cinematic inspirations. It has always been difficult, for instance, to gauge the exact extent of the influence filmmakers such as Saless, as well as the numerous other European directors with whose films Kiarostami's cinema seems to share such an affinity, have had upon Kiarostami. (Though Kiarostami clearly did intend to pay homage to Saless with his short never-to-be-made-into-a-film script entitled *Love and the Wall*, set in Germany, and which featured Saless as the film's main character.)[43] On the other hand, it may also be due to the fact that the similarities between films such as *A Simple Event* and *Where Is the Friend's House?* are so apparent, that any attempt at analysing them inevitably runs the risk of stating the obvious.

There is not sufficient space here to trace fully all of the parallels between these two films, let alone the entire *oeuvres* of Saless and Kiarostami. It is worthwhile noting briefly, however, the similarities between *A Simple Event* and *Where Is the Friend's House?*, to give an intimation of not only where these two important filmmakers begin to cross paths, stylistically and thematically, but also where they begin to diverge. By highlighting the differences as well as the similarities between the two filmmakers, therefore, and by finally bringing this analysis of post-revolutionary Iranian filmmaking full circle as it were, this book as a whole aims to contribute to the further study of the numerous connections between the New Iranian Cinema and Iranian émigré filmmaking. Hopefully it will also provide the groundwork for future, more detailed comparisons between the films of Saless and Kiarostami.

Both *A Simple Event* and *Where Is the Friend's House?* take a young boy as the central character. Both boys display tremendous resilience in their respective endeavours, despite the concerns noted by Farahmand in chapter 1 that the portrayals of children in Iranian cinema of the 1970s and early 1980s, characterized as they were by a 'synthesis of aggressiveness and innocence, the adult world's and the child's, as well as vulnerability and pride', have been replaced by 'purified prototypes of children'[44] throughout the 1990s. In *A Simple Event* the boy is forced to cope with the death of his mother, while his counterpart in *Where Is the Friend's House?* doggedly perseveres until he successfully returns his friend's homework book.

Although Ahmad from *Where Is the Friend's House?* is clearly a far easier character to identify with overall, by virtue of the concerted action he takes in order to solve the dilemma that confronts him, in addition to quite simply how he speaks and interacts more frequently with the people around him (in contrast to the largely muted and seemingly detached response of the boy in *A Simple Event* to the events unfolding around him), both films align the viewer's perspective with that of their central characters to an equally strong degree. Indeed, as the above analysis of Saless's work reveals, the lack of emotion his characters usually display is not generally reflective of the tenderness and care with which Saless portrays them as a director. Whether this can be described as 'humanism' or outright sentimentalism, both films clearly present their central child characters as thoroughly sympathetic figures. Moreover, both films also embody a critique, if not of absolute totalitarianism per se, then at the very least of authority figures in general, via the depiction of their young central characters. In *A Simple Event*, the boy's troubled relationship with his schoolteacher, as well as his own father, is paralleled in *Where Is the Friend's House?* by Ahmad's fraught relationship with his equally condescending schoolteacher, as well as the various elders who hinder his efforts to find the house of his friend Mohammed.

It is the use of repetition, however, which most clearly links the two directors as well as differentiates one from the other. Both Saless and Kiarostami clearly rely upon the device of repetition as a means of structuring the narratives of all their films. This reliance upon repetition can encompass many aspects of the filmmaking process, from the use of particular shots and shot duration, to dialogue and the use of music. More often than not, this repetition serves to give their films a similarly rounded, circular feel, which can be seen as contributive to the sense of open-endedness and irresolution that characterizes the endings of many of their films. As explained above, however, Saless's use of repetition is specifically designed to 'shock' the viewer, to surprise the audience with the unexpected occurrence of a traumatic event that interrupts his characters' daily routines and deeply affects their lives. The abruptness with which these traumatic events take place as well as the particular point at which they occur in the narrative (typically at the very end of the film) have the effect of bringing his films to an abrupt halt, as is the case with *A Time of Maturity* and *Utopia*, though it is not so much the case with a film like *The Willow Tree*, in which the traumatic event in question (a murder) occurs a mere twenty minutes into the film. Although Saless's films are often devised to leave the viewer in a kind of psychological limbo, uncertain as to how these traumatic events will affect his characters' lives, they do also paradoxically provide his films with a narrative 'climax', and hence an abstract sense of closure or finality that is largely absent from Kiarostami's cinema. Kiarostami's films by contrast often employ repetition to defer and confound the viewer's expectations of narrative resolution, pointing to a conclusion that may or may not occur beyond the end of the film in the minds of the audience themselves.

Although the analogies between the works of Saless and Kiarostami may be apparent to many, there exist some important differences that need to be teased out and explored in greater detail, so as to be able to better understand the nature of the connection between these two filmmakers, and by extension between the New Iranian Cinema and Iranian émigré filmmaking. Despite these differences, Kiarostami's cinema and the cinema of the younger generation of Iranian filmmakers such as Babak Payami (who has explicitly credited Saless as one of his major influences)[45] strongly bear traces of Saless's work, confirming Saless as perhaps the key link between these two cinemas, between the past and the future, between Iran and the rest of the world.

Between the new waves

Saless once remarked in an interview with Naficy,

> I must admit with extreme sadness that I have no nostalgic longing for Iran. When each morning I set foot outside my house, whether it was in Germany, France, Venice, or the Soviet Union – the places where I have lived and made films – I would feel at home, because I had no difficulties. I am essentially not a patriot... I think one's homeland is not one's place of birth, but the country that gives one a place to stay, to work, and to make a living... Germany was my home for a long time.[46]

It is particularly striking that Saless does not express regret over the loss of his homeland as such, but rather over *his own incapacity* to feel the weight of this loss – in other words, his sadness over not actually feeling sad. His comments betray an absence of sentimentality in the man himself that manifests itself on an aesthetic and thematic level in many of his films. This absence is not the same, however, as a lack of emotion, for I find many of Saless's films very moving. It is also striking that despite the sombre and critical nature of his émigré works, Saless refers to Germany as his 'home'. His outlook is perhaps even more understandable given the similarities between the film industries in Iran and Germany. As Saless himself has noted, in terms of censorship there was very little to choose between working in Iran and working in Germany: 'Censorship does exist here,' he observes of Germany, 'the only difference is in the methods.'[47] Indeed it is difficult to imagine such a supremely uncompromising and socially conscious filmmaker as Saless finding it particularly easy to practice his craft anywhere in the world.

In addition to examining the defining characteristics of Saless's cinema, primarily his portrayal of the 'everyday', and the limitations of regarding his works exclusively as examples of exilic and/or diasporic filmmaking, this chapter has aimed to illustrate the ways in which Saless can be regarded as both an Iranian filmmaker *and* a German filmmaker. Suspended between the New Iranian Cinema and the New German Cinema and yet at the same time deeply implicated in the development and history of both, Saless represents a powerful link between indigenous post-revolutionary Iranian cinema and Iranian émigré filmmaking. If the typically auteurist understandings of Kiarostami's works, discussed in the opening chapter of this book, frequently serve to essentialize and ultimately impoverish his films, closing them off to the multitude of possible interpretations that Kiarostami himself strives to provoke in the viewer, then in Saless's case recognizing the director's personal vision as a defining structure running throughout all of his works serves by contrast to *open up* his films to the very kind of alternative readings that defy any attempt to pigeonhole them exclusively as exilic, or Iranian, or German. With Saless and Kiarostami this paradox is deeply informed by the way in which both directors and their respective *oeuvres* have traditionally been conceived of in European and North American film circles, Kiarostami as the quasi-European art cinema director par excellence, and Saless, in the limited literature that exists on his work, as the exiled Iranian filmmaker par excellence. Therefore, although the question of national cinema cannot simply be reduced to an issue of authorship, authorship remains an absolutely integral factor when considering and attempting to understand the national 'belonging' or cultural 'identity' of any film or filmmaker.

It seems appropriate, therefore, to conclude with a brief analysis of a scene from the Saless film *Addressee Unknown*, in which the wife (Iris von Reppart-Bismarck), who has left her husband (Manfred Zapatka) to begin an affair with a Turkish 'guest worker' (or *gastarbeiter*), examines a photo of Jewish prisoners in a concentration camp in Nazi Germany. Eventually the faces of the Jewish prisoners are replaced by those of anonymous *gastarbeiteren*, the faces of the latter being superimposed over those of the former. This scene, which draws an explicit parallel between the racist treatment of Jews in Germany during the Second World War and the racist treatment of the *gastarbeiteren* in contemporary Germany, illustrates, perhaps more strongly than any other scene or film in Saless's entire *oeuvre*, Saless's dual status as a German filmmaker and an Iranian émigré filmmaker, as an insider and an outsider, as a filmmaker who tackled the most topical and taboo issues in German society as well as issues which were extremely personal to him as a foreigner living and working in Germany.

Conclusion: Iranian Cinema in Long Shot

This book has attempted to paint a broader, more nuanced picture of post-revolutionary Iranian filmmaking, by way of an analysis of how the existence of a diffuse and eclectic Iranian émigré cinema challenges the artistic, historical and geographical integrity of the New Iranian Cinema. It is the contention of this book that a better understanding of both cinemas is attained when they are viewed in relation to each other, rather than as entirely discrete phenomena.

In the opening chapter we looked at how the New Iranian Cinema has been received and constructed as a quintessential 'New Wave' art cinema in Europe and North America. I argued that although many of the analogies drawn between the New Iranian Cinema and European art cinema frequently serve to hide rather than illuminate the political, historical and cultural particularities of the former's gradual rise to international prominence, on an aesthetic and thematic level many post-revolutionary Iranian films do indeed invite such comparisons, due to the undeniable similarities they share with their post-Second World War European counterparts. At the same time, many Iranian filmmakers have successfully resisted the attempt by critics, academics and audiences in Europe and North America to define their cinema as just another in a long line of 'New Wave' art cinemas, just as they have successfully resisted the attempt of their own government to determine the ideological nature of post-revolutionary Iranian cinema. Iranian filmmakers have achieved this success through what can perhaps best be described as a strategy of considered open-endedness and polysemy, defying overly simplistic and categorical readings of their films.

The Iranian émigré filmmakers considered in chapter 2 display a markedly similar aversion to being pinned down, or neatly categorized. Despite the itinerant and contradictory nature of most Iranian émigré cinema, this heterogeneous group of filmmakers are capable of being conceived of collectively by the way in which their films deal with the experience of displacement, displaying a gradual shift from a myopic and exclusive focus on the experience of exile, typically autobiographical in nature, to a more open and inclusive pan-diasporic perspective. Rather than threatening to fragment irretrievably the notion of a culturally identifiable, indigenous Iranian cinema, however, the existence of a prolific and diverse Iranian émigré cinema promises to enrich and expand not only our knowledge of post-revolutionary Iranian filmmaking, but also our understanding of the concept of national cinema in general.

Finally, the analyses of the New York and German films of Naderi and Saless in chapters 3 and 4 highlight the dangers of consistently imposing an exclusively exilic and/or diasporic reading upon the works of Iranian émigré filmmakers. Despite the manifest differences between Naderi and Saless, in terms of how their émigré works resemble (or, in Naderi's case, do *not* resemble) their Iranian films, both directors defy absolutist interpretations of their individual *oeuvres*. Naderi does so by explicitly tackling numerous issues and themes in his films (such as the role or place of women in the city in *A, B, C... Manhattan*), an appreciation of which is by no means contingent upon an understanding of Naderi as an Iranian émigré filmmaker. Saless by contrast does so by consistently and visibly refining throughout his German works the artistic vision clearly evident in his first two Iranian feature films – *A Simple Event* and *Still Life*. In this book I have chosen to describe this artistic vision as Saless's portrayal of the 'everyday.' As such, Saless represents a vital and perhaps the most compelling link between the New Iranian Cinema and Iranian émigré filmmaking, helping this overview of post-revolutionary Iranian filmmaking return to where it began. His influence is discernible not only in the recent works of long-standing Iranian directors such as Kiarostami, but also in the works of the emerging generation of Iranian filmmakers, some of whom directly acknowledge Saless as an influence on their own filmmaking style. It should be stressed nevertheless that the analyses of the émigré works of Naderi and Saless in this volume are not intended to overlook or undermine the validity of regarding these works as important and valuable examples of émigré filmmaking.

But what of the very concept of national cinema itself? The limitations of Andrew Higson's initial theorization of national cinema are well known. Subsequent revisions of this theorization by Higson and others have thus far failed to come up with a suitably nuanced and comprehensive definition of national cinema which would be capable of accommodating the geographically dispersed understanding of post-revolutionary Iranian cinema that this book proposes. What other term can possibly hope to encompass the multi-sited and itinerant nature of much contemporary filmmaking, Iranian and non-Iranian, local and global, 'accented' and Hollywood, minority and mainstream?

The introduction to Kathleen Newman's essay, entitled 'National Cinema after Globalization', on the films *Tangos: The Exiles of Gardel* (Fernando Solanas, 1985) and *Sur* (Solanas, 1988) suggests some interesting possibilities. In the introduction, the editors, Manuel Alvarado and Anna M. Lopez – referring to the large number of Latin American filmmakers who went into forced or self-imposed exile during the 60s and 70s – observe that in the case of Chile, this massive migration had an 'unexpected side-effect': namely, the creation of a 'prolific "national" cinema produced *outside* the boundaries of the nation-state' (my emphasis).[1] But what exactly makes a film 'Chilean' if it is not made in Chile? Or in the case of this discussion, what exactly makes a film 'Iranian' if it is not made in Iran? Despite the fact that both of the films considered in Newman's essay are directed by Fernando Solanas, an Argentinian émigré, this book has argued that such questions cannot simply be reduced to a matter of authorship. Constantly viewing the works of émigré filmmakers through the potentially distorting prism of displacement can be impoverishing and exclude alternative interpretations of these works. As this book has tried to illustrate, other factors such as content and form need to be taken into account as well. Which is not to say, with regard to the formal properties of émigré cinema, that there is anything inherently exilic and/or diasporic about a close-up or a long shot, for instance, other than that the use of such devices can appear to be informed by a distinctly exilic and/or diasporic sensibility, in a manner akin to the 'Islamic' sensibility discerned in films of the New Iranian Cinema.

Authorship nevertheless remains an absolutely integral factor in any consideration of émigré cinema. It would have been impossible to include, for example, the film *House of Sand and Fog* in the analysis of Iranian émigré cinema conducted in chapter 2, had there not been any Iranians involved in the overall making of the film outside of the primary creative role of director. An Iranian presence in the making of the film is, therefore, a prerequisite.

The fact that Alvardo and Lopez's statement serves as a precursor to an essay that focuses on the film *Tangos: The Exiles of Gardel* – which, as well as being directed by an Argentinian exile, portrays the experience of displacement for a group of Argentinian émigrés living in Paris – would perhaps suggest that any effective answer to the question posed above must involve a combination of authorship and content, if not necessarily form. It does not automatically follow, however, that the Iranian émigré films considered in this book can accurately be described as forming an 'extra-national' cinema produced outside of Iran. What becomes of émigré filmmakers such as Naderi and Saless who do not take the experience of cultural displacement as their subject matter? Excluding them from the group of filmmakers regarded as making up an extra-national cinema would be to expose the concept of such a cinema to the kind of criticisms levelled at the 'limiting imagination' of national cinema. Conversely, it would hardly be sound, theoretically or ethically, to include these filmmakers purely on the basis of their national origins, or even to employ a degree of selectiveness when discussing their films, picking and choosing from their *oeuvres* those films that most readily offer themselves up to exilic and/or diasporic readings. Indeed, there are even more variables to take into account, such as the degree of artistic cooperation and geographical cohesiveness, which characterize certain extra-territorial film movements, not to mention the different ways in which different émigré filmmakers may choose to portray their experiences of displacement, in spite of any (extra)national, (pan)diasporic solidarity they may share with each other. In contrast to a great deal of Latin American émigré filmmaking, for instance, Iranian cinema in exile and diaspora is characterized by a general lack of collaboration between its creators, as well as the geographically diffuse nature of its make-up.

Positing the term 'extra-national cinema' as some kind of counterpoint to 'national cinema', in addition to setting up a potentially reductive binary opposition, ultimately risks eliding many of the geographical and cultural differences that may separate the particular group of émigré filmmakers in question. It also risks overlooking the complex interrelationships between a particular group of émigré film-makers and the indigenous cinema of their adopted homelands or host countries. The term 'intra-national' cinema that Pick suggests implies a more nuanced understanding of these interrelationships and yet at the same seems far too technically clunky a label.[2]

Tim Bergfelder by contrast favours the term 'transnational' as a means of characterizing and examining the varied and numerous cinematic exchanges between different European countries throughout the twentieth century and beyond. Indeed the concept of 'transnational cinema' has gained a great deal of currency in Film Studies in recent years, seeming as it does to be the logical successor to the outmoded and geographically limited concept of 'national cinema.' Bergfelder, for instance, rightly observing that the study of 'European cinema' usually means the study of 'discreet' 'national cinemas' *within* Europe, argues that

> rather than focusing exclusively on separate national formations, a history of European cinema might well begin by exploring the inter-relationship between cultural and geographical centres and margins, and by tracing the migratory movements between these poles. In this context, the various waves of migration into and across Europe, motivated by the two world wars, national policies and ethnic exclusion, and the post-war legacy of colonialism and economic discrepancy between Europe and its others are fundamentally linked to the development of European cinema. Equally important to consider is the facilitating and concentrating function provided throughout European history by metropolitan cities (e.g. Berlin, Paris, London, Vienna), which became focal points and destinations for migrant film-makers at certain historical moments, and which thus transcend their status as purely 'national' locations ... national film cultures and migrant perspectives (themselves rarely 'pure') are always locked in a reciprocal process of interaction.[3]

Bergfelder's argument is equally applicable to the study of cinemas outwith Europe and points toward the need for a more open-ended understanding of the formation and development of most national cinemas. Alastair Phillips's work on the cinematic exchanges between the filmmaking metropolises of Paris and Berlin from 1929 to 1939 is a consummate example of the kind of 'transnational' approach to cinema studies that Bergfelder proposes.[4] Naficy's understanding of the term 'transnational', as discussed in chapter 2, by comparison seems more restrictive. In his writings on exilic television in Los Angeles, he describes as 'transnational' those programmes that are imported from the homeland *into* the United States. In *An Accented Cinema*, he also describes as 'transnational' those films that are made by 'hyphenated Iranians', which do 'not necessarily deal with Iranian issues but instead with universal issues of love and displacement.'[5] In Naficy's work, the term 'transnational' thus lacks the sense of exchange and bilateralism that it possesses in other contexts.

Although it promises to do away with the stale Hollywood/non-Hollywood binary opposition, the term 'transnational' has connotations of 'transcendence' attached to it that are not necessarily reflective of the situation in which many émigré filmmakers find themselves today on the ground, subject as they often are to the very real geographic pressures of national borders and economic pressures of inadequate funding. Therefore , efforts at semantic ingenuity aside, in this respect I find (perhaps somewhat surprisingly given the amorphous nature of the term) Chaudhuri's theorization of 'world cinema' quite an inviting alternative to traditional concepts of 'national cinema.' Although 'world cinema', as Chaudhuri acknowledges, is frequently employed as a 'catch-all term, designating all cinemas around the world, including Hollywood', she interprets it as referring primarily, though not *exclusively*, to 'national cinemas outside Hollywood.' More significantly, Chaudhuri sees the concept of 'world cinema' as a means of 'placing the national *within* regional and global perspectives' (my emphasis), pointing towards not only a way of retaining the concept of national cinema whilst exploring the various cinematic exchanges between different countries all around the world, but also a way of recognizing the cultural and economic hegemony of Hollywood cinema without automatically *re-inscribing* it at a theoretical level.[6]

In the conclusion to his book *Postnationalism Prefigured: Caribbean Borderlands*, Charles V. Carnegie utilizes the religious and philosophical nineteenth-century writings of Bahá'u'lláh (Mirza Hoseyn Ali

Nuri), the Iranian-born founder of the Bahai faith, as a means of envisioning a future world community. Carnegie is especially critical of influential nationalist scholars such as Gellner, Anderson, and even Hobsbawm, for what he describes as their inability to think beyond the restrictive binary opposition of national sovereignty versus globalization. The latter force, Carnegie insists, is typically and narrow-mindedly synonymous with increased consumerism, capitalism and Americanization. The suspicion of any form of 'world community' that such reductive binary thinking entails, claims Carnegie, hinders the realization of unifying global systems that recognize the fundamental equality between nations without sacrificing their cultural particularity and diversity.

> Scholars who have articulated the ideological contradictions of nationalism as the dominant form of modern community also frequently lament its resilience and the lack of viable alternatives...for most social thinkers, a world culture, if it can be envisaged at all, must consist of little more than spin-offs of from global capitalism... such a hodegpodge of elements lacks the centredness, the historical grounding to have any lasting impact on our most deeply felt sense of identity and belonging. A global culture of this sort has no memory; it is too eclectic a construct to take root in the minds and hearts of the world's peoples... Thus, in spite of widespread acknowledgement of and increasing attention to transnational cultural flows, scholars are generally sceptical about achieving any overarching, hegemonic cultural system... Unity and diversity of culture, then, are viewed as mutually exclusive. Binary thinking persists in spite of calls for its abandonment... We are left with the bleak prognosis that the only likely prospect for anything resembling a global culture would come in the form of an eclectic embrace of consumer capitalism and that such a culture, by definition, spells doom for human cultural variety.[7]

This dystopic outlook, Carnegie goes on to argue, has its basis in the extent to which traditional understandings of nationalism and globalization are strongly rooted in 'Western' thought and essentialist conceptual frameworks of race, gender and class. Such views, claims Carnegie, are in stark contrast to the teachings of Bahá'u'lláh, which envision a world community (that Carnegie does not attempt to depict as inherently utopian) by recognizing cultural diversity *through* unity.

Many of the problems Carnegie identifies as detrimental to the realization of a 'world community' are reflective of the conceptual crossroads at which Film Studies currently finds itself as an academic discipline. Reluctant to discard the seemingly outmoded concept of national cinema, on the one hand, for fear of losing sight of the particular historical, social and political contexts out of which most more or less geographically discrete cinematic formations emerge, and yet keenly aware, on the other hand, of the need for a more flexible theoretical framework that is more capable of accommodating the decentred and culturally interconnected nature of much filmmaking, there is no clear indication as to which direction Film Studies will take as a whole.

As for this book, it does not aim or presume to rehabilitate the concept of 'national cinema.' What seems to me to be much more important, than endlessly tying ourselves up in linguistic knots, is the need to carefully yet decisively liberate the term 'national cinema' from the sense of geographical belonging and/or rootedness with which it has traditionally, but by no means exclusively, been associated. What this book proposes, therefore, is in effect a post-national conception of 'national cinema', one that enables us to think more widely about the ways in which the various forces and discourses that give shape to different national cinemas coalesce and disseminate over given periods of time. Indeed, as Dimitris Eleftheriotis observes in his study of popular European cinemas, 'The study of the discursive formation around a national cinema, then, will not strive to discover and impose a coherence and unity where none exists, but to expose both the contradictory aspects of the discourse and how it achieves apparent unity.'[8]

Irrespective of whether the various manifestations of post-revolutionary Iranian filmmaking considered in this book are better encapsulated by the term 'extra-national', 'intra-national', 'supra-national' or 'transnational', the attempt to reconcile the existence of a rich and heterogeneous Iranian émigré cinema with the canon of films that are perceived to constitute the New Iranian Cinema exposes many of the problems with the way in which Film Studies as an academic discipline traditionally imagines its object of analysis. As I have learnt while writing this book, these are problems that can never be fully resolved, but merely resolved in different ways, for all studies of 'national' cinemas employ a degree of selectiveness as a matter of necessity. It is, however, worth noting the dangers of automatically dubbing the appearance on the international film scene of any and all hitherto 'undiscovered' cinemas as the sudden emergence of some 'new wave.' The New Iranian Cinema has a history after all, a history that needs to be better understood if it is to have any kind of future. For just how much longer can the 'New' Iranian Cinema remain 'new'?

Such a question might seem disingenuous. History has proven that very few national cinemas are capable of sustaining indefinitely the interest of foreign audiences. The decline in popularity of the New Iranian Cinema is, therefore, perhaps an inevitability. For just how much longer will film audiences in the 'West' consider Iranian cinema worthy of attention? The fall in critical standing of both French and German cinema following the decline of each country's so-called new wave movement provides a stark warning for Iranian filmmakers. Certain auteurs such as Kiarostami and the Makhmalbafs have undoubtedly cemented their reputations to the extent that their individual careers hinge little upon the larger fate of Iranian cinema itself. But Film Studies has already witnessed a shift of interest from Iranian cinema to other 'new waves' in recent years. A deeper appreciation of how exactly the New Iranian Cinema came about can, therefore, only lead to a better understanding of where it is headed and, more importantly, to echo Godfrey Cheshire, to a better appreciation of where it currently is.

* * *

Postscript: Iranian Cinema after 9/11

The similarity in response to the terrorist attacks in New York City on 11 September 2001 constitutes another major link between the New Iranian Cinema and Iranian émigré filmmaking, or, to be more precise, between two of their foremost directors, Samira Makhmalbaf of

11'09"01 – September 11 (2002) and Caveh Zahedi of *Underground Zero* (2002). Both directors made contributions to these collaborative film projects which explore the effects of the terrorist attacks from a number of different perspectives. Whereas *September 11* is comprised of eleven short films by some of the world's most prominent and highly acclaimed auteurs, *Underground Zero* is comprised of eleven short films made by little-known independent US filmmakers. Whereas the films that comprise *September 11* were all shot in 2002, the films that comprise *Underground Zero* were all shot in the weeks immediately following the terrorist attacks on the World Trade Centre and the Pentagon. Whereas Makhmalbaf's film is primarily a work of fiction, Zahedi's film is a documentary-cum-video diary.

Despite these differences, the similarities between the two films are startling. Both films, for instance, are set in a classroom. In Makhmalbaf's film, a young female teacher arrives at an Afghan refugee camp close to the Iran-Afghanistan border, where the inhabitants are frantically trying to make enough bricks to build shelters in preparation for the impending US bombing of their homeland. Zahedi's film is composed of footage he shot during the filmmaking classes he taught at the San Francisco Institute of Art shortly before and after 9/11.

In both films the teacher occupies an ambiguous position. The teacher in Makhmalbaf's film unfairly chastises her young pupils for failing to comprehend the enormity of the events that have transpired on the other side of the world in New York City. When she asks her pupils whether any of them know of the events that she is referring to, some of the children respond by mentioning the rumour that has been circulating prior to the class, that two local men may have fallen down a well and died. She also berates them when they fail to observe a minute's silence and instead chatter amongst themselves, debating in a seemingly naïve yet deceptively philosophical discussion the concept of a God who would intentionally kill his own creations. In Zahedi's film, entitled 'The World Is a Classroom', conflict breaks out between Zahedi and a young student named Daniel, after the latter refers to Zahedi's somewhat-less-than-orthodox teaching methods as 'stupid.' The power struggle that ensues between Zahedi and Daniel, between the teacher and his student, gradually becomes a metaphor for the wider struggle taking place in the world, as each

CONCLUSION

one tries to constantly impose his will upon the other, Zahedi trying to throw Daniel out of his class, and Daniel obstinately refusing to leave. It is not entirely clear, however, in Zahedi's film who is the terrorist and who is the terrorized. If there are any victims, it is the other students who have their classes disrupted as a result of the conflict between their teacher and one of their fellow classmates.

The methods that the two teachers adopt in order to resolve the dilemmas they find themselves confronted with are, however, radically different. In Makhmalbaf's film, the teacher orders her pupils to go and stand beneath a nearby chimney tower (see figure 9), which she uses as a stand-in for the World Trade Centre, in order to try to more strongly impose upon her pupils the scale of the tragedy that occurred in New York City. When one of the pupils sheepishly asks what they should do if they feel the urge to talk, the teacher responds curtly by saying, 'Just bite your lips and look at the chimney.' The authoritarian attitude of Makhmalbaf's teacher is in stark contrast to Zahedi's more conciliatory approach. After an allegedly hour-long

Figure 9   *11'09"01 – September 11*

telephone conversation with Daniel, Zahedi reveals that Daniel has agreed to participate fully in his classes once again and has given his permission to Zahedi to use the footage he shot of their conflict for his short film. All he needed to do, Zahedi explains to the viewer, was simply use the word 'Please.' Later, in front of the other students, Zahedi acknowledges that he was also at fault and apologizes to Daniel.

Makhmalbaf's film points towards the need for education as an alternative to authoritarianism, represented here by the teacher's very refusal to engage with her pupils and forcing of her own will upon them. Zahedi's film by contrast demonstrates the ability of acceptance and compromise to overcome hatred and confrontation. Taken together, in a world that has witnessed in the media a renewed demonization of Iran and Iranians living at home and abroad, it is no mere coincidence that both Samira Makhmalbaf's film and 'The World Is a Classroom' constitute impassioned pleas for greater tolerance and understanding.

Notes

Introduction

1. Chaudhuri, Shohini, *Contemporary World Cinema: Europe, The Middle East, East Asia and South Asia* (Edinburgh: Edinburgh University Press, 2005), pp. 3–4.

1 Putting the 'New' in the New Iranian Cinema: Post-Revolutionary Iranian Cinema as Art Cinema

1. Lopate, Philip, 'New York', *Film Comment* vol. 33, no. 6 (November–December 1997), p. 60.
2. Holden, Stephen, 'Of Passion and Paradox in the Ruins', *New York Times* (17 February 1995), http://www.nytimes.com/1995/02/17/movies/film-review-of-passion-and-paradox-in-the-ruins.html (no pagination).
3. Front cover of *Cahiers du Cinéma*, no. 493 (July–August 1995).
4. Mulvey, Laura, 'Kiarostami's Uncertainty Principle', *Sight & Sound* vol. 8, no. 6 (June 1998), p. 24.
5. Willemen, Paul, *Looks and Frictions: Essays in Cultural Studies and Film Theory* (London: British Film Institute, 1994), p. 211.
6. Egan, Eric and Mohammadi, Ali, 'Cinema and Iran: Culture and Politics in the Islamic Republic', *Asian Cinema* vol. 12, no. 1 (Spring/Summer 2001), p. 26.
7. Willemen, pp. 209–12.
8. Naficy, Hamid, 'Islamizing Film Culture in Iran: A Post Khatami Update', in Richard Tapper (ed.), *The New Iranian Cinema: Politics, Representation and Identity* (London; New York: I.B.Tauris, 2002), p. 34.
9. Ibid., pp. 39–52.
10. Ibid., p. 53.
11. The film was initially released but after two weeks withdrawn from cinemas when some clerics deemed it offensive.
12. *A Selection of Iranian Films 2003* (Tehran: Farabi Cinema Foundation, 2003), p. 99.
13. Naficy, pp. 40–54.

14. Neale, Steve, 'Art Cinema as Institution', *Screen* vol. 22, no. 1 (1981), pp. 35–7.
15. Mulvey, p. 24.
16. Bordwell, David, 'The Art Cinema as a Mode of Film Practice', *Film Criticism* vol. 4, no. 1 (Fall 1979), p. 57.
17. Ibid., p. 58.
18. Ibid.
19. Elena, Alberto, Belinda Coombes (trans.) *The Cinema of Abbas Kiarostami* (London: Saqi, 2005), p. 128.
20. Nayeri, Farah 'Iranian Cinema: What Happened in Between', *Sight & Sound* vol. 3, no. 12 (1993), p. 28.
21. Hamid, Nassia, 'Near and Far', *Sight & Sound* vol. 7, no. 2 (1997), p. 24.
22. Mulvey, p. 24.
23. See Hamid, p. 24.
24. Mulvey, p. 27.
25. Bordwell, p. 61.
26. Ibid., pp. 59–60.
27. Ibid., p. 59.
28. Nayeri, p. 28.
29. Bordwell, pp. 60–1.
30. Mulvey, p. 27.
31. Andrew, Geoff, *10* (London: British Film Institute, 2005), pp. 21–2.
32. Dabashi, Hamid, 'Re-Reading Reality: Kiarostami's *Through the Olive Trees* and the Cultural Politics of Postrevolutionary Aesthetics', *Critique* vol. 7 (1995), pp. 78–86.
33. Dabashi, *Close Up – Iranian Cinema: Past, Present and Future* (London; New York: Verso, 2001), p. 256.
34. Ibid., p. 252.
35. Totaro, Donato, 'Susan Sontag: Against Interpretation?', *Offscreen* vol. 9, issue. 1 (31 January 2005), http://www.offscreen.com/biblio/phile/essays/against_interpretation/ (no pagination).
36. Dabashi, *Close Up...*, p. 256.
37. Ibid., pp. 253–5.
38. Rosenbaum, Jonathan and Saeed-Vafa, Mehrnaz, *Abbas Kiarostami* (Urbana and Chicago: University of Illinois Press, 2003), p. 34.
39. Dabashi *Close Up...*, p. 257.
40. Elena, p. 115.

41. Ciment, Michel and Goudet, Stephane 'Entretien avec Abbas Kiarostami: Les six faces du cube', *Positif* no. 499 (September 2002), p. 18 (quoted in Elena, pp. 112–3).
42. Dabashi, 'Re-Reading Reality...', p. 71.
43. Cheshire, Godfrey, 'Where Iranian Cinema Is', *Film Comment* vol. 29, no. 2 (1993), p. 38.
44. Orgeron, Devin, 'The Import/Export Business: The Road to Abbas Kiarostami's *Taste of Cherry*', *Cineaction* no. 58 (June 2002), p. 46.
45. Ibid., p. 49.
46. Ibid., p. 51.
47. Ibid., p. 50.
48. See Said, Edward W., *Covering Islam: How the Media and the Experts Determine How We See the Rest of the World* (London: Vintage, 1997).
49. Naficy, Hamid, 'Mediawork's Representation of the Other: The Case of Iran', in Jim Pines and Paul Willeman (eds) *Questions of a Third Cinema* (London: British Film Institute, 1989), p. 232.
50. Fischer, Michael M. J., *Mute Dreams, Blind Owls, and Dispersed Knowledges: Persian Poesis in the Transnational Circuitry* (Durham & London: Duke University Press, 2004), p. 235.
51. Nichols, Bill, 'Discovering Form, Inferring Meaning: New Cinemas and the Film Festival Circuit', *Film Quarterly* vol. 47, no. 3 (Spring 1994), pp. 16–20.
52. *A Selection of Iranian Films 2003*, p. 98.
53. Higson, Andrew, 'The Concept of National Cinema', *Screen* vol. 30, no. 4 (1989), p. 38.
54. For a comprehensive list of these guidelines, see Naficy (2002), pp. 36–7.
55. Sadr, Hamid Reza, 'Contemporary Iranian Cinema and Its Major Themes', in Rose Issa and Sheila Whitaker (eds), *Life and Art: The New Iranian Cinema* (London: National Film Theatre, 1999), pp. 31–2.
56. Higson, 'The Limiting Imagination of National Cinema', in Mette Hjort and Scott Mackenzie (eds), *Cinema & Nation* (London: Routledge, 2000), pp. 63–7.
57. Bordwell, David, Staiger, Janet and Thompson, Kristin, *The Classical Hollywood Cinema: Film Style and Mode of Production to 1960* (London: Routledge and Kegan Paul, 1985).
58. Naficy (2002), p. 46. See also Naficy's essay 'Veiled Voice and Vision in Iranian Cinema: The Evolution of Rakhshan Bani-Etemad's Films', reprinted in several volumes, but most recently in Murray Pomerance (ed.), *Ladies and Gentlemen, Boys and Girls: Gender in Film at the End of the Twentieth Century* (Albany, NY: State University of New York Press,

2001), pp. 36–53. See also Shahla Lahiji's essay 'Chaste Dolls and Unchaste Dolls: Women in Iranian Cinema', *The New Iranian Cinema: Politics, Representation and Identity*, pp. 215–26.
59. Grabar, Oleg, *The Formation of Islamic Art* (New Haven and London: Yale University Press, 1973), pp. 1–3.
60. Egan and Mohammadi, p. 19.
61. See Farahmand, Azadeh, 'Perspectives on Recent (International Acclaim for) Iranian Cinema', *The New Iranian Cinema: Politics, Representation and Identity*, pp. 86–108.
62. Egan and Mohammadi, p. 20.
63. Naficy, Hamid, 'Iranian Cinema', in Oliver Leaman (ed.), *Companion Encyclopaedia of Middle Eastern and North African Film* (London: Routledge, 2001), p. 179.
64. Fischer, p. 223.
65. Grabar, p. 18.
66. Fischer, pp. 225–6.
67. Ibid., pp. 250–7.
68. Grabar, p. 5
69. Ridgeon, Lloyd, 'The Islamic Apocalypse: Mohsen Makhmalbaf's A Moment of Innocence', in Brent S. Plate (ed.), *Representing Religion in World Cinema: Filmmaking, Mythmaking, Culture Making* (New York: Palgrave MacMillan, 2003), pp. 155–7.
70. Naficy, 'Islamizing Film Culture in Iran...', p. 53.
71. Haghighi, Ali Reza, 'Politics and Cinema in Post-revolutionary Iran: An Uneasy Relationship', *The New Iranian Cinema: Politics, Representation and Identity*, p. 109.
72. Chaudhuri, Shohini and Finn, Howard, 'The Open Image: Poetic Realism and the New Iranian Cinema', *Screen* vol. 44, no. 1 (Spring 2003), p. 56.
73. Ibid., p. 43.
74. Ibid., p. 57.
75. Ali, Tariq, 'Fight the Power', *Guardian* (23 April 2005), http://www.guardian.co.uk/books/2005/apr/23/ featuresreviews.guardianreview11 (no pagination).

2 From Iran to Hollywood and Some Places In-Between: Iranian Émigré Filmmaking

1. Sullivan, Zohreh C., *Exiled Memories: Stories of Iranian Diaspora* (Philadelphia; England: Temple University Press, 2001), p. XVI.

2. Gramsci, Antonio, Frank Rosengarten (ed.), Raymond Rosenthal (trans.), *Letters from Prison: Volume 1* (New York: Columbia University Press, 1994), p. 70.
3. Naficy, Hamid, *An Accented Cinema: Exilic and Diasporic Filmmaking* (Princeton, NJ: Princeton University Press, 2001), p. 152.
4. Stam, Robert, 'Beyond Third Cinema: The Aesthetics of Hybridity', in Wimal Dissanayake and Anthony R. Gunaratne (eds), *Rethinking Third Cinema* (New York and London: Routledge, 2003), pp. 37–8.
5. Naficy, *An Accented Cinema...*, pp. 83–7.
6. Naficy, Hamid, 'Iranian Émigré Cinema as a Component of Iranian National Cinema', in Mehdi Semati (ed.), *Media, Culture and Society in Iran: Living with Globalization and the Islamic State* (London and New York: Routledge, 2007), p. 168.
7. Hall, Stuart, 'Culture, Community, Nation', *Cultural Studies* vol. 7, no. 3 (1993), p. 362.
8. Naficy, *An Accented Cinema...*, p. 10.
9. Ibid., pp. 3–4.
10. Ibid., p. 45.
11. See Getino, Octavio and Solanas, Fernando, 'Towards a Third Cinema: Notes and Experiences for the Development of a Cinema of Liberation in the Third World', in Michael T. Martin (ed.), *New Latin American Cinema – Volume 1: Theory, Practices, and Transcontinental Articulations* (Detroit: Wayne State University Press, 1997), pp. 33–58.
12. Naficy, *An Accented Cinema...*, pp. 30–1.
13. Ibid., p. 152.
14. Ibid., p. 188.
15. Ibid., p. 213.
16. Ibid., p. 221.
17. Ibid., pp. 12–5.
18. See Naficy, Hamid, 'Narrowcasting in Diaspora: Iranian Television in Los Angeles', in Lisa Parks and Kumar Shanti (ed.), *Planet TV: A Global Television Reader* (New York: New York University Press, 2003), pp. 376–401.
19. Said, *Reflections on Exile: And Other Literary and Cultural Essays* (London: Granta, 2001), pp. 178–82.
20. For his distinction between these two terms, see Martin Michael T., 'Framing the "Black" in Black Diasporic Cinemas', in Michael T. Martin (ed.), *Cinemas of the Black Diaspora* (Detroit: Wayne State University Press, 1995), p. 3.

21. Pick, Zuzana M., 'Chilean Cinema in Exile, 1973–1986', in Michael T. Martin (ed.), *New Latin American Cinema: Volume 2 – Studies of National Cinemas* (Detroit: Wayne State University Press, 1997), p. 431.
22. Marks, Laura U., 'A Deleuzian Politics of Hybrid Cinema', *Screen* vol. 35, no. 3 (1994), p. 262.
23. McLennen, Sophia A., *The Dialiectics of Exile: Nation, Time, Language, and Space in Hispanic Literatures* (West Lafayette, IN: Purdue University Press, 2004), p. 1.
24. Woodhull, Winifred, 'Exile', *Yale French Studies* no. 81 (1993), p. 8.
25. Barkan, Elazar and Shelton, Marie-Denise, *Borders, Exiles, Diasporas* (Stanford, CA: Stanford University Press, 1998), p. 4. Also, as Edward Said remarks rather romantically, '"exile" carries with it, I think, a touch of solitude and spirituality'. See *Reflections on Exile...*, p. 181.
26. For the six criteria Safran sets out, see Safran, William, 'Diasporas in Modern Societies: Myths of Homeland and Return', *Diaspora* vol. 1, no. 1 (Spring 1991), p. 91.
27. Clifford, James, 'Diasporas', *Cultural Anthropology* vol. 9, no. 3 (1994), pp. 306–8.
28. Ibid., p. 321.
29. Brah, Avtar, *Cartographies of Diaspora: Contesting Identities* (London: Routledge, 1996), p. 203.
30. Naficy, *An Accented Cinema...*, p. 17.
31. Ibid., p. 46.
32. Phillips, Alastair, 'An Accented Cinema', *Screen* vol. 44, no. 3 (2003), p. 344.
33. Bhabha, Homi K., *The Location of Culture* (London and New York: Routledge, 1994), pp. 148–9.
34. Johnston, Sheila, 'The Mission', *Monthly Film Bulletin* vol. 51, no. 604 (1984), p. 155.
35. Ibid.
36. The poems are a mixture of original compositions by Chinese-American writer Fae Myenne Ng and excerpts from Kenneth Rexroth and Ling Chung (eds), *Women Poets of China* (New York: New Directions Publishing, 1972). They are recited not by Mabel Kwong, but by Lois Taylor.
37. Wolff, Janet, 'On the Road Again: Metaphors of Travel in Cultural Criticism', *Cultural Studies* vol. 7, no. 2 (1993), p. 230. 'By "intrinsic", though, I do not mean "essential"; rather my interest is in the centrality of travel/mobility to *constructed* masculine identity'.

38. Clifford, p. 314.
39. Ganguly, Keya, 'Migrant Identities: Personal Memory and the Construction of Selfhood', *Cultural Studies* vol. 6, no. 1 (1992), p. 38.
40. Hall, Stuart, 'Cultural Identity and Diaspora', in Padmini Mongia (ed.), *Contemporary Postcolonial Theory: A Reader* (London and New York: Arnold, 1996), p. 120.
41. Mordler, Michael, 'Privacy Last', *Filmmaker* vol. 2, no. 3 (1994), p. 41.
42. Sadr, Hamid Reza, '... and the World Became His: An Exclusive Interview with Sohrab Shahid Saless', *Film International* vol. 5, no. 3–4 (1998), p. 55.
43. Zaatari, Akram, 'Abbas Kiarostami', *Bomb: Place Unknown* vol. 50 (1994–5), p. 13. Naficy also mentions in *An Accented Cinema*... (p. 324) how Zahedi revealed to him in an interview that Kiarostami's films had affected him deeply.
44. Naficy, *An Accented Cinema*, p. 256.
45. Mordler, p. 58.
46. Naficy, *An Accented Cinema*, p. 210.
47. Hall, 'Culture, Community, Nation', p. 362.
48. Holden, '*Before the Storm*: Parallel Predicaments on a Collision Course', *New York Times* (30 March 2001), http://www.nytimes.com/2001/03/30/movies/film-festival-review-parallel-predicaments-on-a-collision-course.html (no pagination).
49. Ibid.
50. See Gherami, Shahin, 'Mullahs, Martyrs, and Men: Conceptualizing Masculinity in the Islamic Republic of Iran', *Men & Masculinities* vol. 5, no. 3 (January 2003), pp. 257–74.
51. Huston, Johnny Ray, 'Long Story Short: Notes on the S.F. International Asian American Film Festival's 2002 Programs', *San Francisco Bay Guardian* (12 June 2002), http://www.sfbg.com/36/23/ art_notes.html (no pagination).
52. Roger, Ebert, 'Maryam', *Chicago Sun Times* (12 April 2002), http://rogerebert.suntimes.com/apps/pbcs.dll/article?AID=/20020412/REVIEWS/204120305/1023 (no pagination).
53. Langford, Michelle, 'Dreams, Disco and Politics: An Interview with Babak Shokrian', *Senses of Cinema* (March 2002), http://archive.sensesofcinema.com/contents/02/20/shokrian.html (no pagination).
54. Fassihian, Dokhi and Sarafan, Lily, 'NIAC Interviews Iranian American Writer-Director Ramin Serry on His Debut Film Maryam' (10 September 2003), http://payvand.com/news/03/sep/1053.html (no pagination).

55. Langford.
56. Kimiavi is one of Iran's most influential pre-revolutionary filmmakers, director of *P is for Pelican* (1972), *The Mongols* (1973) and *Gardens of Stone* (1976).

3 Close Up I – Amir Naderi

1. Naficy, *An Accented Cinema...*, p. 47.
2. Stone, Judy, *Eye on the World: Conversations with International Filmmakers* (Los Angeles: Silman-James Press, 1997), pp. 382–4.
3. See the introductions to David B. Clarke (ed.), *The Cinematic City* (London: Routledge, 1997), pp. 1–18 and Mark Shiel and Tony Fitzmaurice (eds), *Cinema & the City: Film and Urban Societies in a Global Context* (Oxford: Blackwell, 2001), pp. 1–18.
4. Mahoney, Elisabeth, '"The People in Parentheses": Space Under Pressure in the Postmodern City', in *The Cinematic City...*, pp. 168–85.
5. Mahoney, pp. 169–70.
6. Ibid., p. 181.
7. Ibid., pp. 181–2.
8. Levy, Emanuel, 'A, B, C...Manhattan', *Variety* (26 May – 1 June 1997), p. 179.
9. Kehr, David, 'Marathon', *New York Times* (2 April 2004), http://www.nytimes.com/2004/04/02/ movies/film-in-review-marathon.html (no pagination).
10. Sadr, '...and the World Became His...', p. 54.
11. Quart, Leonard, 'New York City in American film', in Philip John Davies and Paul Wells (eds), *American Film and Politics from Reagan to Bush Jr.* (Manchester: Manchester University Press, 2002), pp. 102–3.
12. Sarris, Andrew, 'Manhattan by Numbers: True Grit and an Orwellian Spirit', *The New York Observer* (November 1994), http://www.ifvc.com/the-new-york-observer.htm (no pagination).

4 Close Up 2 – Sohrab Shahid Saless

1. Rosenbaum and Saeed-Vafa, *Abbas Kiarostami*, p. 98.
2. See Saeed-Vafa, 'Sohrab Shahid Saless: A Cinema of Exile', in *Life and Art...*, pp. 136–4.
3. Naficy, *An Accented Cinema...* p. 200.

NOTES

4. Sadr, '...and the World Became His...', p. 51.
5. Naficy, *An Accented Cinema*, pp. 203–4.
6. Ibid., p. 200.
7. Ibid., p. 206.
8. Ibid., p. 205.
9. See Margulies, Ivone, *Nothing Happens: Chantal Akerman's Hyperrealist Everyday* (Durham: Duke University Press, 1996), pp. 21–41.
10. Chow, Rey, 'Sentimental Returns: On the Uses of the Everyday in the Recent Films of Zhang Yimou and Wong Kar-wai', *New Literary History* vol. 33, no. 4 (Autumn 2002), p. 639.
11. Saless, Sohrab Shahid, 'Sohrab Shahid Saless and a Private Agony', *Film International* vol. 1, no. 4 (Autumn 1993), p. 60.
12. Sadr, '...and the World Became His...', p. 55.
13. Saless, 'Culture as Hard Currency or: Hollywood in Germany', in Eric Rentschler (ed.), *West German Filmmakers on Film: Visions and Voices* (New York; London: Holmes and Meier, 1988), p. 57.
14. Klevan, Andrew, *Disclosure of the Everyday: Undramatic Achievement in Narrative Film* (Trowbridge: Flicks Books, 2000), pp. 1–2.
15. Ibid., p. 114.
16. Maghsoudlou, Bahman, 'Naderi on Naderi', http://www.ifvc.com/naderi-on-naderi.htm (no pagination).
17. Klevan, p. 61.
18. Ibid., p. 62.
19. *Far from Home* was an Iranian-German co-production.
20. As Saless has elaborated: 'In *Diary of a Lover* the character, who is a continuation of the one from *Time of Maturity* in his utter confusion, finds these four walls of the house to be the perimeter of his world. He's a prisoner escaped from society... Between the house of *Time of Maturity* in which the mother defines the child's world and that of *Diary of a Lover* in which the character enters into a sick, anxious world, the boy has passed through puberty, then he collapses; it's at this point that the house is no longer a place of security.' See Haghighat, Mamad and Rahgozar, Timothy S. Murphy (trans.), 'This Isn't Pessimism: Interview with Sohrab Shahid Saless', *Discourse* vol. 21, no. 1 (Winter 1999), p. 179.
21. Saeed-Vafa, 'Sohrab Shahid Saless...', p. 143.
22. Margulies, p. 78.
23. Heath, Stephen, *Questions of Cinema* (London: MacMillan, 1981), pp. 167–9.

24. Möller, Olaf, 'Olaf's World: Sohrab Shahid Saless', *Film Comment* (July–August 2004), p. 13.
25. Margulies, p. 75.
26. Chekov, Anton, 'The Willow', in Frances H. Jones (intro. and trans.), *St. Peter's Day and Other Tales* (New York: Capricorn Books, 1959), p. 40.
27. Santner, Eric L., *Stranded Objects: Mourning, Memory, and Film in Postwar Germany* (Ithaca, NY; London: Cornell University Press, 1990), p. 112.
28. Ibid., p. 147.
29. Ibid., p. 143.
30. Bartov, Omer, ' "Seit die Juden weg sind..." Germany, History, and Representations of Absence', in Scott Denhan, Irene Kacandes and Johnathan Petropoulous (eds), *A User's Guide to German Cultural Studies* (Ann Arbor: University of Michigan Press, 1997), p. 220.
31. See Robertson, Richie in Richie Robertson (ed.), *The German-Jewish Dialogue: An Anthology of Literary Texts – 1749–1993* (Oxford: Oxford University Press, 1999), p. xxvi.
32. 'Certainly the attempt to redeem the memory of those Germans who had taken incredible personal risks to fight the Nazi terror was a necessary act of redemptive historiography for the young Republic; and neither was it a bad idea to show German youths that there were some positive role models in recent German history and that resistance is possible even under the most repressive political circumstances. The problem is that, until the mid-seventies the preponderance of programs dealing with the resistance was so pronounced that a casual observer might wonder how the regime managed to stay in power with so many Germans engaged in active resistance.' Geisler, Michael E., 'The Disposal of Memory: Fascism and the Holocaust on West German Television', in Bruce A.Murray and Christopher J. Wickham (eds), *Framing the Past: The Historiography of German Cinema and Television* (Carbondale: Southern Illinois University Press, 1992), pp. 224–5.
33. Koch, Gertrud, Miriam Hansen and Andy Spencer (trans.), 'Torments of the Flesh, Coldness of the Spirit: Jewish Figures in the Films of Rainer Werner Fassbinder', in Terri Ginsberg and Kristen Moana Thompson (eds), *Perspectives on German Cinema* (New York; London: G. K. Hall; Prentice Hall International, 1996), p. 224.
34. Note also Thomas Elsaesser's pertinent question: 'How can it be possible in relation to the signifier "Jewish" within a discourse about Germany

not to have recourse to the figure of the Other?'; from *Fassbinder's Germany: History, Identity, Subject* (Amsterdam: Amsterdam University Press, 1996), p. 192.
35. Bartov, pp. 211–2.
36. Ibid., p. 221.
37. Ibid., pp. 215–6.
38. Santner, p. 52.
39. Klevan, p. 172.
40. Insdorf, Annette, *Indelible Shadows: Film and the Holocaust* (Cambridge: Cambridge University Press, 1989) p. 81.
41. Geisler, p. 233.
42. The American miniseries *Holocaust* (Marvin J. Chomsky, 1978) was broadcast on West German television in 1979. Geisler has written on how the miniseries itself singlehandedly sparked a nationwide public debate about the place of the Holocaust and the rise of fascism in German history, and the regard in which both were held in contemporary German society. See Geisler, pp. 220–6.
43. See Kiarostami, Abbas, 'Love and the Wall', *Film International* vol. 6, no. 1 (1998), pp. 61–5.
44. Farahmand, 'Perspectives on Recent...', in *The New Iranian Cinema: Politics, Representation and Identity*, p. 104.
45. Akrami, Jamsheed, 'Babak Payami on *Secret Ballot*', http://www.sonyclassics.com/secretballot/ secretballotpressbook.pdf, p. 10.
46. Naficy, *An Accented Cinema*, p. 200.
47. Saless, 'Sohrab Shahid Saless...', p. 65.

Conclusion: Iranian Cinema in Long Shot

1. Newman, Kathleen, 'National Cinema After Globalization: Fernando Solanas's *Sur* and the Exiled Nation', in Manuel Alvarado and Anna M. Lopez (eds), *Mediating Two Worlds: Cinematic Encounters in the Americas* (London: British Film Institute, 1993), p. 243.
2. Pick, 'Chilean Cinema in Exile...', p. 439.
3. Bergfelder, Tim, 'National, transnational or supranational cinema? Rethinking European film studies', *Media, Culture, Society* vol. 27, no. 3 (2005), p. 320.
4. Phillips, Alastair, *City of Darkness, City of Light: Émigré Filmmakers in Paris 1929–1939* (Amsterdam: Amsterdam University Press, 2004).
5. Naficy, *An Accented Cinema...*, p. 78.

6. Chaudhuri, *Contemporary World Cinema...*, p. 1.
7. Carnegie, Charles V., *Postnationalism Prefigured: Caribbean Borderlands* (New Brunswick, NJ; London: Rutgers University Press, 2002), pp. 191–2.
8. Eleftheriotis, Dimitris, *Popular Cinemas of Europe: Studies of Texts, Contexts and Frameworks* (London, New York: Continuum, 2001), pp. 35–6.

Bibliography

Akrami, Jamsheed, 'Babak Payami on *Secret Ballot*', http://www.sonyclassics.com/ secretballot/secretballotpressbook.pdf.

Akrami, Jamsheed, 'The Blighted Spring: Iranian Cinema and Politics in the 1970s', John D. H. Downing (ed.), *Film and Politics in the Third World* (New York: Autonomedia, 1987), pp. 131–44.

Ali, Tariq, 'Fight the Power', *Guardian* (23 April 2005), http://www.guardian.co.uk/books/2005/apr/23/featuresreviews.guardianreview11.

Anderson, Benedict, *Imagined Communities: Reflections on the Origins and Spread of Nationalism* (London: Verso, 1983).

Andrew, Geoff, *10* (London: British Film Institute, 2005).

Aufderheide, Pat, 'Real Life Is More Important Than Art: An Interview with Abbas Kiarostami', *Cineaste* vol. 21, no. 3 (1993), pp. 31–3.

Bakhtin, Mikhail, Michael Holquist (trans.), Caryl Emerson and Holquist (eds), *The Dialogic Imagination: Four Essays* (Austin: University of Texas Press, 1981).

Barkan, Elazar and Shelton, Marie-Denise (eds), *Borders, Exiles, Diasporas* (Stanford, CA: Stanford University Press, 1998).

Barthes, Roland, Stephen Heath (ed.), *Image Music Text* (London: Fontana Press, 1977).

Bartov, Omer, ' "Seit die Juden weg sind..." Germany, History, and Representations of Absence', in Scott Denhan, Irene Kacandes and Johnathan Petropoulous (eds), *A User's Guide to German Cultural Studies* (Ann Arbour: University of Michigan Press, 1997), pp. 209–26.

Bergfelder, Tim, 'National, Transnational or Supranational Cinema? Rethinking European Film Studies', *Media, Culture, Society* vol. 27, no. 3 (2005), pp. 315–31.

Bhabha, Homi K., *Nation and Narration* (London: Routledge, 1990).

Bhabha, Homi K., *The Location of Culture* (London and New York: Routledge, 1994).

Bordwell, David, 'The Art Cinema as a Mode of Film Practice', *Film Criticism* vol. 4, no. 1 (Fall 1979), pp. 56–63.

Bordwell, David, Staiger, Janet and Thompson, Kristin, *The Classical Hollywood Cinema: Film Style and Mode of Production to 1960* (London: Routledge and Kegan Paul, 1985).

Brah, Avtar, *Cartographies of Diaspora: Contesting Identities* (London: Routledge, 1996).

Cahiers du Cinéma no. 493 (July–August 1995).

Carnegie, Charles V., *Postnationalism Prefigured: Caribbean Borderlands* (New Brunswick, NJ; London: Rutgers University Press, 2002).

Caughie, John (ed.), *Theories of Authorship: A Reader* (London: Routledge, 1981).

Chaudhuri, Shohini, *Contemporary World Cinema: Europe, The Middle East, East Asia and South Asia* (Edinburgh: Edinburgh University Press, 2005).

Chaudhuri, Shohini and Finn, Howard, 'The Open Image: Poetic Realism and the New Iranian Cinema', *Screen* vol. 44, no. 1 (Spring 2003), pp. 38–57.

Chekhov, Anton, 'The Willow', in Frances H. Jones (intro. and trans.), *St. Peter's Day and Other Tales* (New York: Capricorn Books, 1959), pp. 37–41.

Cheshire, Godfrey, 'Where Iranian Cinema Is', *Film Comment* vol. 29, no. 2 (March–April 1993), pp. 38–43.

Cheshire, Godfrey, 'Abbas Kiarostami: A Cinema of Questions', *Film Comment* vol. 32, no. 4 (July–August 1996), pp. 34–40.

Cheshire, Godfrey, 'Abbas Kiarostami: Seeking a Home', in John Boorman and Walter Donohue (eds), *Projections 8: Filmmakers on Filmmaking* (London: Faber and Faber, 1998), pp. 209–28.

Cheshire, Godfrey, 'How to Read Kiarostami', *Cineaste* vol. 25, no. 4 (2000), pp. 9–15.

Chow, Rey, *Writing Diaspora: Tactics of Intervention in Contemporary Cultural Studies* (Bloomington: Indiana University Press, 1993).

Chow, Rey, 'Sentimental Returns: On the Uses of the Everyday in the Recent Films of Zhang Yimou and Wong Kar-Wai', *New Literary History* vol. 33, no. 4 (Autumn 2002), pp. 639–54.

Ciecko, Anne, 'Representing the Spaces of Diaspora in Contemporary British Films by Women Directors', *Cinema Journal* vol. 38, no. 3 (1998–9), pp. 67–90.

Claassen, Jo-Marie, *Displaced Persons: The Literature of Exile from Cicero to Boethius* (London: Great Duckworth, 1999).

Clifford, James, 'Travelling Cultures', in Lawrence Grossberg, Cary Nelson and Paula A. Treichler (eds and intro.), *Cultural Studies* (New York; London: Routledge, 1992), pp. 96–116.

Clifford, James, 'Diasporas', *Cultural Anthropology* vol. 9, no. 3, (1994), pp. 302–38.

Crofts, Stephen, 'Reconceptualising National Cinema/s', *Quarterly Review of Film and Video* vol. 14, no. 3 (1993), pp. 49–67.

Crofts, Stephen, 'Concepts of National Cinema', in John Hill and Pamela Church Gibson (eds), *The Oxford Guide to Film Studies* (Oxford: Oxford University Press, 1998), pp. 385–94.

Dabashi, Hamid, 'Re-Reading Reality: Kiarostami's *Through the Olive Trees* and the Cultural Politics of Postrevolutionary Aesthetics', *Critique* vol. 7 (1995), pp. 63–89.

Dabashi, Hamid, *Close Up – Iranian Cinema: Past, Present and Future* (London; New York: Verso, 2001).

Deleuze, Gilles and Polan, Dana (trans.), *Kafka: Towards a Minor Literature* (Minneapolis; Oxford: University of Minnesota Press, 1986).

Deleuze, Gilles, Habberjam, Barbara and Tomlinson Hugh (trans.), *Cinema 1: The Movement Image* (London: Athlone Press, 1986).

Deleuze, Gilles, Habberjam, Barbara and Tomlinson, Hugh (trans.), *Cinema 2: The Time Image* (London: Athlone Press, 1989).

Derrida, Jacques and Vattimo, Gianni (eds), *Religion* (Cambridge: Polity Press, 1998).

Ebert, Roger, 'Maryam', *Chicago Sun Times* (12 April 2002), http://rogerebert.suntimes.com/apps/pbcs.dll/article?AID=/20020412/REVIEWS/204120305/1023.

Egan, Eric, *Films of Makhmalbaf: Cinema, Politics and Culture in Iran* (Washington, D.C.: Mage, 2005).

Egan, Eric and Mohammadi, Ali, 'Cinema and Iran: Culture and Politics in the Islamic Republic', *Asian Cinema* vol. 12, no. 1 (Spring–Summer 2001), pp. 14–28.

Eleftheriotis, Dimitris, *Popular Cinemas of Europe: Studies of Texts, Contexts and Frameworks* (London; New York: Continuum, 2001).

Elena, Alberto and Coombes, Belinda (trans.), *The Cinema of Abbas Kiarostami* (London: Saqi, 2005).

Elsaesser, Thomas, *The New German Cinema: A History* (New Brunswick, NJ: Rutgers University Press, 1989).

Elsaesser, Thomas, *Fassbinder's Germany: History Identity Subject* (Amsterdam: Amsterdam University Press, 1996).

Farahmand, Azadeh, 'Perspectives on Recent (International Acclaim for) Iranian Cinema', in Richard Tapper (ed.), *The New Iranian Cinema: Politics, Representation and Identity* (London; New York: I.B.Tauris, 2002), pp. 86–108.

Fassihian, Dokhi and Sarafan, Lily, 'NIAC Interviews Iranian American Writer-Director Ramin Serry on His Debut Film Maryam' (10 September 2003), http://payvand.com/news/03/sep/1053.html.

Fischer, Michael M.J., *Mute Dreams, Blind Owls, and Dispersed Knowledges: Persian Poesis in the Transnational Circuitry* (Durham and London: Duke University Press, 2004).

Fitzmaurice, Tony and Shiel, Mark (eds), *Cinema & the City: Film and Urban Societies in a Global Context* (Oxford: Blackwell, 2001).

Foster, Gwendolyn Audrey, *Women Filmmakers of the African and Asian Diaspora: Decolonizing the Gaze, Locating Subjectivity* (Carbondale, IL: Southern Illinois University Press, 1997).

Foucault, Michel, Bouchard, Donald F. and Simon, Sherry (eds), Bouchard (trans.), *Language, Counter-Memory, Practice: Selected Essays and Interviews* (Ithaca, NY: Cornell University Press, 1977).

Ganguly, Keya, 'Migrant Identities: Personal Memory and the Construction of Selfhood', *Cultural Studies* vol. 6, no. 1 (1992), pp. 27–50.

Geisler, Michael E., 'The Disposal of Memory: Fascism and the Holocaust on West German Television', in Bruce A. Murray and Christopher J. Wickham (eds), *Framing the Past: The Historiography of German Cinema and Television* (Carbondale, IL: Southern Illinois University Press, 1992), pp. 220–60.

Gellner, Ernest, *Nations and Nationalism* (Oxford: Basil Blackwell, 1983).

Gellner, Ernest, *Nationalism* (London: Phoenix, 1998).

Getino, Octavio and Solanas, Fernando, 'Towards a Third Cinema: Notes and Experiences for the Development of a Cinema of Liberation in the Third World', in Michael T. Martin (ed.), *New Latin American Cinema – Volume 1: Theory, Practices, and Transcontinental Articulations* (Detroit: Wayne State University Press, 1997), pp. 33–58.

Gherami, Shahin, 'Mullahs, Martyrs, and Men: Conceptualizing Masculinity in the Islamic Republic of Iran', *Men & Masculinities* vol. 5, no. 3 (January 2003), pp. 257–74.

Ghosh, Bishnupriya and Sarkar, Bjaskar, 'The Cinema of Displacement: Towards a Politically Motivated Poetics', *Film Criticism* vol. 20, no. 1–2 (Fall–Winter 1995–96), pp. 102–113.

Grabar, Oleg, *The Formation of Islamic Art* (New Haven and London: Yale University Press, 1973).

Gramsci, Antonio, Rosengarten, Frank (ed.) and Raymond Rosenthal (trans.), *Letters from Prison: Volume 1* (New York: Columbia University Press, 1994).

Grossvogel, David I., *Scenes in the City: Film Visions of Manhattan Before 9/11* (New York: Peter Lang, 2003).

Haghighat, Mamad, 'Itinerary 1944–83: Interviews with Sohrab Shahid Saless', *Discourse* vol. 21, no. 1 (Winter 1999), pp. 162–74.

Haghighat, Mamad, and Rahgozar, Timothy S. Murphy (trans.), 'This Isn't Pessimism: Interview with Sohrab Shahid Saless', *Discourse* vol. 21, no. 1 (Winter 1999), pp. 175–80.

Haghighi, Ali Reza, 'Politics and Cinema in Post-revolutionary Iran: An Uneasy Relationship', in Richard Tapper (ed.), *The New Iranian Cinema: Politics, Representation and Identity* (London; New York: I.B.Tauris, 2002), pp. 109–116.

Hamid, Nassia, 'Near and Far', *Sight & Sound* vol. 7, no. 2 (1997), pp. 22–24.

Hall, Stuart, 'Culture, Community, Nation', *Cultural Studies* vol. 7, no. 3 (1993), pp. 349–63.

Hall, Stuart, 'Cultural Identity and Diaspora', in Padmini Mongia (ed.), *Contemporary Postcolonial Theory: A Reader* (London and New York: Arnold, 1996), pp. 110–21.

Heath, Stephen, *Questions of Cinema* (London: MacMillan, 1981).

Hobsbawm, Eric J., *Nations and Nationalism since 1780: Programme, Myth, Reality* (Cambridge: Cambridge University Press, 1990).

Holden, Stephen, '*Before the Storm*: Parallel Predicaments on a Collision Course', *New York Times* (30 March 2001), http://www.nytimes.com/2001/03/30 movies/film-festival-review-parallel-predicaments-on-a-collision-course.html.

Higson, Andrew, 'The Concept of National Cinema', *Screen* vol. 30, n. 4 (1989), pp. 36–46.

Higson, Andrew, 'The Limiting Imagination of National Cinema', in Mette Hjort and Scott Mackenzie (eds), *Cinema & Nation* (London: Routledge, 2000), pp. 63–74.

Holden, Stephen, 'Of Passion and Paradox in the Ruins', *New York Times* (17 February 1995), http://www.nytimes.com/1995/02/17/movies/film-review-of-passion-and-paradox-in-the-ruins.html.

Huston, Johnny Ray, 'Long Story Short: Notes on the S.F. International Asian American Film Festival's 2002 programs', *San Francisco Bay Guardian* (12 June 2002), http://www.sfbg.com/36/23/art_notes.html.

Insdorf, Annette, *Indelible Shadows: Film and the Holocaust* (Cambridge: Cambridge University Press, 1989).

Issari, Ali M., *Cinema in Iran, 1900–79* (Metuchen, NJ; London: Scarecrow Press, 1989).

Johnston, Sheila, 'The Mission', *Monthly Film Bulletin* vol. 51, no. 604, (1984), p. 155.

Kehr, David, 'Marathon', *New York Times* (2 April 2004), http://www.nytimes.com/2004/04/02/movies/film-in-review-marathon.html.

Kiarostami, Abbas, 'Love and the Wall', *Film International* vol. 6, no. 1 (1998), pp. 61–5.

Klevan, Andrew, *Disclosure of the Everyday: Undramatic Achievement in Narrative Film* (Trowbridge: Flicks Books, 2000).

Koch, Gertrud, 'Torments of the Flesh, Coldness of the Spirit: Jewish Figures in the Films of Rainer Werner Fassbinder', in Terri Ginsberg and Kristen Moana Thompson (eds), Miriam Hansen and Andy Spencer (trans.), *Perspectives on German Cinema* (New York: G. K. Hall; London: Prentice Hall International, 1996), pp. 221–30.

Lahiji, Shahla, 'Chaste Dolls and Unchaste Dolls: Women in Iranian Cinema', in Richard Tapper (ed.), *The New Iranian Cinema: Politics, Representation and Identity* (London; New York: I.B.Tauris, 2002), pp. 215–26.

Landy, Marcia, *Cinematic Uses of the Past* (Minneapolis: University of Minnesota Press, 1996).

Langford, Michelle, 'Dreams, Disco and Politics: An Interview with Babak Shokrian', *Senses of Cinema* (March 2002), http://archive.sensesofcinema.com/contents/02/20/shokrian.html.

Levy, Emanuel, 'A, B, C...Manhattan' *Variety* (26 May–1 June 1997) p. 179.

Lopate, Philip, 'New York', *Film Comment* vol. 33, no. 6 (November–December 1997), pp. 60–5.

Maghsoudlou, Bahman, 'Naderi on Naderi', http://www.ifvc.com/naderi-on-naderi.htm.

Mahoney, Elisabeth, '"The People in Parentheses": Space under Pressure in the Postmodern City', in David. B Clarkes (ed.), *The Cinematic City* (London: Routledge, 1997), pp. 168–85.

Margulies, Ivone, *Nothing Happens: Chantal Akerman's Hyperrealist Everyday* (Durham: Duke University Press, 1996).

Marks, Laura U., 'A Deleuzian Politics of Hybrid Cinema', *Screen* vol. 35, no. 3 (1994), pp. 244–64.

Marks, Laura U., *The Skin of Film: Intercultural Cinema, Embodiment, and the Senses* (Durham and London: Duke University Press, 2000).

Martin, Michael T., 'Framing the "Black" in Black Diasporic Cinemas', Martin (ed.), *Cinemas of the Black Diaspora* (Detroit: Wayne State University Press, 1995), pp. 1–21.

McLennen, Sophia A., *The Dialiectics of Exile: Nation, Time, Language, and Space in Hispanic Literatures* (West Lafayette, IN: Purdue University Press, 2004).

Mohammadi, Ali, 'The Impact of Globalization upon Iranian Cinema', *Asian Cinema* vol. 13, no. 1 (Spring–Summer 2002), pp. 3–16.

Möller, Olaf, 'Olaf's World: Sohrab Shahid Saless', *Film Comment*, (July–August 2004), pp. 12–3

Mordler, Michael, 'Privacy Last', *Filmmaker* vol. 2, no. 3 (1994), pp. 41–2.

Mulvey, Laura, 'Kiarostami's Uncertainty Principle', *Sight and Sound* vol. 8, no. 6 (June 1998), pp. 24–7.

Naficy, Hamid, 'Mediawork's Representation of the Other: The Case of Iran', in Jim Pines and Paul Willeman (eds), *Questions of a Third Cinema* (London: British Film Institute, 1989), pp. 227–39.

Naficy, Hamid, *The Making of Exile Cultures: Iranian Television in Los Angeles* (Minneapolis: University of Minnesota Press, 1993).

Naficy, Hamid, 'Veiled Visions/Powerful Presences: Women in Post-revolutionary Iranian Cinema', in Mahnaz Afkhami and Erika Friedl (eds), *In the Eye of the Storm* (London; New York: I.B.Tauris, 1994).

Naficy, Hamid (ed.), *Home, Exile, Homeland: Film, Media, and the Politic of Space* (New York; London: Routledge, 1999).

Naficy, Hamid, 'Self-Othering: A Postcolonial Discourse on Cinematic First Contacts', in Fawzia Afzal-Khan and Kalpana Seshadri-Crooks (eds), *The Pre-Occupation of Postcolonial Studies* (Durham and London: Duke University Press, 2000), pp. 292–310

Naficy, Hamid, 'Veiled Voice and Vision in Iranian Cinema: The Evolution of Rakhshan Bani-Etemad's Films', in Murray Pomerance (ed.), *Ladies and Gentlemen, Boys and Girls: Gender in Film at the End of the Twentieth Century* (Albany, NY: State University of New York Press: 2001), pp. 36–53.

Naficy, Hamid, 'Iranian Cinema', in Oliver Leaman (ed.), *Companion Encyclopaedia of Middle Eastern and North African Film* (London: Routledge, 2001), pp. 130–222.

Naficy, Hamid, *An Accented Cinema: Exilic and Diasporic Filmmaking* (Princeton, NJ: Princeton University Press, 2001).

Naficy, Hamid, 'Islamizing Film Culture in Iran: A Post Khatami Update', in Richard Tapper (ed.), *The New Iranian Cinema: Politics, Representation and Identity* (London; New York: I.B.Tauris, 2002), pp. 26–65.

Naficy, Hamid, 'Narrowcasting in Diaspora: Iranian Television in Los Angeles', in Lisa Parks and Kumar Shanti (eds), *Planet TV: A Global Television Reader* (New York: New York University Press, 2003), pp. 376–401.

Nayeri, Farah, 'Iranian Cinema: What Happened in Between', *Sight & Sound* vol. 3, no. 12 (1993), pp. 26–8.

Neale, Steve, 'Art Cinema as Institution', *Screen* vol. 22, no. 1 (1981), pp. 11–39.

Newman, Kathleen, 'National Cinema after Globalization: Fernando Solanas's *Sur* and the Exiled Nation', in John King and Ana M. Lopez (eds), *Mediating Two Worlds: Cinematic Encounters in the Americas* (London: British Film Institute, 1993), pp. 242–57.

Nichols, Bill, 'Discovering Form, Inferring Meaning: New Cinemas and the Film Festival Circuit', *Film Quarterly* vol. 47, no. 3 (Spring 1994), pp. 16–30.

Orgeron, Devin, 'The Import/Export Business: The Road to Abbas Kiarostami's *Taste of Cherry*', *Cineaction* no. 58 (June 2002), pp. 46–51.

Phillips, Alastair, 'An Accented Cinema', *Screen* vol. 44, no. 3 (2003), pp. 343–6.

Phillips, Alastair, *City of Darkness, City of Light: Émigré Filmmakers in Paris 1929–1939* (Amsterdam: Amsterdam University Press, 2004).

Pick, Zuzana M., 'The Dialectical Wanderings of Exile', *Screen* vol. 30, no. 4 (1989), pp. 48–64.

Pick, Zuzana M., 'Chilean Cinema in Exile, 1973–1986', in Michael T. Martin (ed.), *New Latin American Cinema: Volume Two – Studies of National Cinemas* (Detroit: Wayne State University Press, 1997), pp. 420–1.

Quart, Leonard, 'New York City in American Film', in Philip John Davies and Paul Wells (eds), *American Film and Politics from Reagan to Bush Jr* (Manchester: Manchester University Press, 2002), pp. 91–104.

Reiter, Andrea and Calimmer, Patrick (trans.), *Narrating the Holocaust* (London; New York: Continuum, 2000).

Ridgeon, Lloyd, 'The Islamic Apocalypse: Mohsen Makhmalbaf's A Moment of Innocence', Brent S. Plate (ed.), *Representing Religion in World Cinema: Filmmaking, Mythmaking, Culture Making* (New York: Palgrave MacMillan, 2003), pp. 145–58.

Robertson, Ritchie (ed.), *The German-Jewish Dialogue: An Anthology of Literary Texts – 1749–1993* (Oxford: Oxford University Press, 1999).

Rosenbaum, Jonathan and Saeed-Vafa, Mehrnaz, *Abbas Kiarostami* (Urbana and Chicago: University of Illinois Press, 2003).

Sadr, Hamid Reza, '…and the World Became His: An Exclusive Interview with Sohrab Shahid Saless', *Film International* vol. 5, no. 3 (Spring 1998), pp. 50–5.

Sadr, Hamid Reza, 'Contemporary Iranian Cinema and Its Major Themes', in Rose Issa and Sheila Whittaker (eds), *Life and Art: The New Iranian Cinema* (London: National Film Theatre, 1999), pp. 26–43.

Saeed-Vafa, Mehrnaz, 'Sohrab Shahid Saless: A Cinema of Exile', in Rose Issa and Sheila Whittaker (eds), *Life and Art: The New Iranian Cinema* (London: National Film Theatre, 1999), pp. 136–45.

Safran, William, 'Diasporas in Modern Societies: Myths of Homeland and Return', *Diaspora* vol. 1, no. 1, (Spring 1991), pp. 83–99.

Said, Edward W., *Covering Islam: How the Media and the Experts Determine How We See the Rest of the World* (London: Vintage, 1997).

Said, Edward W., *Reflections on Exile: And Other Literary and Cultural Essay* (London: Granta, 2001).

Santner, Eric L., *Stranded Objects: Mourning, Memory, and Film in Postwar Germany* (Ithaca, NY; London: Cornell University Press, 1990).

Sarris, Andrew, '*Manhattan by Numbers*: True Grit And An Orwellian Spirit', *The New York Observer* (November 1994), see http://www.ifvc.com/the-new-york-observer.htm. Selection of Iranian Films 2003, A (Tehran: Farabi Cinema Foundation, 2003).

Saless, Sohrab Shahid, 'Culture as Hard Currency or: Hollywood in Germany', in Eric Rentschler (ed.), *West German Filmmakers on Film: Visions and Voices* (New York; London: Holmes and Meier, 1988), pp. 57–9.

Saless, Sohrab Shahid, 'Sohrab Shahid Saless and a Private Agony', *Film International* vol. 1, no. 4 (Autumn 1993), pp. 60–5.

Schrader, Paul, *Transcendental Style in Film* (Berkeley; London: University of California Press, 1972).

Shohat, Ella and Stam, Robert, *Unthinking Eurocentrism: Multiculturalism and the Media* (London: Routledge, 1994).

Soja, Edward, *Thirdspace: Journeys to Los Angeles and Other Real-and-Imagined Places* (Cambridge, MA; Oxford: Blackwell, 1996).

Sontag, Susan, *Against Interpretation, and Other Essays* (New York: Farrar, Strauss & Giroux, 1967).

Sontag, Susan, *Styles of Radical Will* (London: Vintage, 2001).

Stam, Robert, 'Beyond Third Cinema: The Aesthetics of Hybridity', in Wimal Dissanayake and Anthony R. Gunaratne (eds), *Rethinking Third Cinema* (Routledge: New York and London, 2003), pp. 31–48.

Stone, Judy, *Eye on the World: Conversations with International Filmmakers* (Los Angeles: Silman-James Press, 1997).

Sullivan, Zohreh C., *Exiled Memories: Stories of Iranian Diaspora* (Philadelphia; England: Temple University Press, 2001).

Tololyan, Khachig, 'The Nation-State and Its Others: In Lieu of a Preface', *Diaspora* vol. 1, no. 1 (Spring 1991), pp. 3–7.

Tololyan, Khachig, 'Rethinking Diaspora(s): Stateless Power in the Transnational Moment', *Diaspora* vol. 5, no. 1 (1995), pp. 3–36.

Totaro, Donato, 'Susan Sontag: Against Interpretation?', Offscreen vol. 9, issue 1, (31 January 2005), http://www.offscreen.com/biblio/phile/essays/against_ interpretation/.

Walsh, Maria, 'Intervals of Flight: Chantal Akerman's *News from Home*', *Screen* vol. 45, no. 3 (2004), pp. 190–225.

Willemen, Paul, *Looks and Frictions: Essays in Cultural Studies and Film Theory* (London: British Film Institute, 1994).

Wollen, Peter, *Signs and Meanings in the Cinema* (London: British Film Institute, 1998).

Woodhull, Winifred, 'Exile', *Yale French Studies*, no. 81 (1993), pp. 7–24.

Woolf, Janet, 'On the Road Again: Metaphors of Travel in Cultural Criticism', *Cultural Studies* vol. 7, no. 2 (1993), pp. 224–39.

Woolf, Janet, *The Social Production of Art* (London: MacMillan, 1993).

Zaatari, Akram 'Abbas Kiarostami', *Bomb* no. 50 (1994–5), pp. 12–4.

Filmography

10 (Abbas Kiarostami, 2002)
11'09"01 – 11 September ('Iran' segment, Samira Makhmalbaf, 2002)
400 Blows, The/Les quatre cents coups (François Truffaut, 1959)
A, B, C...Manhattan (Amir Naderi, 1997)
Addressee Unknown/Empfänger Unbekannt (Sohrab Shahid Saless, 1983)
All Hell Let Loose/Hus I Helvete (Susan Taslimi, 2002)
America So Beautiful (Babak Shokrian, 2001)
And Life Goes On... aka *Life and Nothing More/Zendegi va digar Hich* (Abbas Kiarostami, 1991)
Apple, The/Sib (Samira Makhmalbaf, 1998)
Baran (Majid Majidi, 2001)
Bashu, the Little Stranger/Bashu, Gharibeh-ye Kuchak (Bahram Beyza'i, 1988)
Before the Storm/Före Stormen (Reza Parsa, 2000)
Bread and Alley/Nan va Kucheh (Abbas Kiarostami, 1970)
Close Up/Nama-ye Nazdik (Abbas Kiarostami, 1989)
Colour of Paradise, The/Rang-e Khoda (Majid Majidi, 1999)
Dash Akol (Masoud Kimia'i, 1971)
Day of the Jackal, The (Fred Zinnemann, 1973)
Diary of a Lover/Tagebuch eines Liebenden (Sohrab Shahid Saless, 1977)
Djomeh (Hassan Yektapaneh, 2000)
Driver, The (Walter Hill, 1978)
Far from Home/In Der Fremde aka *Dar Ghorbat* (Sohrab Shahid Saless, 1975)
Five (Abbas Kiarostami, 2005)
Girl in the Sneakers, The/Dokhtari ba Kafsh-haye Katani (Rassul Sadr-Ameli, 1999)
Guests of the Hotel Astoria (Reza Allahmehzadeh, 1989)
Hans – A Boy in Germany/Hans – Ein Junge in Deutschland, (Sohrab Shahid Saless, 1985)
Heimat – a German Chronicle/Heimat – eine Deutsche Chronik (Edgar Reitz, 1984)
Hitler – A Film from Germany/Hitler – ein Film aus Deutschland (Hans Jürgen Syberberg, 1978)
House Is Black, The/Khaneh Siah Ast (Farough Farrokhzad, 1963)

House of Sand and Fog, The (Vadim Perelman, 2003)
I Don't Hate Las Vegas Anymore (Caveh Zahedi, 1994)
I'm Taraneh, 15/Man, Taraneh, Panzdah Sal Daram (Rassul Sadr-Ameli, 2001)
In the Bathtub of the World (Caveh Zahedi, 2001)
Iran Is My Home (Fariborz David Diaan, 2003)
Jeanne Dielman, 23 Quai du Commerce, 1080 Bruxelles (Chantal Akerman, 1975)
Just Another Girl on the I. R. T. (Leslie Harris, 1992)
Letter from An Unknown Woman (Max Ophüls, 1948)
Little Stiff, A (Caveh Zahedi, 1994)
Lizard, The/Marmulak (Kamal Tabrizi, 2004)
Manhattan by Numbers (Amir Naderi, 1993)
Marathon (Amir Naderi, 2000)
Maryam (Ramin Serry, 2000)
Mean Streets (Martin Scorsese, 1973)
Meeting Evil (Reza Parsa, 2002)
Mission, The (Parviz Sayyad, 1983)
Moment of Innocence, A/Nan va Goldun (Mohsen Makhmalbaf, 1996)
Never aka *Border/Gränsen* (Reza Parsa, 1995)
News from Home (Chantal Akerman, 1977)
Nightsongs (Marva Nabili, 1984)
Order/Ordnung (Sohrab Shahid Saless, 1980)
Prince Etehjab/Shazdeh Etehjab (Bahman Farmanara, 1974)
Report, The/Gozaresh (Abbas Kiarostami, 1978)
Roses for Africa/Rüsen fur Afrika (Sohrab Shahid Saless, 1991)
Rhythm Thief (Matthew Harrison, 1994)
Runner, The/Davandeh (Amir Naderi, 1985)
Saturday Night Fever (John Badham, 1977)
Saless, Far from Home (Mehrnaz Saeed-Vafa, 1998)
Silence, The/Sokut (Mohsen Makhmalbaf, 1998)
Simple Event, A/Yek Ettefaq-e Sadeh (Sohrab Shahid Saless, 1973)
Still Life/Tabi'ate Bijan (Sohrab Shahid Saless, 1974)
Taste of Cherry/Ta'm-e Gilas (Abbas Kiarostami, 1997)
Taxi Driver (Martin Scorsese, 1976)
Through the Olive Trees/Zir-e Derakhtan Zeytun (Abbas Kiarostami, 1994)
Time for Drunken Horses, A/Zamani baraye Masti Ashba (Bahman Ghobadi, 2000)
Time of Maturity, A/Reifezeit, (Sohrab Shahid Saless, 1976)

FILMOGRAPHY

Turtles Can Fly/Lakposht-ha ham Parvaz Mikonand (Bahman Ghobadi, 2004)
Wind Will Carry Us, The /Bad Ma ra Khahad Bord (Abbas Kiarostami, 1999)
Under the Skin of City/Zir-e Poost-e Shar (Rakhshan Bani-Etemad, 2001)
Underground Zero ('The World Is a Classroom' segment, Caveh Zahedi, 2002)
Utopia (Sohrab Shahid Saless, 1983)
Walls of Sand (Erica Jordan, 1994)
Water, Wind and Dust/Ab, Khak va Bad (Amir Naderi, 1988)
Where Is the Friend's House?/Khaneh-ye Dust Kojast? (Abbas Kiarostami, 1987)
White Balloon, The/Badkonak-e Sefid (Jafar Panahi, 1995)
Willow Tree, The/Der Weidenbaum (Sohrab Shahid Saless, 1983)
Women's Prison/Zedan-e Zanan (Manijeh Hekmat, 2001)

Index

9/11, 41, 108, 116, 199–202
10 (2002), 36
11'09"01 – September 11 (2002), 199–202
400 Blows, The (1959), 49

A, B, C... Manhattan (1997), 128–39, 143–4, 146, 192
Addressee Unknown (1983), 150, 188
Aghdashloo, Sohreh, 87–121
Akerman, Chantal, 152, 164, 165, 169
Ali, Tariq, 58
All Hell Let Loose (2002), 111–14, 123
Allahmehzadeh, Reza, 82
Allahyari, Houshang, 67, 149
Allen, Woody, 144
Alvardo, Manuel, 193–4
America So Beautiful (2001), 67, 95, 114–21, 126
And Life Goes On... (1991), 1, 19–22, 24–5, 27
Andrew, Geoff, 28
Antonioni, Michelangelo, 22
art cinema, 3–7, 10–13, 16–44, 49–50, 54–5, 57–8, 188, 191; and ambiguity, 26–39, 55; and authorship, 3, 6–7, 21–7, 150, 188, 193–4; and realism, 18–21, 24, 27
avant-garde filmmaking, 18, 165

Badham, John, 116
Bakhtin, Mikhail, 62, 68
Band Wagon, The (1953), 145
Bani-Etemad, Rakhshan, 43
Baran (2001), 47
Barkan, Elazar, 74
Bartov, Omer, 176, 178
Bashu, the Little Stranger (1988), 42, 46, 50, 107
Before the Storm (2000), 108–9
Bergfelder, Tim, 195
Bergman, Ingmar, 22
Berlin Alexanderplatz (1980), 177–8
Bhabha, Homi K., 80
Blue Scarf, The (1995), 52
Bordwell, David, 17–19, 21–2, 26–7, 39, 47, 55
Brah, Avtar, 76
Bread and Alley (1970), 28
Bresson, Robert, 155
Broken Hearts (1978), 120
Broszat, Martin, 176
Bunuel, Luis, 22
Bus Stop (1956), 85–6

Calendar (1993), 70
Carnegie, Charles V., 196–8
Cars, The, 115
Carter, Jimmy, 114
Cassavetes, John, 146
censorship, 14, 16, 47, 56, 58, 188
Chaudhuri, Shohini, 4–5, 55–6, 196

Chekov, Anton, 153–4, 172
Cheshire, Godfrey, 39–40, 199
children, portrayal of, 49–51, 185–6
Chilean cinema, 72, 193
Chomsky, Marvin J., 181
Chow, Rey, 152–3
Cimarosa, Domenico, 1
Clifford, James, 75–6, 93
Close Up (1989), 24, 55
Colour of Paradise, The (1999), 44, 50

Dabashi, Hamid, 6, 28–33, 36–9, 55, 57
Dash Akol (1974), 48
Davies, Terence, 44
Davoudnezad, Ali Reza, 52
Day of the Jackal, The (1973), 82
De Sica, Vittorio, 40
Deer, The (1976), 14
Deleuze, Gilles, 55–6
Derrida, Jacques, 51
Diaan, Fariborz David, 116, 125–6
Diary of a Country Priest (1950), 155
Diary of a Lover (1977), 150, 157, 168
diaspora, theories of, 71–7; see also exile, theories of
Djomeh (2000), 47
Donen, Stanley, 145
Driver, The (1978), 82–3

Ebadi, Shirin, 121
Ebert, Roger, 116
Egan, Eric, 2, 11–12, 50
Egoyan, Atom, 70
Eleftheriotis, Dimitris, 198
Elena, Alberto, 19, 37, 184

Ephron, Nora, 144
Etessam, Shirin, 96, 103, 106
exile, theories of, 71–7; see also diaspora, theories of

Falling Down (1993), 131
Far From Home (1975), 150
Farabi Cinema Foundation, 15
Farahmand, Azadeh, 49–50, 185
Farmanara, Bahman, 48
Farrokhzad, Farough, 3, 31
Fassbinder, Rainer Werner, 33, 177–8
Fellini, Federico, 22
Fels, Ludwig, 154
film festivals, 42–4, 49
Finn, Howard, 55–7
Fischer, Michael M. J., 42, 51–2
Five (2005), 26
Forman, Milos, 155
French New Wave, 4, 6, 10, 21, 41, 43
Frick, Hans, 154, 175

Geisler, Michael E., 181
Getino, Octavio, 68
Ghaffari, Farokh, 153
Ghobadi, Bahman, 47, 184
Girl in Sneakers, The (1999), 44
Glass Agency, The (1997), 52
Godard, Jean-Luc, 9, 21, 39–40, 43
Grabar, Oleg, 48, 51–3
Gramsci, Antonio, 61
Great Sadness of Zohara, The (1983), 70
Grosz, Elizabeth, 131
Guests of the Hotel Astoria (1989), 82, 87–92, 95–6, 106, 121
Güney, Yilmaz, 70

INDEX

Haghighi, Ali Reza, 55
Hall, Stuart, 66, 96, 107
Hamid, Nassia, 20, 24
Hans – A Boy in Germany (1985), 150, 154, 157, 166, 175–83
Harmonica (1974), 50, 144
Harris, Leslie, 130–1, 133
Harrison, Matthew, 144
Harvey, David, 131
Hatami, Ali, 120
Hatamikia, Ebrahim, 52
Heimat – a German Chronicle (1984), 176
Hekmat, Manijeh, 44
Herzog, Werner, 43
Higson, Andrew, 45–6, 192–3
Hill, Walter, 82
Hitler – A Film from Germany (1978), 175–6, 179
Holden, Stephen, 9, 108
Hollywood, 4, 10–13, 15, 17–18, 20–1, 36, 40, 42–3, 47, 68, 77–81, 85–6, 125, 129, 144–5, 150, 153, 193, 196
Holocaust, 175–82
Holocaust (1978), 181
hostage crisis, 41–2, 114–19
House Is Black, The (1962), 3
House of Sand and Fog (2003), 81, 120–2
Houston, Thelma, 116
Huston, Johnny Ray, 115

I Don't Hate Las Vegas Anymore (1994), 96–103, 106–7
I'm Taraneh, 15 (2001), 44
In a Year with Thirteen Moons (1978), 177–8

In the Bathtub of the World (2001), 98
In The Mood for Love (2000), 152
Insdorf, Annette, 180
Iran Is My Home (2003), 125–6
Iran Is My Land (1999), 125
Islam; in art, 48–9; in cinema, 45–54
Italian neo-realism, 10, 41, 52
Iven, Joris, 70

Jarmusch, Jim, 131, 146
Jeanne Dielman, 23 Quai du Commerce, 1080 Bruxelles (1975), 164, 169
Jews, portrayal of, 177–9
Johnston, Sheila, 83
Jordan, Erica, 96, 106
Just Another Girl on the I. R. T. (1992), 130–2

Kaes, Anton, 181
Kanun (Centre for the Intellectual Development of Children and Young Adults), 28
Kehr, David, 140
Kelly, Gene, 145
Keshavarz, Mohammad Ali, 20
Khatami, Seyyed Mohammad, 15
Khomeini, Ayatollah, 41, 114–15
Kiarostami, Abbas, 1–5, 7, 9–11, 13, 18–41, 43, 56–7, 96, 101, 120, 130, 146, 152, 167, 183–8, 192, 199
Kimia'i, Massoud, 14, 48, 148
Kimiavi, Parviz, 67, 125, 148
Kingsley, Ben, 120
Klevan, Andrew, 155–6, 173, 180
Koch, Gertrud, 177

231

Kolah, Ghermezi and Sarvenaz (2001), 44
Kubler-Ross, Elisabeth, 107
Kurosawa, Akira, 43

Langford, Michelle, 118
Late Spring (1949), 155
Lefebvre, Henri, 130
Leigh, Mike, 44
Letter from An Unknown Woman (1948), 150
Levy, Emanuel, 139
Lili Marleen (1981), 177
Little Stiff, A (1991), 129
Lizard, The (2004), 16
Loach, Ken, 44
Logan, Joshua, 85
Lopate, Philip, 9
Lopez, Ana M., 193–4
Lost, Lost, Lost (1976), 79
Loves of a Blonde (1965), 155

Made in Iran (1978), 128
Mahoney, Elisabeth, 130–1
Majidi, Majid, 43–4, 47
Makhmalbaf, Mohsehn, 3, 22, 24, 39, 43, 50, 53–4
Makhmalbaf, Samira, 43, 55, 199–202
Manhattan, portrayal of, 129–43; see also New York City
Manhattan (1978), 144
Manhattan by Numbers (1993), 126, 138, 145
Marathon (2001) 126, 128–9, 139–45
Margulies, Ivone, 197, 211, 217
Mark, Laura U., 92

The Marriage of Maria Braun (1979), 177
Maryam (2000), 114–21, 144–51
masculinity, 111–12, 134; see also patriarchy
Massey, Doreen, 131
McLennen, Sophia A., 73–4
Mean Streets (1973), 116
media portrayal of Iran, 41–2
Meeting Evil (2002), 108–11
Mehrjui, Dariush, 43, 148
Mekas, Jonas, 79
Menkes, Nina, 70
Milani, Tahmineh, 43
Ministry of Culture and Islamic Guidance, 14–15, 45
Minnelli, Vincente, 145
Mission, The (1983), 67, 82–92, 95, 106, 109, 117
Mohammadi, Ali, 11–13, 50
Moller, Olaf, 66–7
Moment of Innocence, A (1996), 53–5
Monroe, Marilyn, 85–6
Mullen, Peter, 44
Mulvey, Laura, 11, 18, 20, 26, 28

Nabili, Marva, 64, 90
Naderi, Amir, 4, 7, 50, 67, 81, 107, 125–46, 148, 155, 192, 194
Naficy, Hamid, 4, 6, 14–16, 41–2, 47–8, 50, 54, 62–3, 66–72, 77–80, 102, 104, 117, 124, 128, 148–51, 187, 196; and 'accented cinema', 4, 66–72, 77–81, 124, 129, 193, 196

national cinema, 4, 6–7, 10–13, 43, 45–8, 57, 59, 63–6, 80, 82, 124, 146–7, 150, 188, 192–9
Nayeri, Farah, 20, 25
Neale, Steve, 17–18
Need (1992), 52
Never (1995), 107–9
New German Cinema, 10, 41, 43, 147–8, 150–1, 154, 183, 188
New York City, portrayal of, 86–7, 91, 116, 129–46; and independent filmmaking, 144–6; *see also* Manhattan, portrayal of
Newman, Kathleen, 193
News from Home (1977), 91
Nichols, Bill, 42–4, 49
Night on Earth (1991), 131
Nightsongs (1984), 64, 82, 90–6, 106

On the Town (1949), 145
Ophüls, Max, 149–50
Order (1980), 157
Orgeron, Devin, 39–41
Ozu, Yasujiro, 155

Panahi, Jafar, 43, 47, 57, 167, 184
Parsa, Reza, 107–11, 113, 118
Pasolini, Pier Paolo, 55
patriarchy, 93–4, 111–12, 123; *see also* masculinity
Perlman, Vadim, 81
Phillips Alastair, 77–8, 196
Pick, Zuzana M., 72–4, 195
Prince Etehjab (1974), 48

Quart, Leonard, 144

Rafsanjani, Ali Akbar Hashemi, 15
Ramsey, Lynne, 44
Ray, Satyajit, 43
Reitz, Edgar, 175–6
Report, The (1978), 22, 120
revolution, aftermath of, 13–17
Rex Cinema, Abadan, 14
Rhythm Thief (1994), 144
Ridgeon, Lloyd, 53–4
Road Home, The (2000), 152
Robertson, Richie, 177
Rohmer, Eric, 22, 155
Rose, Gillian, 130–1
Rosenbaum, Jonathan, 32
Roses for Africa (1991), 149–50, 154, 157
Runner, The (1985), 50, 127, 129–30

Sadr-Ameli, Rassul, 44
Saeed-Vafa, Mehrnaz, 32, 147–9, 151, 157
Safran, William, 75
Said, Edward, 41–2, 72, 74
Saless, Sohrab Shahid, 2, 4, 7, 27, 39, 49, 58, 67, 81, 101, 107, 125–7, 144, 146–89, 192, 194; and the 'everyday', 151–75
Santner, Eric L., 175–6, 179
Sarris, Andrew, 145
Saturday Night Fever (1977), 116
Sayyad, Parviz, 67, 82–3, 107
Schrader, Paul, 55
Schumacher, Joel, 131
Scorsese, Martin, 116
Second World War, 3, 13, 45, 175, 189, 191
Serry, Ramin, 114, 119
Shelton, Marie-Denise, 74–5

Shokrian, Babak, 67, 118–19, 126
The Silence (1998), 50
Simple Event, A (1973), 49–50, 156–7, 173–5, 184–6, 192
Snow, Michael, 70
Soja, Edward, 88, 70, 130–1
Solanas, Fernando, 68, 193
Solution, The (1978), 40
Sontag, Susan, 30
Staiger, Janet, 47
Stam, Robert, 62–3, 69
Still Life (1974), 157, 192
Sufism, 53–4
Sullivan, Zohreh. C, 61
Sur (1988), 193
Sweden, 67, 107–9, 111
Syberberg, Hans Jürgen, 175–6

Tabrizi, Kamal, 16
Tahmasb, Iraj, 44
Tale of Springtime, A (1990), 155
Tale of the Wind (1988), 70
Tangos: The Exiles of Gardel (1985), 193
Tapper, Richard, 2
Taslimi, Susan, 4, 107–8, 111, 113
Taste of Cherry (1997), 2, 19–20, 23, 27–8, 36, 40, 47, 50
Taxi Driver (1976), 116
Tehran, 9–10, 14, 19, 33–4, 44, 107, 114–15, 117, 125–6
Thompson, Kristin, 47
Through the Olive Trees (1994), 1–2, 8–9, 20–4, 28–9, 31–2, 36–9, 96
Time for Drunken Horses, A (2000), 47, 50

Time of Maturity, A (1976), 150, 157–68, 171–2, 174–5, 179, 186
Totaro, Donato, 30
Touzie, Houshang, 82–3, 88, 115
Travolta, John, 116
Truffaut, François, 9, 21–2, 25, 39, 43, 49
Turkey, 70, 82, 88–9
Turtles Can Fly (2004), 47

Under the Skin of City (2001), 44
Underground Zero (2002), 199–202
Utopia (1983), 166, 172, 186

Veronika Voss (1982), 177
Vossoughi, Behrouz, 14, 120

Wai, Wong Kar, 91
Walls of Sand (1994), 96, 103–7, 123–4
Water, Wind and Dust (1988), 50, 127, 130
Wavelength (1967), 70
Wedding of the Blessed (1989), 53
Wenders, Wim, 40, 43
Where Is the Friend's House? (1989), 1, 3–4, 10, 19–20, 22, 27–8, 36, 49, 130, 183–6
White Balloon, The (1995), 47, 55–6
Willemen, Paul, 11–12
Willow Tree, The (1983), 150, 154, 169–73, 186
Wind Will Carry Us, The (1999), 9–10, 19, 24, 29–36, 38, 47, 52, 55, 58
Wolff, Janet, 93

women, portrayal of, 47–8
Women's Prison (2001), 44
Woodhull, Winifred, 74

Yektapaneh, Hassan, 47
Yimou, Zhang, 152

Yol (1982), 70
You've Got Mail (1998), 144

Zahedi, Caveh, 96–103, 106, 119, 199–202
Zinnemann, Fred, 82

www.ingramcontent.com/pod-product-compliance
Lightning Source LLC
Chambersburg PA
CBHW051520230426
43668CB00012B/1682